本著作的研究与出版获国家社会科学基金（教育学）"大学推动人类命运共同体建设的理论依据与实践研究"（BIA200176）项目资助

Research and publication of this book were supported by the Project of "Research on the Rationale and Practice for Universities to Promote the Building of A Community with a Shared Future for Mankind" (BIA200176) under the National Social Science Fund of China (NSSFC) (Education)

人类命运共同体
构建进程指标体系研究

The Indicators System on the Process of Building a Community with a Shared Future for Mankind

汪明义 等 著

中国出版集团
中译出版社

四川师范大学全球治理与区域国别研究丛书

人类命运共同体
构建进程指标体系研究

四川师范大学课题组

组　长　汪明义

副组长　高中伟　张海东

成　员　汪明义　高中伟　张海东　吕　京　孙　勇
　　　　谭光辉　雷　勇　郑　涛　陈丽静　甘　娜

The Indicators System on the Process of Building a Community with a Shared Future for Mankind

Task Force on the Community with a Shared Future for Mankind, Sichuan Normal University

Team leader: Wang Mingyi

Deputy team leaders: Gao Zhongwei   Zhang Haidong

Members:

Wang Mingyi	Gao Zhongwei	Zhang Haidong	Lyu Jing	Sun Yong
Tan Guanghui	Lei Yong	Zheng Tao	Chen Lijing	Gan Na

目 录

绪 论　　　　　　　　　　　　　　　　　　　002

第一章　人类命运共同体构建进程
　　　　　政治维度指标体系　　　　　　　　012

第二章　人类命运共同体构建进程
　　　　　经济维度指标体系　　　　　　　　056

第三章　人类命运共同体构建进程
　　　　　文化维度指标体系　　　　　　　　088

第四章　人类命运共同体构建进程
　　　　　安全维度指标体系　　　　　　　　168

第五章　人类命运共同体构建进程
　　　　　生态维度指标体系　　　　　　　　192

附　录　人类命运共同体构建进程
　　　　　安全维度指标体系排序案例　　　　222

后　记　　　　　　　　　　　　　　　　　324

Contents

Introduction 003

Chapter I An Indicator System for Measuring the Process of Building a Community with Shared Future for Mankind: Political Dimension 013

Chapter II An Indicator System for Measuring the Process of Building a Community with a Shared Future for Mankind: Economic Dimensio 057

Chapter III An Indicator System for Measuring the Process of Building a Community with a Shared Future for Mankind: Cultural Dimension 089

Chapter IV An Indicator System for Measuring the Process of Building a Community with a Shared Future for Mankind: Security Dimension 169

Chapter V An Indicator System for Measuring the Process of Building a Community with a Shared Future for Mankind: Ecological Dimension 193

Appendix Ordering of the Indicator System for Measuring the Process of Building a Community with a Shared Future for Mankind: Security Dimension 223

Postscript 325

人类命运共同体
构建进程指标体系研究

The Indicators System on the Process of Building a Community with a Shared Future for Mankind

绪　论

目前，人类已经进入一个高度相互依存的社会。

人类命运共同体理念的提出既是中华优秀传统文化的当代反映，也是中国共产党人 100 年来实践经验的升华，引领着人类文明进步的方向。"人类命运共同体，顾名思义，就是每个民族、每个国家的前途命运都紧紧联系在一起，应该风雨同舟、荣辱与共，努力把我们生于斯、长于斯的这个星球建成一个和睦的大家庭，把世界各国人民对美好生活的向往变成现实"。[①]

人类命运共同体理念为当代社会提供了"平等互信、持久和平、普遍安全、共同繁荣、开放包容、清洁美丽"的人类共同愿景。然而，愿景并非等于现实。由于国情不同、文化差异等诸多因素，当今世界依然是一个不安宁的世界，面临和平、

---

① 习近平. 携手建设更加美好的世界 [N]. 人民日报, 2017-12-02. http://politics.people.com.cn/n1/2017/1202/c1024-29681216.html

Introduction

The human beings are living in a world where people are highly interdependent on each other.

The proposing of the concept of the community with a shared future for mankind not merely reflects the Chinese traditional culture in modern sense, but raises the best practices of the Communist Party of China (CPC) over the past century to a higher level, showing the way for the development of civilization for the mankind. "As the term suggests, the community with a shared future for mankind means that the future of each and every nation and country is interlocked. We are in the same boat, and we should stick together, share weal and woe, endeavor to build this planet of ours into a single harmonious family, and turn people's longing for a better life into reality". [1]

The concept of a Community with a Shared Future for Mankind provides the world today with a common vision featuring "equality, mutual trust, lasting peace, universal security, common prosperity, openness, tolerance, cleanliness and beauty". However, this vision does not necessarily turn into reality. Due to national and cultural differences, unrest is still a major

---

[1] Xi Jinping. Working together to Build a Better World [N]. People's Daily. 2017-12-02. http://politics.people.com.cn/n1/2017/1202/c1024-29681216.html

发展、治理、信誉"四大赤字"。其具体表现为：一是极端的国家权力观依然盛行，霸权主义和强权政治还在世界范围横行；二是狭隘的国家利益观依然盛行，贸易保护主义和逆全球化势力开始抬头；三是西方文明中心论与文化多元的现实冲突激烈；四是片面的国家安全观依然盛行，以扩张谋求安全和以孤立逃避风险的心态依旧；五是功利的生态观依然盛行，对发展中国家的生态破坏、资源掠夺与生态危机输出未能得到有效遏制。所以，"人类命运共同体"不仅是要共享发展的成果，也意味着共同分担责任，共渡难关。

2019年底开始全球范围内爆发的新冠疫情，现已导致上亿人感染成百万人死亡。风雨同舟、患难与共的人类命运共同体意识在抗击疫情中释放出强大感召力。

大学理应成为构建人类命运共同体的中流砥柱。[①] 大学在人才培养、科学研究、服务社会、文化传承与创新、国际交流合作等方面的独特优势，为构建人类命运共同体夯实教育基础。大学通过培养具有世界眼光和专业素质的时代新人，为构建人类命运共同体提供强有力的人才支撑。大学通过提供科学研究和创新技术支撑，为构建人类命运共同体创造强大驱动。大学通过推进人类文明的传承与创新，为构建人类命运共同体筑牢

---

① 汪明义. 大学理应成为构建人类命运共同体的中流砥柱 [J]. 探索与争鸣，2019 (09): 8-11.

threat to today's world. Mankind runs peace, development, governance, and credibility deficits. First, an extreme view on state power is prevalent — hegemonism and power politics are rampant worldwide; second, a narrow view on national interests is prevalent — trade protectionism and anti-globalization sentiment are on the rise; third, Western-centrism runs totally contrary to the reality of cultural diversity; fourth, a one-sided view on national security is prevalent — the mentality to ensure security through expansion and avoid risks through isolation is as strong as ever; fifth, a utilitarian view on ecological improvement is prevalent — ecological damage, resource plundering and eco-crisis export to the detriment of developing countries continue unbated. "A Community with a Shared Future for Mankind" is built for mankind to share not only the fruits of development, but also the responsibility for tiding over difficulties.

The worldwide outbreak of COVID-19 at the end of 2019 has left hundreds of millions of people infected and millions dead. "Stand together through storm and stress", "come together through thick and thin" and similar ideas associated with the Community with a Shared Future for Mankind have held considerable appeal in the fight against COVID-19.

Universities should be the chief builder of the Community with a Shared Future for Mankind.[①] Universities, with intellectual superiority in talent production, scientific research, social services, cultural inheritance and innovation, and international communication and cooperation, lay a solid educational foundation for building a Community with a Shared Future for Mankind. Universities produce professionals with a global vision; they are the talent necessary for the building of a Community with a Shared Future for Mankind. Universities conduct innovative scientific research to provide momentum for building a Community with a Shared Future for Mankind.

---

① Wang Mingyi. Universities As the Chief Builder of the Community with a Shared Future for Mankind [J]. Exploration and Free Views, 2019 (09) :8-11.)

思想根基。大学通过服务经济社会需求，为构建人类命运共同体增添新动力。大学通过国际间的交流合作，为构建人类命运共同体营造良好氛围。①

习近平总书记在第二届"一带一路"国际合作高峰论坛开幕式上发表主旨演讲时指出："我们要积极架设不同文明互学互鉴的桥梁，深入开展教育、科学、文化、体育、旅游、卫生、考古等各领域人文合作，加强议会、政党、民间组织往来，密切妇女、青年、残疾人等群体交流，形成多元互动的人文交流格局。"这为包括大学在内的教育领域人文交流合作指明了方向，也为大学在推动构建人类命运共同体中发挥重要作用提出了新的更高要求。

综上所述，由大学来开展相关研究，对构建人类命运共同体进程中的诸多要素进行探讨，如构建人类命运共同体进程中面临的风险挑战、相配套的国际机制和国际平台、相关的国际制度等，并对如何建构世界秩序进行思考，创建操作性较强的指标体系，进行科学测评，提出切实可行的能够调动各国积极有效参与的对策已成为一个很有价值的课题。

为此，四川师范大学成立了"人类命运共同体构建进程指标体系研究"课题组，在建构指标体系时，坚持以下原则：

---

① 杜玉波. 大学在构建人类命运共同体中的使命担当[J]. 探索与争鸣，2019 (09): 5-7.

Universities inherit and innovate human civilization to lay an ideological foundation for building a Community with a Shared Future for Mankind. Universities serve economic and social needs to add impetus to the building of a Community with a Shared Future for Mankind. Universities promote international communication and cooperation to create a premium environment for the building of a Community with a Shared Future for Mankind.[①]

In his keynote speech at the opening ceremony of The Second Belt and Road Forum for International Cooperation, General Secretary Xi Jinping said, "We will build bridges for mutual learning between civilizations, promote people-to-people cooperation in education, science, culture, sports, tourism, healthcare, and archeology, and increase exchanges between parliaments, political parties and non-governmental organizations, as well as between women, youth and the disabled, to promote diversified interaction." This points people-to-people exchanges and cooperation in the education sector (universities included) in the right direction and lays down new and higher requirements for universities' role in building a Community with a Shared Future for Mankind.

In a nutshell, universities are well positioned to conduct research into the Community with a Shared Future for Mankind. They can consider the multiple factors involved in the building of a community with a shared Future for Mankind, such as the risks and challenges facing it and the international systems, mechanisms, and platforms necessary for it, explore ways of maintaining the world order, build an operable indicator system, carry out scientific evaluations, and suggest practical measures that appeal to all countries.

To this end, Sichuan Normal University (SICNU) has established the Task Force on the Indicators System on the Process of Building a Community with a Shared Future for Mankind (the Task Force). The following principles

---

① Du Yubo. Universities' Mission in Building a Community with a Shared Future for Mankind [J]. Exploration and Free Views, 2019 (09): 5-7.

（1）全面性原则。人类命运共同体的构建在覆盖面上较为广泛，它要求所需构建的指标体系可以综合全面地呈现出某一时期内人类命运共同体的总体发展水平和进程，能从多角度展现出人类命运共同体的新图景。

（2）科学性原则。指标体系在构建时应充分考虑到不同国家尤其当前世界一些中等收入国家以及欠发达国家发展的平均水平来制定构建人类命运共同体的评价标准。

（3）可比性原则。由于人类命运共同体建设评价指标体系不仅要能够对某一确定国家人类命运共同体构建的快慢进行纵向比较，还要能够揭示横向国家之间构建人类命运共同体的差距。

（4）可操作性原则。鉴于指标体系构建的目的在于应用，所以在设计指标体系时应充分考虑相关数据资料是否具备可获得性、共有性、可操作性。

人类命运共同体构建进程指标体系框架包括政治、经济、文化、安全以及生态等五个维度。五个维度自成五章，每章包括目的和意义、指导思想、构建原则、指标体系框架以及指标赋权方法等五个部分。每个维度包括一级指标（范畴）、二级指标（测度）、三级指标（观测点）及备注。一级指标体系下设 N 个二级指标、二级指标下设 N 个三级指标及备注构成。在选取二级指标、三级指标及权数确定时，尽可能统筹各国政治、经济、文化、安全以及生态相关因素。

任何的量化指标只能显现构建人类命运共同体在某一个方面的发展水平和发展状态，不能反映构建人类命运共同体的全

must be observed in developing the indicators system:

(1) The principle of comprehensiveness. The building of a Community with a Shared Future for Mankind involves a wide range of factors. So the indicator system to be built must comprehensively reflect the overall development across time and present its new image from multiple perspectives.

(2) The principle of scientificity. The indicator system being established should factor in the average of development-related indicators of different countries especially middle-income countries and that of underdeveloped countries.

(3) The principle of comparability. The indicator system for measuring the building of the Community with a Shared Future for Mankind should be able to compare the speed of the building processes of specific countries and discover the gap between them.

(4) The principle of operability. Since the purpose of building the indicator system is application, the availability, commonality, and operability of relevant data should be fully considered in the design of the indicator system.

This research includes political, economic, cultural, security and ecological dimensions. Each dimension constitutes one chapter, and each chapter includes five parts: purpose and significance, guiding ideology, guiding principles, framework of indicator system and indicator weighting. Each dimension includes Tier 1 indicators (categories), Tier 2 indicators (measures), Tier 3 indicators (observation points) and the remarks on them. The Tier 1 indicators include N Tier 2 indicators, and the Tier 2 indicators consist of N Tier 3 indicators and the remarks on them. The Tier 2 and Tier 3 indicators are selected and their weights are assigned in such a way as to cover the political, economic, cultural, security and ecological factors of all countries.

A quantitative indicator can only partially measure the quality and level of building a Community with a Shared Future for Mankind; it cannot capture what is happening on all dimensions because evaluation involves

部内涵，况且评测涉及到许多层面的指标。本研究在于创建人类命运共同体构建进程评价指标体系，并试着应用该评价指标体系去评估和引导世界主要国家以及国际组织为推动构建人类命运共同体做出应有的贡献。

需要指出的是，人类命运共同体作为全球治理进程中的一种社会状态，不是孤立存在和静止不动的。因此，在确立各项评价指标时，既要能综合地反映出比原有水平的明显进步与全面发展，又要保证与人类命运共同体构建目标的衔接性和连贯性，用发展的眼光看待问题，使之成为一个动态评价系统。在研究过程中，各个维度尽可能在指标体系风格上保持基本一致，同时又根据研究问题及其选取指标的差异性，各自保留了适当灵活度。这样有助于指标体系对人类命运共同体构建进程的评价更加科学。

a large number of indicators. This study is innovative in that it creates an indicator system for measuring the process of building a Community with a Shared Future for Mankind and endeavors to use this indicator system to inspire major countries and international organizations to get actively involved in this worldwide project.

It should be stressed, however, that the Community with a Shared Future for Mankind is a state of society in global governance; it's not an isolated phenomenon, nor is it still. Therefore, the indicators should reflect obvious progress and overall development and maintain coherence with the goal of building a Community with a Shared Future for Mankind. We should make sure to observe the evolution of problems and make it a dynamic evaluation system. In our research, we make sure all the communities follow basically the same style, and at the same time allow for some flexibility depending on the problems under study and the difference between the indicators. This will make our indicator system scientific in evaluation.

第一章
人类命运共同体构建进程政治维度指标体系

一、目的和意义

党的十九大报告指出:"世界正处于大发展大变革大调整时期,和平与发展仍然是时代主题。同时,世界面临的不稳定性不确定性突出,人类面临许多共同挑战。"一方面,随着经济全球化和信息技术的发展,各国之间的联系和交流不断加强,人类世界已经成为一个命运休戚与共、利益密切相关的有机整体,任何一个国家都不可能在封闭的状态下求得发展。另一方面,人类也面临着诸多挑战,如一些发展中国家和发达国家之间的差距不断拉大,霸权主义和强权政治也逐渐显现,恐怖主义和极端主义、难民危机、重大传染性疾病以及气候变化等问题持续蔓延,领土争端、地区冲突时有发

Chapter I
An Indicator System for Measuring the Process of Building a Community with Shared Future for Mankind: Political Dimension

I. Purpose and Significance

According to the report at the 19th CPC National Congress, "The world is undergoing major developments, transformation, and adjustment, but peace and development remain the call of our day. And yet, as a world we face growing uncertainties and destabilizing factors. As human beings we have many common challenges to face." As the economy globalizes and information technology develops, countries around the world are establishing effective communication, and the human world is becoming an organic whole where we share weal and woe and act in common interest. No one country can hope to achieve development without seeking cooperation with others. Mankind is also faced with a cornucopia of challenges. The gap between some developing countries and the developed world continues to widen, hegemonism and power politics are rampant, terrorism, extremism, refugee crises, major communicable diseases and climate change are making their impact increasingly felt, and territorial disputes and regional conflicts surface from time to time to threaten world peace

生，威胁世界的和平与稳定。具体表现在以下几个方面。

第一，文化和制度差异未被包容。一些西方国家不能真正包容文化、制度差异。西方国家奉行自由主义的政策，坚持个人主义的原则，重视个人自由、个人权利、个人利益，奉行优胜劣汰、成王败寇规则。信奉"人人为自己，上帝为大家""走自己的路，让别人无路可走"的极端个人主义座右铭。因此，在当代国际关系实践中，一些西方大国就抱着零和思维、冷战思维、修昔底德陷阱思维不放，对合作共赢理念不屑一顾，用经济民族主义对抗全球主义，带着资本主义的有色眼镜诋毁社会主义，不能真正包容世界其他文化和社会制度的差异，唯我独尊。与此相对，以中国为代表的东方国家的传统观念以及现在作为社会主义国家的价值取向则是社会本位的。他人、集体、国家乃至世界相对个人、家庭而言是优先考虑的，信奉着"大河里涨水小河里满""身无半亩，心忧天下"这样的道理。

第二，和平与安全理念未得到认可。自20世纪90年代初始，东欧剧变，苏联解体，冷战结束，世界呈现多极化发展态势。特别是以"金砖国家"为代表的新兴经济体迅速崛起，世界和平发展有了越来越大的保障。但是，美国垄断集团感到自己的霸权地位受到挑战，霸权红利（Hegemony Bonuses）岌岌可危，于是把斗争矛盾直接对准中国、俄罗斯等所谓"竞争对手"。这样，使得世界和平局面波诡云谲，风险重重。在安全观上，中国奉行"综合安全""共同安全"和"合作安全"的新安全观，核心内容是国家之间互信、互利、平等和协

and stability. The specific causes of these challenges are listed as follows.

1. Intolerance to cultural and institutional differences. Some western countries do not really tolerate cultural and institutional differences. They follow a policy of liberalism, adhere to the principle of individualism, value individual freedom, rights and interests, and pursue a "survival of the fittest" and "winner takes all" strategy. They use ultra-individualistic "Every man for himself, and God for us all" and "Go your own way even if it leaves others with no choice" as their mottoes. As a result, some western powers adopt a zero-sum mentality, Cold War thinking and a Thucydides trap mindset when handling contemporary international relations. They shrug off the concept of win-win cooperation, confront globalism with economic nationalism, and denigrate socialism indiscriminatingly. All these reflect their egotistic streak and intolerance to cultural and institutional differences. In contrast, eastern countries with China as the leading representative endorse traditional views and socialist values in which society is established as the sole criterion. In their view, others, the collective, the country and even the world take precedence over individuals and families. They see truth in sayings like "The big river in flood supplies water to small ones" and "One must put his country first however impoverished he is."

2. Marginalization of peace and security. The drastic changes in Eastern Europe, the disintegration of the former Soviet Union and the end of the Cold War in the early 1990s brought the world into multi-polarization. The rapid rise of emerging economies like the BRICS countries has offered the world a firm guarantee of peace and development. However, the United States and its followers see this as a challenge to their supremacy and a threat to their hegemony bonuses. They put China and Russia, the so-called "competitors", in the crosshairs, causing sudden and perplexing changes to world peace and stability. China has formulated new concepts of security such as "comprehensive security," "common security," and "cooperative security" with mutual trust, mutual benefit, equality and cooperation at the core. However, a handful of western countries, especially the United States, hold the stereotyped view that security is a zero-sum

作。然而，以美国为首的少数西方国家却秉持安全关系是零和的陈腐观念，追求军事优势和绝对安全，大力发展军事实力。在实践上，美国特朗普政府上台加快了谋求单极霸权的步伐。2019年美国国防预算高达7 163亿美元，比上年增加12%，相当于其他9个军费开支位居前列国家的总和。不仅如此，美国2018年退出《伊核协议》，2019年又退出与苏联签署的《中导条约》，以朝核问题为借口对朝鲜极限施压，派遣航母侵扰中国南海，等等。美国种种所为，打破全球战略平衡，破坏了地区和全球安全稳定，致使世界和平面临极大风险。

第三，南北发展差距未有机会弥合。这种差距主要表现在三个方面：其一是人类发展差距。联合国开发计划署（UNDP）曾经提出"人类发展指数（HDI）"这一概念，用以衡量国别人类的发展程度。这些发展指数主要包括：预期寿命指数，用以衡量过上健康生活的能力；受教育年限指数，用以衡量获取知识的能力；人均国民收入指数，用以衡量过上体面生活的能力。近30年来，经多方努力，全球人类发展已经取得了实质性进展。2017年全球HDI是0.728，比1990年的0.598上升21.7%，但是国别差距仍然很大。HDI最高的挪威（0.953）是最低的尼日尔（0.354）的2.7倍。在预期寿命上，最高的中国香港（84.1岁）是最低的塞拉利昂（52.2）的1.6倍；在平均受教育年限上，最高的德国（14.1年）是最低的布基纳法索（1.5年）的9.4倍；在人均国民收入上，按2011年为基期的购买力评价计算，最高的卡塔尔（116 818美元）是最低的中非共和国（663美元）的176倍。其二是发展速度差距。霸权主义、不合理的国际经济

game. They seek to establish military superiority and ensure absolute security through military expansion. In effect, the Trump administration went further towards unipolar hegemony. The 2019 US defense budget reached up to $716.3 billion, an increase of 12% over the previous year and equivalent to the sum of the military spending of the other top nine military spenders. Moreover, the United States withdrew from the *Iranian Nuclear Deal* in 2018, and in 2019, it withdrew from the *Intermediate-Range Nuclear Forces Treaty* signed with the former Soviet Union. It exerted maximum pressure on North Korea under the pretext of the North Korea nuclear issue and sent aircraft carriers to the South China Sea to "contain" China. All these actions have upset the global strategic balance, undermined regional and global stability, and posed a real risk to world peace.

3. Widening gap between North and South. The gap is manifest first in human development. The United Nations Development Program (UNDP) compiled the "Human Development Index (HDI)" to rank countries into four tiers of human development. These indices include the life expectancy index which measures the ability to live a healthy life, the education index which measures the ability to acquire knowledge, and the per capita national income index which measures the ability to live a decent life. Thanks to the joint efforts of multiple sides, substantial progress has been made in global human development over the past 30 years. In 2017, the global HDI was 0.728, up 21.7% from 0.598 in 1990, but the gap across countries remained large. Norway had the highest HDI (0.953), 2.7 times that (0.354, the lowest) of Niger. Hong Kong, China, had the highest life expectancy (84.1), 1.6 times that (52.2, the lowest) of Sierra Leone; Germany had the highest mean years (14.1) of schooling, 9.4 times that (1.5, the lowest) of Burkina Faso; in terms of purchasing power parity with 2011 as the base period, Qatar had the highest per capita national income ($116,818), 176 times that ($663, the lowest) of Central African Republic. The gap is manifest secondly in the speed of development. Hegemonism and the irrational old international economic order are the major reasons behind inequality in global development. In order to seek hegemony

旧秩序是导致全球发展不平等的重要原因。以美国为首的西方发达国家发动伊拉克战争、阿富汗战争、利比亚战争，以及直接插手叙利亚内战，是为了争夺中东、中亚的霸权，其后果是严重阻碍了这些地区的发展。其三是经济话语权大小的差距。2008年西方爆发金融、经济危机，发达国家通过减少进口和对外投资，直接向发展中国家转嫁危机。美国还联合少数发达国家对中国、印度等发展中国家发起了大规模的贸易战。通过提高关税、严格高技术产品出口管制等措施，实行贸易保护主义和贸易霸凌主义，导致全球经济放缓，以致广大发展中国家雪上加霜。在全球性国际经济组织、行业协会上，发达国家也在一定程度上掌握了贸易规则、贷款条件、技术标准的制定权、表决权，形成制度霸权（Institutional Hegemony），导致不公平、不合理的国际经济旧秩序，获取不正当利益。

第四，人类与自然关系未能和谐共生。生态环境是人类的生存家园。一方面，越来越多的发展中国家在工业化、现代化的过程中，在取得经济社会进步的同时，其生态环境也在一定程度上遭到破坏。另一方面，越来越多的发展中国家已跨入中等收入国家行列。追求美好生活开始成为发展的重要目标，形成良好的生态环境正在成为世界大多数国家的共识。但是，全球生态环境治理却步履艰难，困难重重。经济上产业结构转型升级面对科技研发、大量不熟练劳动力等因素的约束，不可能一蹴而就。在发展经济、扩大就业、增加收入与保护环境之间，在生存权、发展权与环境权之间存在一定程度的尖锐矛盾。更为重要的原因是，并非所有的人和国家

in the Middle East and Central Asia, developed western countries, with the United States as the head, fought the Iraq War, the Afghanistan War, and the Libya War and intervened in the Syrian Civil War. As a result, development in these areas was hindered. The gap is manifest thirdly in economic discourse power. In 2008, a financial and economic crisis arose in the West. Developed countries shifted the burden of the crisis to developing countries by reducing imports and investments abroad. The United States started a full-scale trade war against developing countries such as China and India in collaboration with a handful of other developed countries. They raised tariffs and tightened high-tech export controls in the pursuit of trade protectionism and trade bullying, resulting in global economic slowdown and casting a shadow on the economic prospects of developing countries. To a certain degree, developed countries dominate the formulation and approval of trade rules, terms of credit and technical standards in international economic organizations and global industry associations. Their institutional hegemony in an unfair, unreasonable old international economic order brought them ill-gotten gains.

4. Failure on the part of mankind and nature to coexist. Mankind depends on the eco-environment for survival. On the one hand, a growing number of developing countries have wrecked their eco-environment in their industrialization and modernization drive, though they have achieved some socio-economic progress. On the other hand, more developing countries are joining the ranks of middle-income countries. A better life is beginning to become one of the major goals of development, and a favorable eco-environment is becoming the consensus of most countries in the world. However, the governance of the global eco-environment is struggling to overcome a horde of difficulties. The transformation and upgrading of the industrial structure will not happen overnight due to, among others, the lack of technological achievements and an experienced labor force. Economic development, employment expansion, and income increase are found to be incongruous with environmental protection; the right to subsistence and the right to development are found to contradict the right

都能以积极的态度对待生态环境问题。"吉登斯悖论"(Giddens Paradox)表明,既然气候变化在人们的生活中不直接、不具体、不可见,也就很少有人认识到它的严重性进而采取行动。美国本来有财力、技术在全球气候治理上做出更大的贡献,却把应对全球气候变暖当作制约别国发展和维持自己霸权的战略手段。美国颇为明显的损招是,2001年小布什政府退出了减少温室气体排放的《京都议定书》。2017年特朗普政府又退出了应对气候变化的《巴黎协定》,使得全球气候治理机制再次遭到重创。

总的说来,以上全球性问题集中表现为全球公共产品供给短缺。无论是国际安全体系,还是国际货币制度、自由贸易体系、世界气候协调、国际知识产权保护、国际技术标准形成等等,因为作为国际公共产品,其收益和成本的非对称性,以美国为首的少数西方国家从一己之私出发,不愿意承担全球公共产品供给责任,有将整个世界拖入全球性问题泛滥国际失序的"金德尔伯格陷阱"(Kindleberger Trap)的风险。

因此,构建人类命运共同体的政治维度指标体系就具有十分重要的理论价值和现实意义。

其一,和谐国与国的关系。构建人类命运共同体的政治维度指标体系有利于妥善处理不同国家之间的政治差异和政治分歧,寻求共识以及求同存异、彼此尊重的公共理性,维护世界和平。世界是多样的,不同国家在地理位置、历史条件、文化传统、民族构成等方面存在较大的差异,所选择的

to the environment. More importantly, not all people and countries maintain a positive attitude towards ecological and environmental issues. According to the Giddens Paradox, climate change is not direct, concrete or visible in people's lives, therefore few appreciate its gravity and take action accordingly. With the financial resources and technologies it has available, the United States could have made greater contributions to global climate governance. However, it seeks to contain the development of others and maintain its hegemony under the pretext of responding to global warming. In 2001, the US government under George W. Bush made a downright sinister move. It withdrew from the *Kyoto Protocol* on reducing greenhouse gas emissions. In 2017, the Trump administration withdrew from the *Paris Agreement* on self-imposed targets for emissions reduction, dealing another blow to the global mechanism for climate governance.

To sum up, the above global issues arise from the short supply of global public goods. The returns on and the costs of global public goods, whether they are the international security system, the international monetary system, the world free trade system, global climate coordination, the protection of intellectual property rights, or the establishment of international technical standards, are asymmetrical. Some western countries, the United States in particular, are reluctant to assume the responsibility for supplying global public goods. This inundates the world with global issues and catches it in the "Kindleberger Trap," which stands for international disorder.

The building of a political indicator system for a community with a shared future for mankind, therefore, is of great theoretical value and practical significance.

1. Harmonious relations among countries. It contributes to the handling of political differences and disputes among countries, the reaching of consensus, the listening to public reason that prioritizes common points over differences and values mutual respect, and the safeguarding of world peace to build a political indicator system for a community with a shared future for mankind. The world is diverse, and countries show vast differences in not only their geographical locations, historical circumstances, cultural traditions, and ethnic makeup,

政治制度和政治发展模式通常也存在较大的不同。当今世界，存在资本主义和社会主义两种社会制度。即使在资本主义世界，不同国家的政治模式也存在着较大的差异。如英国施行的是君主立宪制，美国施行的是总统制。构建人类命运共同体，不是建立以某种政治制度或某种政治发展模式为模版的同一政治，不是用一种政治模式取代其他政治模式，进而建立统一的帝国模式。换言之，人类命运共同体之"同"不是绝对的同一，完全的相同，而是寻求政治发展的相同点和最大公约数。世界上没有完全相同的两片树叶。人类命运共同体是建立在不同社会制度和不同政治发展模式基础之上的共同体，是建立在多样性基础之上的共同体。构建人类命运共同体的政治维度指标体系，有利于超越不同国家政治制度的差异，彼此尊重，以实现世界的和平。

其二，协调各国利益诉求。构建人类命运共同体的政治维度指标体系有利于协调不同国家之间的利益以及国家利益和全球利益的关系，实现共同发展。民族国家是当今世界国际关系的行为主体，维护国家的核心利益是一个国家进行外交活动的主要目标。不同国家存在不同的利益诉求，不同诉求之间有些时候甚至存在矛盾。但是，国家与国家之间是否仅存在竞争关系？或者说一国的发展是否必然影响其他国家利益的实现？构建人类命运共同体的政治维度指标体系，可以更好地解读这样的问题。该指标体系有利于协调不同国家的利益关系，使国家之间摆脱零和博弈的思维，看到其利益的共同点而非分歧点，看到国家之间不只存在竞争关系，更重

but also the political systems and models of political development they choose. Capitalism and socialism are the two social systems in today's world. Political models differ across countries; those in the capitalist world are no exception. For example, Britain is a constitutional monarchy, while the United States has a presidential system of government. The building of a community with a shared future for mankind is not the building of one and the same political system or model of political development, nor the replacement of one political model by another one for the purpose of creating a unified model of empire. In other words, the concept of "community" in the term "community with a shared future for mankind" does not suggest unconditional sameness. It refers to the common ground and the greatest common divisor of political development. No two leaves are absolutely identical in the world. The community with a shared future for mankind is built upon diverse social systems and models of political development. It is based on diversity. It bypasses the differences in political systems, builds mutual respect, and contributes to world peace to build a political indicator system for a community with a shared future for mankind.

2. Coordination of the interests and appeals of all countries. It facilitates better coordination in interests between nations and between nations and the globe and promotes common development to build a political indicator system for a community with a shared future for mankind. Nation states play central roles on the current world stage, and countries undertake diplomatic activities mainly to safeguard their core interests. Different countries have different interests and appeals. These interests and appeals are sometimes mutually contradictory. Yet is competition the only thing going on between countries? Does the development of one country necessarily act against the interests of others? A political indicator system for a community with a shared future for mankind will offer adequate answers to these questions. This indicator system will help to coordinate the interests of countries, urge them to ditch zero-sum mentality, and put common interests and cooperation opportunities before differences and competitive relationships. In addition, the relationship between national interests and global interests can be put in terms of one between the part and

要的是合作关系。此外,国家利益和全球利益的关系是部分与整体的关系。部分离不开整体,整体功能的好坏决定了部分功能的好坏。构建人类命运共同体政治维度指标体系,有利于实现国家利益和全球利益的有机统一。

其三,促进国际关系民主化。构建人类命运共同体政治维度指标体系有利于实现国际关系的民主化,增强各国人民在国际事务中的主体性,建立公平、正义的国际政治新秩序。在当今世界政治舞台上,以美国为代表的少数西方国家企图主宰世界,它们向发展中国家推销自己的政治制度和发展模式,干涉别国内政,推行其霸权主义和强权政治。这不仅不利于国际社会的稳定,而且不利于国际关系的民主化。世界历史是各国人民共同参与创造的,世界事务理应由各国人民共同决定,世界交往的规则理应由各国人民共同制定,发展成果理应由各国人民共同享有。构建人类命运共同体政治维度指标体系,有利于为国际关系提供公平、正义的价值标准和行为准则,反对西方国家的霸权主义,增强发展中国家的代表性和发言权,维护广大发展中国家的权利,真正实现国家不分大小、强弱、一律平等,形成共商共建共享的治理格局,建立公平、正义的国际政治新秩序。

二、指导思想

(一)马克思、恩格斯的人类共同体思想

早在中学时期,马克思就树立了为人类的事业而奋斗的人生理想。人类解放是马克思、恩格斯毕生追求的理想。马克思、恩

the whole. The part is inseparable from the whole, and the performance of the whole determines that of the individual parts. It strikes a balance between national interests and global interests to build a political indicator system for a community with a shared future for mankind.

3. Democracy in international relations. It supports democracy in international relations, promotes national initiative in settling international affairs, and maintains new international political order that is equitable and impartial to build a political indicator system for a community with a shared future for mankind. Some western countries, especially the United States, attempt to dominate the world's political stage today. Active in hegemonism and power politics, they peddle their political systems and models of development to developing countries and interfere in other countries' internal affairs. This is detrimental not only to the stability of the international community, but also to democracy in international relations. World history is written by all, therefore every country is entitled to settle world affairs, formulate rules for contact, and share development achievements with others. It provides a fair, just set of values and codes of conduct for handling international relations, contributes to the opposition of Western hegemonism, builds up developing countries' representativeness, protects their right to speech, safeguards the rights of developing countries, ensures equality for all countries regardless of size or strength, creates a governance structure featuring wide consultation, co-building and sharing, and maintains new international political order that is equitable and impartial to build an indicator system for a community with a shared future for mankind: Political Dimension.

II. Guiding Ideology

(I) Marx and Engels' Thoughts on Community for Mankind

Marx pursued the ideal of furthering the cause of mankind as early as middle school. Human liberation was the life-long goal of Marx and Engels. According to Marx and Engels, "The community is the only place where individuals have the

格斯认为,"只有在共同体中,个人才能获得全面发展其才能的手段。也就是说,只有在共同体中才可能有个人自由"。马克思认为资本主义社会的共同体是"虚假的共同体"。资本主义的基本矛盾,即生产的社会化同生产资料私有制之间的矛盾是无法调和的。它把人与人之间的关系异化为物与物的关系,导致人的个性和共同利益无法获得真正的实现。因此,资本主义国家仅仅是资产阶级进行阶级统治从而实现自己特殊利益的工具,是"虚假共同体"。在批判资本主义社会"虚假共同体"的基础上,马克思、恩格斯提出了"真正的共同体"思想。在他们看来,真正的共同体只有在共产主义社会才能实现;共产主义社会是自由人的联合体,联合起来的个人共同占有生产资料,有计划地分配社会劳动时间,生活资料实行按需分配,劳动者的能力和个性得到全面发展。此外,马克思还提出,社会生产力的发展、社会分工的扩大,必然形成普遍交往,最终使人类由国别历史走向世界历史。构建人类命运共同体政治维度指标体系必须坚持以马克思、恩格斯的人类共同体思想为指导,着眼于整个人类的发展。

(二)党的十九大精神和关于构建人类命运共同体的重要论述

党的十九大精神以及习近平新时代中国特色社会主义思想,尤其是关于构建人类命运共同体的重要论述的精神,对构建人类命运共同体政治维度指标体系有着重要的指导作用。自党的十八大召开以来,习近平总书记对构建人类命运共同体的必要性、基本内涵和主要路径等进行了系统地阐释。党

means to fully tap their talents. In other words, personal freedom is possible only in communities." Marx holds that the capitalist community is a "false community". The fundamental contradiction within capitalism is the reconcilable contradiction between socialized production and the private ownership of the means of production. It downgrades interpersonal relationships to those between objects, making personality and common interests unachievable. In this sense, the capitalist regime is nothing but a tool of the bourgeoisie to rule other classes and exercise their privileges. It is a "false community." Marx and Engels introduced the concept of "true community" and built it upon their critique of the "false community" in the capitalist society. In their view, a true community is achievable only in a communist society; the communist society is a union of free people where united individuals share the means of production, systematically allocate time for social production, and distribute consumer goods on demand. In a true community, laborers have the chance to fully develop their abilities and personality. Marx also pointed out that the development of social productive forces and the further division of labor in society inevitably facilitate widespread contacts and eventually result in globalization. Marx and Engels' thoughts on "community for mankind," which investigate the development of the entire human race, are the guiding principles for building an indicator system for a community with a shared future for mankind: Political Dimension.

(II) The Spirit of the 19th CPC National Congress and Important Remarks on Building a Community with a Shared Future for Mankind

The spirit of the 19th CPC National Congress and Xi Jinping's thoughts on socialism with Chinese characteristics for a new era, especially those on building a community with shared future for mankind, serve to guide the building of a political indicator system for a community with a shared future for mankind. Since the 18th CPC National Congress, General Secretary Xi jinping has systematically elucidated the necessity, basic content and main ways of building a community with shared future for mankind. The twelfth part of the report at the 19th CPC National Con-

的十九大报告的第十二部分"坚持和平发展道路,推动构建人类命运共同体"进一步深入阐释了构建人类命运共同体的丰富内涵和时代价值。

(三)中国优秀传统政治文化

中华民族自古以来热爱和平,崇尚和谐,反对战争,蕴含着丰富的政治智慧。中国的"和"文化蕴涵着协和万邦的世界观、和而不同的交往观、人心向善的道德观。孔子主张"泛爱众,能亲仁","有朋自远方来,不亦乐乎";孟子主张"亲亲而仁民,仁民而爱物";孙子反对战争,他说:"百战百胜,非善之善也;不战而屈人之兵,善之善者也"。墨子主张博爱,提出"兼相爱,交相利"。毫无疑问,如此深邃的中华优秀传统政治文化,对构建人类命运共同体政治维度指标体系具有重要的借鉴意义。

三、构建原则

构建人类命运共同体政治维度指标体系可以遵循下列原则。

第一,科学性原则。指标的选择要以构建人类命运共同体的相关重要论述为基础。从人类政治生活的实际出发,准确地反映国际政治的现实情况和主要特点,注意指标的实证性。

第二,系统性原则。指标的选择要全面、系统地反映当今世界国际政治发展的主要内容,注意分析各种指标之间的内在逻辑关系。

gress, titled "Following a Path of Peaceful Development and Working to Build a Community with a Shared Future for Mankind," further interprets the rich content and contemporary value of building a community with shared future for mankind.

(III) China's Excellent Traditional Political Culture

The politically wise Chinese nation loves peace, fosters harmony and opposes war. China's culture of "harmony" incorporates a world outlook that values peace among all nations, a contact outlook that advocates harmony in diversity, and a moral outlook that endorses the inclination to goodness. Confucius said, "Love all and befriend those who are benevolent ... It's a pleasure to have friends from afar." Mencius said, "The love for your loved ones can extend to all people and objects." Sun Tzu opposed war, saying, "Coming out victorious in every battle is not the ultimate objective; subduing the enemy without fighting is the ideal approach." Mozi advocated love for humanity, saying, "When there is mutual care, the world will be in peace; when there is mutual hatred, the world will be in chaos." Undoubtedly, the profound excellent traditional Chinese political culture provides a frame of reference for the building of an indicator system for a community with a shared future for mankind: Political Dimension.

III. Guiding Principles

The following guiding principles apply to the building of a political indicator system for a community with a shared future for mankind.

(I) Scientificity. The indicators selected should be based on important remarks on building a community with a shared future for mankind, proceed from actual human political life, reflect the status quo and main characteristics of international politics, and be empirical.

(II) Systematicness. The indicators selected should comprehensively and systematically reflect international political developments and apply certain internal logic.

第三，可操作性原则。指标的选择要具体，做到可收集、可量化、可比较，尤其是对世界主要国家或有代表性的国家能进行比较分析。

第四，动态性原则。指标的选择要注意跟踪国际政治形势的变化，反映不同国家在一定历史时期内对人类命运共同体建设的政策变化。

四、指标体系框架

根据推动构建人类命运共同体的相关重要论述，结合当今世界的时代主题和国际政治的主要特点，设立如下人类命运共同体的政治维度指标体系。

（一）和平的范畴

1. 遵守联合国宪章和有关决议（5个观测点）

1.1 缴纳成员国会费，参加联合国所属机构

1.2 维护国际和平与安全，发展友好关系，互相尊重主权和领土完整，不干涉别国内政

1.3 依据联合国宗旨，秉持公平正义，在联合国提出动议和投票表决

1.4 切实履行联合国有关决议，积极参与联合国维和行动、国际反恐行动和联合边防行动

(III) Operability. The indicators selected should be specific, collectable, quantifiable and comparable, and most importantly, can be applied to compare and analyze major or representative countries.

(IV) Dynamicity. The indicators selected should be able to track changes on the international political landscape and reflect the policy changes made by different countries in building a community with a shared future for mankind during a certain period.

IV. Framework of Indicator System

The following indicator system for a community with a shared future for mankind: Political Dimension is devised in line with building a community with a shared future for mankind, the theme of the times, and the main characteristics of international politics.

(I) Sphere of Peace Efforts

1. Compliance with the UN Charter and relevant UN resolutions (5 observation points)

1.1 Payment of membership dues and participation in UN-affiliated institutions

1.2 Maintenance of international peace and security, development of friendly relations, display of respect for each other's sovereignty and territorial integrity, and unwillingness to interfere in other countries' internal affairs

1.3 Achievement of fairness and justice, proposing of motions, and deciding by voting in the United Nations in accordance with its purposes

1.4 Earnest implementation of UN resolutions and active involvement in UN peacekeeping operations, anti-terrorism operations and joint border defense operations

1.5 在联合国框架下加强国际网络安全治理

2. 国防政策和国防力量（3个观测点）

2.1 奉行防御性国防政策，裁减军队数量

2.2 军费占 GDP 的比重，军费增幅情况

2.3 在国外驻军或建立军事基地

3. 对待核生化大规模杀伤性武器的态度（3个观测点）

3.1 参加国际原子能机构、《核不扩散条约》等，防核生化武器扩散

3.2 出台并执行核生化武器出口管制法规

3.3 积极参与朝核问题、伊核等地区核问题的解决

4. 解决国际争端、全球问题的方式（5个观测点）

4.1 反对诉诸武力或武力威胁，主张和平解决国际争端

4.2 坚持全球治理的多边主义，反对单边行动

4.3 军事结盟情况

4.4 针对他国的军演次数

4.5 与他国的军事冲突次数

5. 和平利用外太空情况（4个观测点）

5.1 加入《外空条约》

5.2 主张外太空非军事化，和平利用外太空

1.5 Efforts towards stringent global governance of cybersecurity under the framework of the United Nations

2. National defense policies and national defense capabilities (3 observation points)

2.1 Pursuit of a defense policy that is defensive in nature and the reduction of troops

2.2 The proportion of military spending in GDP and the increase in military spending

2.3 Troops or military bases abroad

3. Attitude towards nuclear, chemical and biological weapons of mass destruction (3 observation points)

3.1 Involvement in the International Atomic Energy Agency and the *Nuclear Non-Proliferation Treaty* to prevent the proliferation of nuclear, chemical and biological weapons

3.2 Introduction and implementation of export control regulations on nuclear, chemical and biological weapons

3.3 Active involvement in the settlement of nuclear issues in the DPRK, Iran and other regions

4. Ways to resolve regional and territorial disputes (5 observation points)

4.1 Opposition to the use of force or the threat of force and advocation of peaceful settlement of international disputes

4.2 Advocation of multilateralism in global governance and opposition to unilateral action

4.3 Military alliance

4.4 Number of military exercises against other countries

4.5 Number of military conflicts with other countries

5. Peaceful use of outer space (4 observation points)

5.1 Accession to the *Outer Space Treaty*

5.2 Advocation of demilitarization and peaceful use of outer space

5.3 加强外太空利用的科技合作，促进空间技术的国际合作

5.4 加强外太空利用的法律合作

（二）合作的范畴

1. 政治沟通（4个观测点）

1.1 领导人热线、访问、会晤

1.2 建立伙伴关系

1.3 举办、参加国际论坛或会议

1.4 参加有关国际人权公约、宣言、行动纲领，参加联合国人权委员会会议

2. 经济合作（8个观测点）

2.1 参与、创建多边国际性经济合作组织

2.2 遵守世贸组织协定情况，贸易、投资自由化程度

2.3 双边贸易额和增幅情况、外贸依存度高低

2.4 贸易、投资对本国和世界GDP的贡献

2.5 货币互换和金融监管

2.6 促成国际货币体系稳定和多元化的努力

2.7 区域性投资银行、投资基金设立

2.8 宏观经济政策协调以克服世界经济下行、危机的努力

3. 能源与环境合作（3个观测点）

3.1 能源贸易、投资合作情况

3.2 制定并实施国内环境保护法、环境保护议程或计划

5.3 Promotion of scientific and technological cooperation in outer space utilization and international cooperation in space technology development

5.4 Encouragement of legal cooperation in outer space utilization

(II) Sphere of Cooperation Efforts

1. Political communication (4 observation points)

1.1 Leader hotlines, visits and summits

1.2 Establishment of partnerships

1.3 Organization of and participation in international forums or conferences

1.4 Ratification of international conventions on human rights, declarations and programs of action, and attendance to meetings of the United Nations Human Rights Commission

2. Economic cooperation (8 observation points)

2.1 Involvement in and establishment of multilateral international economic cooperation organizations

2.2 Compliance with the WTO Agreements and degree of trade and investment liberalization

2.3 Volume of bilateral trade and its growth rate; dependence on foreign trade

2.4 Contribution of trade and investment to domestic and world GDP

2.5 Currency swap and financial supervision

2.6 Efforts to promote the stability and diversification of the international monetary system

2.7 Establishment of regional investment banks and investment funds

2.8 Efforts to tackle economic downturn and crisis through the coordination of macro-economic policies

3. Energy and environment cooperation (3 observation points)

3.1 Energy trade and investment cooperation

3.2 Formulation and implementation of domestic environmental protection laws, environmental protection agendas or plans

3.3 加入《巴黎协定》，承担温室气体减排责任

4. 国际救援（3个观测点）

4.1 帮助发展中国家和地区进行基础设施建设

4.2 向发展中国家地区派出医疗队

4.3 参与国际救灾、赈灾

5. 科教、文化、卫生、体育、旅游合作交流（7个观测点）

5.1 科研论文、科技计划和项目国际合作情况

5.2 互派留学生和访问学者、联合培养人才、跨境办学

5.3 知识产权国际保护的努力

5.4 国际卫生、疾控尤其是传染性疾病方面的合作

5.5 国际体育交流和赛事

5.6 友好城市、文化年、电影节、文化展、民众好感度情况

5.7 签订旅游合作协议

6. 反腐败合作（3个观测点）

6.1 加入《联合国反腐败公约》

6.2 签订引渡条约，遣返罪犯

6.3 提供追逃追赃相关信息

7. 反对"三股势力"合作（3个观测点）

7.1 缔结反对"三股势力"的条约

7.2 联合举行反恐军事演习

7.3 开展反对"三股势力"的会晤或论坛

3.3 Signing of the *Paris Agreement* and assumption of responsibility for reducing greenhouse gas emissions

4. International rescue (3 observation points)

4.1 Assistance to developing countries and regions in infrastructure projects

4.2 Dispatch of medical teams to developing countries and regions

4.3 Involvement in international disaster relief

5. Cooperation and exchange in science, education, culture, health, sports and tourism (7 observation points)

5.1 International cooperation in the publication of scientific papers and the implementation of scientific plans and projects

5.2 Exchange of international students and visiting scholars, joint training of talent, and cross-border education

5.3 Efforts towards the international protection of intellectual property rights

5.4 International cooperation in health and disease (especially infectious diseases) control

5.5 International sports exchanges and events

5.6 Sister cities, culture years, film festivals, culture exhibitions and public favor

5.7 Signing of tourism cooperation agreements

6. Anti-corruption cooperation (3 observation points)

6.1 Accession to the *United Nations Convention Against Corruption*

6.2 Signing of extradition treaties to repatriate criminals

6.3 Provision of information related to pursuit evasion and the recovery of booties

7. Cooperation in fighting the "three forces of terrorism, separatism, and extremism" (3 observation points)

7.1 Conclusion of the treaty on fighting the "three forces of terrorism, separatism, and extremism"

7.2 Joint anti-terrorism military exercises

7.3 Holding of meetings or forums to fight the "three forces of terrorism,

8. 反贫困合作（4 个观测点）

8.1 制定反贫困的长远规划

8.2 参与国际社会扶贫项目

8.3 共建国际社会减贫交流合作平台

8.4 开展减贫项目对外援助

（三）指标体系框架附表

表1.1　人类命运共同体构建进程政治维度指标体系

一级指标	二级指标	三级指标
和平的范畴	遵守联合国宪章和有关决议测度	缴纳成员国经费，参与联合国所属机构观测点
		维护国际和平与安全，发展友好关系，互相尊重主权和领土完整，不干涉别国内政观测点
		依据联合国宗旨，秉持公平正义，在联合国提出动议和投票表决观测点
		切实履行联合国有关决议，积极参与联合国维和行动、国际反恐行动和联合边防行动观测点
		在联合国框架下加强国际网络安全治理观测点
	国防政策和国防力量测度	奉行防御性国防政策，裁减军队数量观测点
		军费占 GDP 的比重，军费增幅情况观测点
		在国外驻军或建立军事基地观测点

separatism, and extremism"

8. Cooperation in poverty eradication (4 observation points)

8.1 Formulation of long-term anti-poverty plans

8.2 Involvement in poverty alleviation projects launched by the international community

8.3 Building of platforms for exchanges and cooperation in poverty reduction in the international community

8.4 Implementation of poverty reduction projects and provision of foreign aid

(III) Schedule of Framework of Indicator System

Schedule 1.1 An Indicator System for Measuring the Process of Building a Community with a Shared Future for Mankind: Political Dimension

Tier 1 indicators	Tier 2 indicators	Tier 3 indicators
The sphere of peace efforts	Measure of compliance with the UN Charter and relevant UN resolutions	Observation point for payment of membership dues and participation in UN-affiliated institutions
		Observation point for maintenance of international peace and security, development of friendly relations, display of respect for each other's sovereignty and territorial integrity, and unwillingness to interfere in other countries' internal affairs
		Observation point for achievement of fairness and justice, proposing of motions, and deciding by voting in the United Nations in accordance with its purposes
		Observation point for earnest implementation of UN resolutions and active involvement in UN peacekeeping operations, anti-terrorism operations and joint border defense operations
		Observation point for efforts towards stringent global governance of cybersecurity under the framework of the United Nations
	Measure of national defense policies and national defense capabilities	Observation point for pursuit of a defense policy that is defensive in nature and the reduction of troops
		Observation point for the proportion of military spending in GDP and the increase in military spending
		Observation point for troops or military bases abroad

续表

一级指标	二级指标	三级指标
和平的范畴	对待核生化大规模杀伤性武器的态度测度	参加国际原子能机构、《核不扩散条约》等，防核生化武器扩散观测点
		出台并执行核生化武器出口管制法规观测点
		积极参与朝核问题、伊核等地区核问题的解决观测点
	解决国际争端、全球问题的方式测度	反对诉诸武力或武力威胁，主张和平解决国际争端观测点
		坚持全球治理的多边主义，反对单边行动观测点
		军事结盟情况观测点
		针对他国的军演次数观测点
		与他国的军事冲突次数观测点
	和平利用外太空情况测度	加入《外空条约》观测点
		主张外太空非军事化，和平利用外太空观测点
		加强外太空利用的科技合作，促进空间技术的国际合作观测点
		加强外太空利用的法律合作观测点
合作的范畴	政治沟通测度	领导人热线、访问、会晤观测点
		建立伙伴关系观测点
		举办、参加国际论坛或会议观测点
		参加有关国际人权公约、宣言、行动纲领，参加联合国人权委员会会议观测点
	经济合作测度	参与、创建多边国际性经济合作组织观测点
		遵守世贸组织协定情况，贸易、投资自由化程度观测点

Continued Schedule

Tier 1 indicators	Tier 2 indicators	Tier 3 indicators
The sphere of peace efforts	Measure of attitude towards nuclear, chemical and biological weapons of mass destruction	Observation point for involvement in the International Atomic Energy Agency and the *Nuclear Non-Proliferation Treaty* to prevent the proliferation of nuclear, chemical and biological weapons
		Observation point for introduction and implementation of export control regulations on nuclear, chemical and biological weapons
		Observation point for active involvement in the settlement of nuclear issues in the DPRK, Iran and other regions
	Measure of ways to solve international disputes and global issues	Observation point for opposition to the use of force or the threat of force and advocacy of peaceful settlement of international disputes
		Observation point for advocacy of multilateralism in global governance and opposition to unilateral action
		Observation point for military alliance
		Observation point for number of military exercises against other countries
		Observation point for number of military conflicts with other countries
	Measure of peaceful use of outer space	Observation point for accession to the *Outer Space Treaty*
		Observation point for advocacy of demilitarization and peaceful use of outer space
		Observation point for promotion of scientific and technological cooperation in outer space utilization and international cooperation in space technology development
		Observation point for encouragement of legal cooperation in outer space utilization
The sphere of cooperation efforts	Measure of political communication	Observation point for leader hotlines, visits and summits
		Observation point for establishment of partnerships
		Observation point for organization of and participation in international forums or conferences
		Observation point for ratification of international conventions on human rights, declarations and programs of action, and attendance to meetings of the United Nations Human Rights Commission
	Measure of economic cooperation	Observation point for involvement in and establishment of multilateral international economic cooperation organizations
		Observation point for compliance with the WTO Agreements and degree of trade and investment liberalization

041

续表

一级指标	二级指标	三级指标
合作的范畴	经济合作测度	双边贸易额和增幅情况、外贸依存度高低观测点
		贸易、投资对本国和世界GDP的贡献观测点
		货币互换和金融监管观测点
		促成国际货币体系稳定和多元化的努力观测点
		区域性投资银行、投资基金设立观测点
		宏观经济政策协调以克服世界经济下行、危机的努力观测点
	能源与环境合作测度	能源贸易、投资合作情况观测点
		制定并实施国内环境保护法、环境保护议程或计划观测点
		加入《巴黎协定》，承担温室气体减排责任观测点
	国际救援测度	帮助发展中国家和地区进行基础设施建设观测点
		向发展中国家地区派出医疗队观测点
		参与国际救灾、赈灾观测点
	科教、文化、卫生、体育、旅游合作交流测度	科研论文、科技计划和项目国际合作情况观测点
		互派留学生和访问学者、联合培养人才、跨境办学观测点
		知识产权国际保护的努力观测点
		国际卫生、疾控尤其是传染性疾病方面的合作观测点
		国际体育交流和赛事观测点
		友好城市、文化年、电影节、文化展、民众好感度情况观测点
		签订旅游合作协议观测点

Continued Schedule

Tier 1 indicators	Tier 2 indicators	Tier 3 indicators
The sphere of cooperation efforts	Measure of economic cooperation	Observation point for volume of bilateral trade and its growth rate and dependence on foreign trade
		Observation point for contribution of trade and investment to domestic and world GDP
		Observation point for currency swap and financial supervision
		Observation point for efforts to promote the stability and diversification of the international monetary system
		Observation point for establishment of regional investment banks and investment funds
		Observation point for efforts to tackle economic downturn and crisis through the coordination of macro-economic policies
	Measure of energy and environment cooperation	Observation point for energy trade and investment cooperation
		Observation point for formulation and implementation of domestic environmental protection laws, environmental protection agendas or plans
		Observation point for signing of the *Paris Agreement* and assumption of responsibility for reducing greenhouse gas emissions
	Measure of international rescue	Observation point for assistance to developing countries and regions in infrastructure projects
		Observation point for dispatch of medical teams to developing countries and regions
		Observation point for involvement in international disaster relief
	Measure of cooperation and exchange in science, education, culture, sports, health and tourism	Observation point for international cooperation in the publication of scientific papers and the implementation of scientific plans and projects
		Observation point for exchange of international students and visiting scholars, joint training of talent, and cross-border education
		Observation point for efforts towards the international protection of intellectual property rights
		Observation point for international cooperation in health and disease (especially infectious diseases) control
		Observation point for international sports exchanges and events
		Observation point for sister cities, culture years, film festivals, culture exhibitions and public favor
		Observation point for signing of tourism cooperation agreements

续表

一级指标	二级指标	三级指标
合作的范畴	反腐败合作测度	加入《联合国反腐败公约》观测点
		签订引渡条约，遣返罪犯观测点
		提供追逃追赃相关信息观测点
	反对"三股势力"合作测度	缔结反对"三股势力"的条约观测点
		联合举行反恐军事演习观测点
		开展反对"三股势力"的会晤或论坛观测点
	反贫困合作测度	制定反贫困的长远规划观测点
		参与国际社会扶贫项目观测点
		共建国际社会减贫交流合作平台观测点
		开展减贫项目对外援助观测点

五、指标赋权方法

推动构建人类命运共同体政治维度指标体系（Political Indicator System），可以从"和平的范畴"和"合作的范畴"两个最基本的方面着手建立一级指标（Tier 1 indicators）。

从理性原则到实践，一级指标"和平的范畴"可以通过5个二级指标（测度）回答如何维护和实现世界和平：遵守联合国宪章和有关决议；国防政策和国防力量；对待核生化大规模杀伤性武器的态度，解决地区争端和领土争端方式，和平利用外太空情况。每一个二级指标又可以通过若干可观察、可调研，从而可操作的三级指标（Tier 3 indicators）来检验和说明。现举例"和平的范畴"下的三级指标（观测点）赋权方法。

Continued Schedule

Tier 1 indicators	Tier 2 indicators	Tier 3 indicators
The sphere of cooperation efforts	Measure of anti-corruption cooperation	Observation point for accession to the *United Nations Convention Against Corruption*
		Observation point for signing of extradition treaties to repatriate criminals
		Observation point for provision of information related to pursuit evasion and the recovery of booties
	Measure of cooperation in fighting the "three forces of terrorism, separatism, and extremism"	Observation point for conclusion of the treaty on fighting the "three forces of terrorism, separatism, and extremism"
		Observation point for joint anti-terrorism military exercises
		Observation point for holding of meetings or forums to fight the "three forces of terrorism, separatism, and extremism"
	Measure of cooperation in poverty eradication	Observation point for formulation of long-term anti-poverty plans
		Observation point for involvement in poverty alleviation projects launched by the international community
		Observation point for building of platforms for exchanges and cooperation in poverty reduction in the international community
		Observation point for implementation of poverty reduction projects and provision of foreign aid

V. Indicator Weighting

An indicator system for a community with a shared future for mankind: Political Dimension includes a set of Tier 1 indicators developed in terms of peace efforts and cooperation efforts — the two basic categories.

The Tier 1 indicator, developed in terms of "peace efforts" and in which rationality governs practice, answers the question of how to maintain world peace through five Tier 2 indicators (measures): compliance with the UN Charter and relevant UN resolutions; national defense policies and national defense capabilities; attitude towards nuclear, chemical and biological weapons of mass destruction, ways to resolve regional and territorial disputes, and peaceful use of outer space. Each Tier 2 indicator can be verified and explained by several observable, available and operable Tier 3 indicators. Below are illustrations of the weighting of Tier 3 indicators (observation points) in the "sphere of peace efforts":

"积极参与国际反恐行动"指加入系列国际反恐公约,在上合组织等地区安全组织中签署系列反恐文件,举行联合反恐演习等。

"维护核安全"指的是除遵守《核不扩散条约》外,还有《全面禁止核试验条约》《国际原子能机构保障监督协定附加议定书》《禁止生物武器公约》《禁止化学武器公约》等。

"反对诉诸武力或武力威胁,和平解决争端"指根据《联合国宪章》原则、双边和多边声明、协定,通过对话谈判,和平解决地区、全球的主权领土、经贸等争端。如中国主张对话谈判,和平解决朝核、伊核问题,并为此做出努力。主张按照"主权归我,搁置争议,共同开发"的战略原则,按照《联合国海洋法公约》《南海各方行为宣言》相关规定,解决南海争端。

另一个一级指标"合作的范畴",是实现"和平的范畴"的经济文化基础和条件,因而是人类命运共同体政治维度指标体系的重点内容。具体从国际社会的重点领域,由表层的政治经济生活深入到深层的国际人道主义救援、文化教育等人类精神情感方面,设计了8个二级指标(测度)来说明:政治沟通;经济合作;能源与环境合作;国际救援;科教、文化、

"Active involvement in international anti-terrorism operations": to ratify international anti-terrorism conventions, sign anti-terrorism agreements in regional security organizations such as the SCO, and hold joint anti-terrorism exercises.

"Safeguarding nuclear safety": to sign the *Comprehensive Nuclear-Test-Ban Treaty, Additional Protocol to the Safeguards Agreement of the International Atomic Energy Agency, Convention on the Prohibition of Biological Weapons, Chemical Weapons Convention* and so on in addition to compliance with the *Nuclear Non-Proliferation Treaty*.

"Opposition to the use of force or the threat of force and advocation of peaceful settlement of international disputes": to peacefully resolve regional and global disputes over sovereignty, economic and trade issues through dialog and negotiation in accordance with the principles of the UN Charter, bilateral and multilateral statements and agreements. For example, China advocates peaceful settlement of the North Korean and Iranian nuclear issues through dialog and negotiation and works towards this end. It came up with the strategic principle of "shelving disputes and joint development despite divergent claims to sovereignty" in a bid to settle the disputes over the South China Sea in accordance with relevant provisions of the *United Nations Convention on the Law of the Sea* and the *Declaration on the Conduct of Parties in the South China Sea*.

Another Tier 1 indicator, developed in terms of "cooperation efforts," is the economic and cultural basis for "peace efforts." It is the core of the political indicator system for a community with shared future for mankind. It covers the key aspects of the international community, which include political and economic life on the surface layer and international humanitarian relief, culture and education on the bottom layer that are concerned with human intellect and emotions, and incorporates eight Tier 2 indicators (measures) to illustrate political communication, economic cooperation, cooperation in energy and the environment, international rescue, cooperation and exchange in science, education, culture, health, sports and tourism, anti-corruption cooperation,

卫生、体育、旅游合作交流；反腐败合作；反对三股势力合作；反贫困合作。针对每个二级指标，又从大量的社会现象中重点选择了若干三级指标进行解析、回应。下面举例说明"合作的范畴"下的三级指标（观测点）赋权方法：

（一）三级指标（观测点）赋权方法

"建立伙伴关系"主要包括中美建设性战略伙伴关系、中俄战略协作伙伴关系、中日致力于和平与发展的友好合作伙伴关系、中欧全面战略伙伴关系等。

"举办、参加国际论坛或会议"主要有博鳌亚洲论坛、中非合作论坛、中拉论坛、中阿合作论坛、上合会议、东盟10＋1或10＋3会议、东亚峰会、亚欧会议、中美战略对话、亚太经合组织（APEC）会议、二十国集团（G20）峰会、联合国大会等。

"有关人权的国际法文件"主要有《经济、社会及文化权利国际公约》《消除一切形式种族歧视国际公约》《儿童权利公约》《残疾人权利公约》《维也纳宣言和行动纲领》等。

"参与、创建多边国际性经济合作组织"主要指世界贸易组织、世界银行、国际货币基金组织、欧盟、东盟等地区性和全球性的政府间组织。

"关于贸易、投资自由化程度"主要指降低进口关税，消除关税壁垒和非关税壁垒，反对贸易霸凌主义和贸易战，减

cooperation in fighting the "three forces of terrorism, separatism, and extremism," and anti-poverty cooperation. Each Tier 2 indicator is split into a number of Tier 3 indicators derived from multiple social phenomena. Below are illustrations of the weighting of Tier 3 indicators (observation points) in the "sphere of cooperation efforts":

(I) Weighting of Tier 3 indicators (observation points)

"Establishment of partnerships": constructive strategic partnership between China and the United States, strategic cooperative partnership between China and Russia, friendly cooperative partnership between China and Japan for peace and development, and comprehensive strategic partnership between China and Europe.

"Organization of and participation in international forums or conferences": Boao Forum for Asia, China-Africa Cooperation Forum, China-Latin America Forum, China-Arab Cooperation Forum, Shanghai Cooperation Organization Conference, China-ASEAN (10+1 or 10+3) Cooperation Mechanism, East Asia Summit, Asia-Europe Meeting, China-US Strategic and Economic Dialog, Asia-Pacific Economic Cooperation (APEC) Meeting, G20 Summit, United Nations General Assembly, etc.

"Documents of international law on human rights": *International Covenant on Economic, Social and Cultural Rights*, *International Convention on the Elimination of All Forms of Racial Discrimination*, *Convention on the Rights of the Child*, *Convention on the Rights of Persons with Disabilities*, and *Vienna Declaration and Program of Action*.

"Involvement in and establishment of multilateral international economic cooperation organizations": regional and global intergovernmental organizations such as the World Trade Organization, the World Bank, the International Monetary Fund, the European Union and ASEAN.

"Degree of trade and investment liberalization": reducing import tariffs, eliminating tariff and non-tariff barriers, opposing trade bullying and trade

少出口管制，反对以产业安全和国家安全为借口对外资进行投资审查，放宽外商投资准入，优化投资环境等。

"减少贸易、投资不平衡的努力"主要指积极扩大进口，实施走出去战略，规范引导企业对外投资。

"货币互换和金融监管"指签订双边货币互换协议、金融监管备忘录，防止汇率波动过大和金融风险。

"促成国际货币体系稳定和多元化的努力"，以人民币为例，央行实行稳健货币政策，保持人民币汇率稳定，2015年人民币"入篮"，人民币向国际化迈出了重要的一步。

"关于区域性投资银行、投资基金设立"，近年来主要有上合银行、亚洲基础设施投资银行、金砖国家开发银行、丝路基金等。

"关于宏观经济政策协调"主要是召开西方七国集团（G7）首脑会议、二十国集团（G20）峰会、金砖国家领导人峰会，协调立场，努力达成共识，就财政货币政策采取一致行动。

"能源贸易、投资合作"主要表现为石油、天然气、电力进出口，石油、天然气勘探、开采、冶炼合作，核电技术贸易和核电站建设合作等。

"加入《巴黎协定》，承担温室气体减排责任"指的是，如加入《联合国气候变化框架公约》《京都协定书》《巴黎协定》等。

"帮助发展中国家地区进行基础设施建设"，如中非十大合作计划，帮助非洲国家建设道路、桥梁，派遣志愿者，减

wars, reducing export controls, opposing foreign investment review under the pretext of industrial security and national security, granting access to foreign investment, optimizing investment environment, etc.

"Efforts to reduce trade and investment imbalance": expanding imports, implementing the strategy of going global, and regulating and guiding Chinese investment abroad.

"Currency swap and financial supervision": signing bilateral currency swap agreements and financial supervision memorandums to prevent excessive exchange rate fluctuations and financial risks.

"Efforts to promote the stability and diversification of the international monetary system": the RMB is an example. The Central Bank of China implemented a prudent monetary policy and kept the RMB exchange rate stable. In 2015, the RMB "entered the basket" and made an important step towards internationalization.

"Establishment of regional investment banks and investment funds": Shanghai Cooperation Organization Bank, Asian Infrastructure Investment Bank, BRICS Development Bank and Silk Road Fund.

"Efforts to tackle economic downturn and crisis through the coordination of macro-economic policies": G7 Summit, G20 Summit and the BRICS Summit were convened to coordinate positions, reach consensus and take concerted actions in the field of fiscal and monetary policies.

"Energy trade and investment cooperation": the import and export of oil, natural gas and electricity, cooperation in the exploration, mining and smelting of oil and natural gas, trade in nuclear power technology and cooperation in the construction of nuclear power plants, etc.

"Signing of the *Paris Agreement* and assumption of responsibility for reducing greenhouse gas emissions": joining the *United Nations Framework Convention on Climate Change*, *Kyoto Protocol* and *Paris Agreement*, etc.

"Assistance to developing countries and regions in infrastructure projects": the 10 Major China-Africa Cooperation Plans were devised to help African

免到期的受援国债务等。

"联合培养人才、跨境办学",如成立孔子学院,对外汉语(英语)教学和考试、国际会计证书培训和考试等。

"科技计划和项目国际合作",如欧盟同意中国参与其研究、技术开发框架计划。中国高技术研发计划(863 计划)和基础研究计划(973 计划)也都向欧盟开放。

"关于知识产权国际保护",以中国为例,依据《专利法》《商标法》《著作权法》等国内法和政府法规,世界贸易组织(WTO)《与贸易有关的知识产权协议》(TRIPS),对国际知识产权进行有效保护。

"国际卫生、疾控合作"主要指加入并参与世界贸易组织(WTO)的相关活动,对传染性疾病与相关国家建立联防联控机制等。

"反腐败合作"主要参考透明国际(Transparency International)的相关数据和世界银行的全球治理指标之腐败控制的相关资料。

"减少贫困合作"主要参考世界银行的相关数据。

(二)三级指标数据来源、分数分布和评分方法

关于三级指标数据来源。一是从我国党和政府的各大网站可以找到外交政策、战略,领导人外事活动,以及大多数经

countries build roads and bridges, send volunteers to Africa, and reduce the due debts of recipient countries.

"Joint training of talent and cross-border education": the establishment of Confucius Institutes, the teaching and testing of Chinese as a foreign language (in English), training and examinations for the conferment of international accounting certificates, etc.

"International cooperation in the implementation of scientific plans and projects: the EU approved China's application for participation in its framework plan for research and the development of technology. China's high-tech research and development program (863 Program) and basic research program (973 Program) are also open to the EU.

"Efforts towards the international protection of intellectual property rights": China effectively protects international intellectual property rights in accordance with domestic laws and government regulations such as the *Patent Law*, *Trademark Law* and *Copyright Law*, as well as the *WTO Agreement on Trade-related Aspects of Intellectual Property Rights* (*TRIPS*).

"International cooperation in health and disease control": participating in activities held by the World Health Organization (WHO), and establishing joint prevention and control mechanisms for infectious diseases with relevant countries.

"Anti-corruption cooperation": discussions in this part are based on relevant data of Transparency International and the global governance indicators of the World Bank on corruption control.

"Cooperation in poverty eradication": discussions in this part are based on relevant data of the World Bank.

(II) Data source, score distribution and scoring method for Tier 3 indicators

Data source Foreign policies and strategies, state leaders' diplomatic activities, data on economic and trade, databases and statistical yearbooks

贸数据、数据库、统计年鉴。例如中国共产党新闻网、人民网、新华网，外交部、商务部、财政部、国务院新闻办公室、国家发改委、国家统计局、中国人民银行、国家外汇管理局、海关总署等网站。二是为了便于国际比较，还可以从著名国际组织网站以及其他国家政府网站找到一些数据。如联合国（UN）、世界银行（WB）、国际货币基金组织（IMF）、世界贸易组织、美国商务部经济分析局（BEA）等网站。三是国内外相关纸质出版物。

关于评分方法。有客观事实、数据作支撑的，根据实际材料给分，正向指标，表现越高，得分越高；逆向指标，表现越高，得分越低。客观依据不充分，带有主观感受的指标，可请多名专家凭经验、认识打分，最后取平均分。也可对社会大众进行访谈或发放问卷调查，再根据结果打分。

on the websites of the party and the government which include the Chinese Communist Party News Network, People's Daily Online, Xinhua Net, Ministry of Foreign Affairs, Ministry of Commerce, Ministry of Finance, State Council Information Office, National Development and Reform Commission, National Bureau of Statistics, People's Bank of China, State Administration of Foreign Exchange, General Administration of Customs. In order to facilitate international comparison, data from the websites of famous international organizations and other government websites were also sourced, such as the United Nations (UN), the World Bank (WB), the International Monetary Fund (IMF), the World Trade Organization, and the Bureau of Economic Analysis (BEA) of the US Department of Commerce. Related Chinese and foreign paper publications.

Scoring Indicators supported by objective facts and data are scored on the basis of the actual supporting materials. For forward indicators, the higher the performance, the higher the score; for contrary indicators, the higher the performance, the lower the score. Subjective indicators that are not sufficiently supported by objective facts are scored by several experts according to their experiences and understanding; the average score is the final measure. The results of interviews and questionnaires can also be used for scoring.

第二章
人类命运共同体构建进程经济维度指标体系

一、目的和意义

"开放带来进步,封闭必然落后。"纵观国际经贸发展史,深刻验证了"相通则共进,相闭则各退"的规律。当今世界正经历着新一轮大发展、大变革和大调整:经济全球化大势不可逆转,但保护主义、单边主义抬头,多边主义和自由贸易体制受到冲击;新科技革命和产业变革蓄势待发,但增长新旧动能转换尚未完成;国际格局深刻演变,但发展失衡未有根本改观;全球治理体系加快变革,但治理滞后仍是突出挑战。当今世界之大变局百年未有,变革催生新机遇的过程中往往充满着风险挑战。

Chapter II

An Indicator System for Measuring the Process of Building a Community with a Shared Future for Mankind: Economic Dimension

I. Purpose and Significance

"Opening up brings about progress, while seclusion results in underdevelopment". The international economy and trade have, over the course of their development, verified the law that "connectivity brings about common progress, while shying away from international intercourse leads to backwardness". The world today is experiencing a new round of development, transformation and adjustment: as the general trend, economic globalization is irreversible, yet protectionism and unilateralism are rising to exert a huge impact on multilateralism and free trade; a new scientific revolution and industrial transformation are gaining momentum, yet some old growth drivers have yet to be replaced by new ones; the international landscape is undergoing profound changes, yet development imbalance keeps arising; the global governance system is adopting reform, yet poor governance remains a significant challenge. We live in a world of unprecedented changes. Change opens up fresh opportunities, but at the same time it often involves risks and presents challenges.

面对当今世界经济的诸多挑战，党的十八大以来习近平总书记在多个场合阐述了构建人类命运共同体的思想。党的十九大报告明确提出：构建人类命运共同体，建设"持久和平、普遍安全、共同繁荣、开放包容、清洁美丽"的世界。作为人类命运共同体的基础平台，构建一个"开放包容、共同繁荣"的人类命运经济共同体尤为关键。这对于中国统筹国内国际两个大局，矢志不渝走和平发展道路、奉行互利共赢的开放战略，坚定不移地"推动打造富有活力的增长模式、开放共赢的合作模式、公正合理的治理模式、平衡普惠的发展模式，促进经济全球化朝着更加开放、包容、普惠、平衡、共赢方向发展"，[①]提高发展的整体性、互惠性与共享性，推动构建涵盖"持久和平、共同繁荣、开放创新、包容互惠、繁荣发展"等核心内涵的人类命运共同体，为实现"'两个一百年'奋斗目标和中华民族伟大复兴的中国梦"营造更加有利的国际环境，具有十分重要的意义。

二、指导思想

人类经济共同体构建进程指标体系的指导思想源于以下三个方面。

---

① 张耀军."一带一路"：全球治理体系变革的中国方案[N].光明日报，2018-10-10. https://news.gmw.cn/2018-10/10/content_31619856.htm

Acutely conscious that the world economy is faced with tough challenges, General Secretary Xi Jinping introduced the concept of "Community with a Shared Future for Mankind" on many occasions since the 18th National Congress of the Communist Party of China. The report delivered at the 19th National Congress of the Communist Party of China calls on the people of all countries to work together to build a community with a shared future for mankind and to build an open, inclusive, clean, and beautiful world that enjoys lasting peace, universal security, and common prosperity. It is crucial to build an open, inclusive Economic Community with a Shared Future for Mankind that enjoys common prosperity. This is the groundwork for the Community with a Shared Future for Mankind and for China to keep in mind both its internal and international imperatives, stay on the path of peaceful development, and continue to pursue a mutually beneficial strategy of opening up. China will unswervingly "build a dynamic growth model, an open and mutually beneficial cooperation model, a fair and reasonable governance model, and a balanced and all-benefiting development model so that economic globalization can move in a more open, inclusive, all-benefiting, balanced and mutually beneficial direction",[1] To create a more favorable international environment for reaching the "'two centennial goals' and realizing the Chinese dream of the great rejuvenation of the Chinese nation," we must improve the globality, reciprocity and shareability of development, build a Community with a Shared Future for Mankind that covers the core concepts of "lasting peace, common prosperity, open innovation, inclusiveness, mutual benefit, prosperity and development".

II. Guiding Ideology

The guiding ideology for the indicator system for measuring the process of building an Economic Community with a Shared Future for Mankind is derived from the following three aspects.

---

[1] Zhang Yaojun Belt and Road Initiative: China's Plan for the Reform of the Global Governance System [N]. Guangming Daily, 2018-10-10. https://news.gmw.cn/2018-10/10/content_31619856.htm

一是马克思主义政治经济学中有关共同体的思想理论阐述。命运共同体的实质是发展共同体。从全世界范围来看，人类社会还远远没有达到马克思意义上"物质财富极大丰富"的状态，发展的不平衡性使一部分人还在为生存问题担忧。发展生产力依然是人类社会的不懈追求，生产力的不断发展也将为构建人类经济共同体提供源源不断的动力。

二是构建人类命运共同体的一系列讲话精神和重要论述。正确义利观，公平、开放、全面、创新的发展观，开放、融通、互利、共赢的合作观，共商、共建、共享的全球治理观都是构建进程指标体系最重要的指导思想。

三是共生理论。共生的概念源自生物学，其基本观点认为，共生是人的基本存在方式。就国际经济与贸易关系而言，任何国家皆存于国际共生关系之中。从消极共生走向积极共生就是共生的优化问题，其本质是发展问题，着力点是如何实现均衡、平衡、和谐的发展，目标是如何建立相互包容、相互克制、互利共赢、共同发展的共生关系。

三、构建原则

以推动构建人类命运共同体系列重要论述中有关经济发展的论述为指导，立足当前世界经济大变局，观测构建开放、创新、包容、互惠、发展的构建进程指标体系，应遵循科学性、

Theories about community in Marxist Political Economics. The Community with a Shared Future for Mankind is essentially the Community of Development. Globally, human society is far from "abundant material wealth" envisioned by Marx, and development imbalance leaves some struggling for survival. The development of productive forces is still the unremitting pursuit of human society, and the continuous development of productive forces will provide a steady stream of power for building an Economic Community with a Shared Future for Mankind.

The remarks and theories about building a Community with a Shared Future for Mankind. The correct concept of moral and profit, the concept of development which highlights fairness, openness, thoroughness and innovation,the concept of cooperation which stresses openness, accommodation, mutual benefit and win-win results, and the concept of global governance which features consultation, co-building and sharing are the most important guiding ideology for build ing the process indicator system.

The Intergrowth Theory. The concept of intergrowth originated in biology, and its basic viewpoint is that intergrowth is the basic form of human existence. All countries have an intergrowth relationship with each other when it comes to international economic and trade relations. Intergrowth is optimized when it shifts from negative intergrowth to positive intergrowth. It's essentially a matter of development that focuses on how to achieve balanced and harmonious development to establish an intergrowth relationship of mutual tolerance, mutual restraint, mutual benefit and common development.

III. Guiding Principles

This indicator system is formulated under theories about economic development in the Community with a Shared Future for Mankind and in the context of the drastically changing world economy. Therefore, the assessment of this open, innovative, inclusive, mutually beneficial, and developing

系统性、动态性、可行性和综合性等原则。

第一，科学性原则。既能充分反映和体现内涵，又能客观全面反映各指标之间的真实关系，最终能够测度出发展状况和水平。

第二，系统性原则。一级指标是一个系统之内的子系统，彼此之间是平行关系且有一定的逻辑关系，不但要从不同的侧面反映出各个子系统的主要特征和状态，且要反映出这些子系统之间的内在联系。

第三，动态性原则。一级指标内容的互动，需要通过一定时间尺度的指标反映出来，要延伸出二级指标，并为三级指标做出框定。

第四，可行性原则。构建评价指标体系应当具有很强的实用性，因而要求具有操作上的可行性。指标的选取不仅要考虑理论依据，也要尽量建立在数据可得的基础上，便于量化、测度和检验。

第五，综合性原则。构建评价指标要求有足够的涵盖面，在整体上要基本反映主要方面，抓住关键点和重点。整体评价指标体系应当呈现出较强的逻辑性和较清晰的层次。

四、指标体系框架

根据构建共同繁荣、开放包容世界的意义，以构建人类命运共同体思想为指导，参考联合国等国际组织已有评价指标体系、"一带一路"大数据报告及习近平总书记在"经济发展"

process indicator system should follow the principle of being scientific, systematic, up-to-date, feasible and comprehensive.

First, Scientificity. It can not only fully reflect and embody the content of a Community with a Shared Future for Mankind, but also objectively and comprehensively demonstrate the true relationships among the indicators and, ultimately, measure the development and level of the Community with a Shared Future for Mankind.

Second, Systematicness. The Tier 1 indicators form a subsystem. They are parallel and logically related to each other. They should display the internal relations among the subsystems while depicting the main characteristics and states of each subsystem from different perspectives.

Third, Dynamicity. The interaction between Tier 1 indicators needs to be reflected by certain time scale indicators. It should be able to develop Tier 2 indicators and define Tier 3 indicators.

Fourth, Feasibility. The assessment indicator system should be highly practical, so it requires operational feasibility. The indicators chosen should have a theoretical basis as well as the support of available data so that they can be quantified, measured and tested.

Fifth, Comprehensiveness. The assessment indicator system should be comprehensive, basically reflect the main aspects, and cover the key points. The entire assessment indicator system should be logical and clear.

IV. Framework of Indicator System

This indicator system is formulated in line with what is meant by a world of common prosperity, openness and tolerance, under the guidance of the idea of building a Community with a Shared Future for Mankind, and based on the assessment indicator systems of international organizations such as the United Nations, the *"Belt and Road Initiative" Big Data Report*, and General Secretary

命题下的讲话内容，将内部指标与外部指标结合，遵循科学性、系统性、动态性、可行性、综合性原则，从开放合作、创新引领、包容互惠、发展繁荣四个维度，构建了包含三个层次，由 4 个一级指标（范畴）、15 个二级指标（测度）、60 个三级指标（观测点）在内的评价指标体系。各级评价指标具体如下：

（一）开放合作

1. 市场准入度（5 个观测点）

1.1 关税总水平变动幅度

1.2 非关税壁垒强度变动幅度观测点

1.3 服务业总体开放水平提高幅度

1.4 通关便利化水平提高幅度

1.5 进口环节制度性成本削减幅度

2. 贸易自由化（4 个观测点）

2.1 外贸依存度

2.2 货物贸易增长率

2.3 服务贸易增长率

2.4 数字贸易增长率

3. 投资便利化（4 个观测点）

3.1 实际利用外资额

3.2 对外直接投资额

3.3 投资环境改善程度

Xi Jinping's speeches on economic development. It is a combination of internal and external indicators that scientifically, systematically, dynamically, feasibly and comprehensively measures the four dimensions of openness and cooperation, innovation-driven development, inclusiveness and mutual benefit, and development and prosperity, comprising three tiers — four Tier 1 indicators (categories), 15 Tier 2 indicators (measures) and 60 Tier 3 indicators (observation points). The assessment indicators are as follows:

(I) Openness and cooperation

1. Level of market access (5 observation points)

1.1 Amplitude of fluctuation in the overall tariff level

1.2 Observation points for change in non-tariff barriers intensity

1.3 Increase in overall openness of the service industry

1.4 Increase in the level of customs clearance facilitation

1.5 Reduction in institutional import cost

2. Trade liberalization (4 observation points)

2.1 Degree of dependence upon foreign trade

2.2 Growth rate of trade in goods

2.3 Growth rate of trade in services

2.4 Growth rate of digital trade

3. Investment facilitation (4 observation points)

3.1 Amount of foreign investment in actual use

3.2 Amount of outward foreign direct investment

3.3 Degree of improvement in the investment environment

3.4 新兴市场参与度

4. 设施联通度（4个观测点）

4.1 交通设施联通度

4.2 通信设施联通度

4.3 能源设施联通度

4.4 移动互联设施联通度

5. 金融开放度（4个观测点）

5.1 利率市场化变动程度

5.2 汇率国际化变动程度

5.3 金融风险可控程度

5.4 金融监管与协调国际化程度

（二）创新引领

1. 创新投入指数（2个观测点）

1.1 研发投入强度

1.2 每百万中研究人员数

2. 创新产出指数（5个观测点）

2.1 专利申请数量

2.2 高新技术产品出口额占比

2.3 知识产权综合发展指数

2.4 创新效率指数

2.5 全球创新指数

3.4 Rate of participation in emerging markets

4. Level of infrastructure connectivity (4 observation points)

4.1 Level of transportation facilities connectivity

4.2 Level of communication facilities connectivity

4.3 Level of energy facilities connectivity

4.4 Level of mobile Internet connectivity

5. Level of financial openness (4 observation points)

5.1 Fluctuation in interest rate liberalization

5.2 Fluctuation in exchange rate internationalization

5.3 Degree of financial risk control

5.4 Degree of internationalization of financial supervision and coordination

(II) Innovation-driven development

1. Innovation input indicator (2 observation points)

1.1 R&D input intensity

1.2 Number of researchers per million people

2. Innovation output indicator (5 observation points)

2.1 Number of patent applications

2.2 Proportion of high-tech products in total exports

2.3 Composite development indicator of intellectual property rights

2.4 Innovation efficiency indicator

2.5 Global innovation indicator

3. 创新活力指数（2个观测点）

3.1 人力资源增长率

3.2 高技术共享程度

（三）包容互惠

1. 包容程度（5个观测点）

1.1 参与国际经济组织数

1.2 高层领导互访次数

1.3 签署双边与区域合作协议文件数

1.4 参与全球经济治理程度

1.5 不推行单边主义、不诉诸保护主义

2. 互惠与共赢程度（5个观测点）

2.1 提供公共产品数

2.2 合作共享平台数

2.3 自由贸易区互惠程度

2.4 维护多边贸易体制程度

2.5 经济全球化指数

（四）发展繁荣

1. 经济活力（3个观测点）

1.1 GDP增长率

1.2 第三产业对GDP贡献增长率

1.3 数字经济增长率

3. Innovation vitality indicator (2 observation points)

3.1 Growth rate of human resources

3.2 Level of the sharing of high-tech

(III) Inclusiveness and reciprocity

1. Level of inclusiveness (5 observation points)

1.1 Number of international economic organizations joined

1.2 Number of exchange visits by senior leaders

1.3 Number of agreements signed on bilateral and regional cooperation

1.4 Degree of participation in global economic governance

1.5 Restraint from unilateralism or protectionism

2. Degree of reciprocity and mutual benefit (5 observation points)

2.1 Number of public goods provided

2.2 Number of cooperation and sharing platforms

2.3 Degree of reciprocity of free trade zones

2.4 Efforts to maintain the multilateral trading system

2.5 Economic globalization indicator

(IV) Development and prosperity

1. Economic vitality (3 observation points)

1.1 GDP growth rate

1.2 Growth rate of the tertiary industry's contribution to GDP

1.3 Growth rate of the digital economy

2. 经济效率（5个观测点）

2.1 劳动生产率增长率

2.2 资本产出率增长率

2.3 技术进步率

2.4 全球竞争力指数

2.5 国家健康指数

3. 可持续发展能力（3个观测点）

3.1 万美元 GDP 能耗

3.2 人均二氧化碳排放量

3.3 碳中和程度

4. 民众幸福指数（5个观测点）

4.1 人口预期寿命

4.2 国际贫困率变动幅度

4.3 幸福指数

4.4 全球最健康国家指数变化率

4.5 恐怖主义指数

5. 经济贡献率（4个观测点）

5.1 对世界经济贡献率

5.2 对国际贸易贡献率

5.3 对国际直接投资贡献率

5.4 对全球科技进步贡献率

（五）指标体系框架附表

2. Economic efficiency (5 observation points)

2.1 Growth rate of labor productivity

2.2 Growth rate of capital output ratio

2.3 Rate of technological progress

2.4 Global competitiveness indicator

2.5 National health index

3. Sustainable development capability (3 observation points)

3.1 Energy consumption per 10 thousand U.S. dollars in GDP

3.2 Per capita CO_2 emissions

3.3 Degree of carbon neutrality

4. General happiness indicator (5 observation points)

4.1 Life expectancy of population

4.2 Change in international poverty rate

4.3. Happiness indicator

4.4 Rate of change in the Indicator of the Healthiest Countries in the World

4.5 Terrorism indicator

5. Economic contribution rate (4 observation points)

5.1 Rate of contribution to the world economy

5.2 Rate of contribution to international trade

5.3 Rate of contribution to direct foreign investment

5.4 Rate of contribution to global scientific and technological progress

(V) Schedule of Framework of Indicator System

表2.1 人类命运共同体构建进程经济维度指标体系

一级指标	二级指标	三级指标	备注
开放合作范畴	市场准入度测度	关税总水平变动幅度观测点	
		非关税壁垒强度变动幅度观测点	
		服务业总体开放水平提高幅度观测点	
		通关便利化水平提高幅度观测点	
		进口环节制度性成本削减幅度观测点	
	贸易自由化测度	外贸依存度观测点	
		货物贸易增长率观测点	
		服务贸易增长率观测点	
		数字贸易增长率观测点	
	投资便利化测度	实际利用外资额观测点	
		对外直接投资额观测点	
		投资环境改善程度观测点	
		新兴市场参与度观测点	新兴市场资本流入额/国际资本流动总额
	设施联通度测度	交通设施联通度观测点	通过航空、公路、铁路和港口的联通度来进行测评
		通信设施联通度观测点	通过移动电话普及率、宽带普及率和跨境通信设施联通度来进行测评

Schedule 2.1 An Indicator System for Measuring the Process of Building a Community with a Shared Future for Mankind:Economic Dimension

Tier 1 indicators	Tier 2 indicators	Tier 3 indicators	Remarks
The sphere of opening up and cooperation	Measure of level of market access	Observation point for amplitude of fluctuation in the overall tariff level	
		Observation point for change in non-tariff barriers intensity	
		Observation point for increase in overall openness of the service industry	
		Observation point for increase in the level of customs clearance facilitation	
		Observation point for reduction in institutional import cost	
	Observation point for measure of trade liberalization	Observation point for degree of dependence upon foreign trade	
		Observation point for growth rate of trade in goods	
		Observation point for growth rate of trade in services	
		Observation point for growth rate of digital trade	
	Measure of investment facilitation	Observation point for amount of foreign investment in actual use	
		Observation point for amount of outward foreign direct investment	
		Observation point for degree of improvement in the investment environment	
		Observation point for rate of participation in emerging markets	Amount of capital flowing to emerging markets/ total amount of international capital flow
	Measure of level of infrastructure connectivity	Observation point for level of transportation infrastructure connectivity	Based on aviation, highway, railway and port connectivity
		Observation point for level of communication facility connectivity	Based on mobile phone penetration rate, broadband penetration rate and cross-border communication facility connectivity

续表

一级指标	二级指标	三级指标	备注
开放合作范畴	设施联通度测度	能源设施联通度观测点	通过跨境输电线路和油气管道的联通度来进行测评
		移动互联设施联通度	通过移动互联网、手机、微信、抖音、快手等短视频应用的联通度来进行测评
	金融开放度测度	利率市场化变动程度观测点	
		汇率国际化变动程度观测点	
		金融风险可控程度观测点	
		金融监管与协调国际化程度观测点	
创新引领范畴	创新投入指数测度	研发投入强度观测点	研发经费支出/GDP（地区生产总值）
		每百万中研究人员数观测点	
	创新产出指数测度	专利申请数量观测点	
		高新技术产品出口额占比观测点	
		知识产权综合发展指数观测点	
		创新效率指数观测点	
		全球创新指数观测点	
	创新活力指数	人力资源增长率观测点	
		高技术共享程度观测点	
	包容程度测度	参与国际组织数观测点	

Continued Schedule

Tier 1 indicators	Tier 2 indicators	Tier 3 indicators	Remarks
The sphere of opening up and cooperation	Measure of level of infrastructure connectivity	Observation point for level of energy infrastructure connectivity	Based on connectivity of cross-border power transmission lines and oil and gas pipelines
		Level of mobile Internet facility connectivity	Based on connectivity of the mobile Internet, mobile phones, WeChat, and short video applications like Tik Tok and Kuaishou
	Measure of level of financial openness	Observation point for fluctuation in interest rate liberalization	
		Observation point for fluctuation in exchange rate internationalization	
		Observation point for degree of financial risk control	
		Observation point for degree of internationalization of financial supervision and coordination	
The sphere of innovation-driven development	Measure of innovation input indicator	Observation point for R&D input intensity	R&D expenditure / GDP (gross regional domestic product)
		Observation point for number of researchers per million people	
	Measure of innovation output indicator	Observation point for number of patent applications	
		Observation point for proportion of high-tech products in total exports	
		Observation point for composite development indicator of intellectual property rights	
		Observation point innovation efficiency indicator	
		Observation point for global innovation indicator	
	Innovation vitality indicator	Observation point for growth rate of human resources	
		Observation point for level of the sharing of high-tech	
	Measure of degree of inclusiveness	Observation point for number of international economic organizations joined	

075

续表

一级指标	二级指标	三级指标	备注
包容互惠范畴	包容程度测度	高层领导互访次数观测点	
		签署双边与区域合作协议文件数观测点	
		参与全球经济治理程度观测点	
		不推行单边主义、不诉诸保护主义观测点	
	互惠与共赢程度测度	提供公共产品数观测点	
		合作共享平台数观测点	
		自由贸易区互惠程度观测点	
		维护多边贸易体制程度观测点	
		经济全球化指数观测点	
发展繁荣范畴	经济活力测度	GDP 增长率观测点	
		第三产业对 GDP 贡献增长率观测点	
		数字经济增长率观测点	
	经济效率测度	劳动生产率增长率观测点	
		资本产出率增长率观测点	
		技术进步率观测点	
		全球竞争力指数观测点	
		国家健康指数观测点	

Continued Schedule

Tier 1 indicators	Tier 2 indicators	Tier 3 indicators	Remarks
The sphere of reciprocity and mutual benefit	Measure of degree of inclusiveness	Observation point for number of exchange visits by senior leaders	
		Observation point for number of agreements signed on bilateral and regional cooperation	
		Observation point for degree of participation in global economic governance	
		Observation point for restraint from unilateralism or protectionism	
	Measure of degree of reciprocity and mutual benefit	Observation point for number of public goods provided	
		Observation point for number of cooperation and sharing platforms	
		Observation point for degree of reciprocity of free trade zones	
		Observation point for efforts to maintain the multilateral trading system	
		Observation point for indicator of economic globalization	
The sphere of development and prosperity	Measure of economic vitality	Observation point for GDP growth rate	
		Observation point for growth rate of the tertiary industry's contribution to GDP	
		Observation point for growth rate of the digital economy	
	Measure of economic efficiency	Observation point for growth rate of labor productivity	
		Observation point for growth rate of capital output ratio	
		Observation point for rate of technological progress	
		Observation point for global competitiveness indicator	
		Observation point for national health indicator	

续表

一级指标	二级指标	三级指标	备注
发展繁荣范畴	可持续发展能力测度	万美元GDP能耗观测点	
		人均二氧化碳排放量观测点	
		碳中和程度观测点	
	民众幸福指数测度	人口预期寿命观测点	
		国际贫困率下降幅度观测点	
		幸福指数观测点	
		全球最健康国家指数变化率观测点	
		恐怖主义指数观测点	
	经济贡献率测度	对世界经济贡献率观测点	
		对国际贸易贡献率观测点	
		对国际直接投资贡献率观测点	
		对全球科技进步贡献率观测点	

五、指标赋权方法

上述指标体系的构建是基于推动构建人类命运共同体思想中与"经济发展"有关的论述，体现着构建人类命运共同体的初衷，重在考量构建进程中取得的成效，以及中国在构建进程中发挥的作用和做出的贡献。

（一）数据来源

本指标体系所涉及的数据主要来源于历年的《中国统计

Continued Schedule

Tier 1 indicators	Tier 2 indicators	Tier 3 indicators	Remarks
The sphere of development and prosperity	Measure of sustainable development capability	Observation point for energy consumption per 10 thousand U.S. dollars in GDP	
		Observation point for per capita CO_2 emissions	
		Observation point for degree of carbon neutrality	
	Measure of general happiness indicator	Observation point for life expectancy of population	
		Observation point for decrease in international poverty rate	
		Observation point for happiness indicator	
		Observation point for rate of change in the Indicator of the Healthiest Countries in the World	
		Observation point for terrorism indicator	Tradingeconomics.com Tradingeconomics.com
	Measure of rate of economic contribution	Observation point for rate of contribution to the world economy	
		Observation point for rate of contribution to international trade	
		Observation point for rate of contribution to direct foreign investment	
		Observation point for rate of contribution to global scientific and technological progress	

V. Indicator Weighting Methods

The above indicator system is built on "economic development" in a Community with a Shared Future for Mankind. It reflects the original aspiration to focus on achievements made in the building process, as well as China's role and contribution.

(I) Data sources

The data referenced in this indicator system is mainly from *China Statistical*

年鉴》《国际统计年鉴》、联合国贸发会议（UNCTAD）数据库、世界贸易组织数据库、《"一带一路"大数据报告》、世界经济论坛的《全球竞争力报告》（*The Global Competitiveness Report*）、《全球贸易促进报告》（*The Global Enabling Trade Report*）、世界银行WDI数据库和全球营商环境报告、《全球创新指数》、联合国《世界幸福指数报告》和全球经济指标数据网（Trading economics.com）等。

由于原始数据的来源、取值范围不同，彼此间不具有可比性。可采用线性变换法对各二级指标的原始数据做指数化处理。经过指数化处理后的数据更具有可比性，并能直观地看出每个国家各个指标所处的位置。

（二）主要评价方法

指标测度过程中主要采用三种评价方法：一是关于指标权重将通过层次分析法和客观的数据分析，对不同层次的分项指标综合主客观方法进行分配。定性指标评分将采用德尔菲法，经过多轮专家评议，最终确定。二是关于定量指标，主要采用无量纲化处理；三是对数值分布极其不均匀的指标，将采取栅格法，依据实际数值划分若干个区间进行分档打分。

（三）指标赋权

1."开放合作"指标

开放合作是建立经济共同体的前提，是经济共同体的第

Yearbook, *International Statistical Yearbook*, UNCTAD database, WTO database, *Belt and Road Initiative Big Data Report*, *Global Competitiveness Report* (GCR) made at the World Economic Forum, *Global Enabling Trade Report* (GETR), World Bank WDI database and *Report on Global Business Environment*, *Global Innovation Index*, UN *World Happiness Index Report*, and Trading Economics. com.

The original data is from different sources and has different value ranges, so it is not comparable to each other. The linear converter technique can be used to index the original data of all Tier 2 indicators. Indexed data is more comparable and can visually show the position of all the indicators of a country.

(II) Main assessment methods

Three assessment methods are used for measuring indicators: First, the AHP and objective data analysis are conducted to objectively and subjectively allocate sub-indicators at all levels to determine indicator weight. The Delphi method is used to score qualitative indicators in several rounds of expert reviews. Second, most quantitative indicators are nondimensionalized; Third, the grid method is adopted to score indicators with an extremely uneven distribution of values; the actual values are grouped, and scores are given by group.

(III) Indicator weighting

1. "Openness and cooperation" indicator

Openness and cooperation are the precondition and No. 1 principle for an Economic Community with a Shared Future for Mankind. Opening up brings

一原则。开放带来进步，封闭必然落后。"相通则共进，相闭则各退"。回顾历史，开放合作是增强国际经贸活力的重要动力。立足当今，开放合作是推动世界经济稳定复苏的现实要求。放眼未来，开放合作是促进人类社会不断进步的时代要求。各国应该坚持开放融通，拓展互利合作空间。开放合作既是人类命运共同体的核心，又是亚洲命运共同体的核心。因此，按照上述指标权重分配方法，将"开放合作"指标权重设定为30%。

2. "创新引领"指标

创新引领是在开放合作基础上派生出来的第二原则，它决定着人类经济共同体的发展速度、效能和可持续性。纵观近代以来世界发展历程，一个国家和民族的创新能力从根本上影响甚至决定着国家和民族的前途命运。当今世界，创新是引领发展的第一动力，造福人类又是科技创新最强大的动力。只有敢于创新、勇于变革，才能突破世界经济的发展瓶颈，共同推动科技创新、共享创新成果。创新引领既是开放合作这一指标在构建经济共同体进程中的关键，又在一定程度上体现着各国间的包容互惠程度，并决定着各国经济的发展繁荣程度。因此，"创新引领"指标按照上述指标权重分配方法，将其权重设定为25%。

about progress, while seclusion results in underdevelopment. "Connectivity brings about common progress, while shying away from international intercourse leads to backwardness". History has shown that openness and cooperation are the major driving force behind international trade and economic vitality. In today's world, openness and cooperation are the specific requirement of a stable world economic recovery. In the future, openness and cooperation are the requirement of an era of continuing social progress. All countries should continue to open up, embrace difference and expand the space for mutually beneficial cooperation. "Openness and cooperation", it is the core of the Community with a Shared Future for Mankind and the Asian Community with a Shared Future. According to the above method for determining indicator weight, the weight of "openness and cooperation" as an indicator is set at 30%.

2. "Innovation-driven development" indicator

Innovation-driven development is the second principle derived from openness and cooperation. It determines the development speed, performance and sustainability of the Economic Community with a Shared Future for Mankind. The development of the world since modern times shows that the innovation ability of a country or nation fundamentally influences or even determines its future and destiny. In today's world, innovation is the No. 1 driving force behind development andtechnological innovation is motivated by the desire to benefit mankind. With the courage to innovate and change, we can remove the bottleneck that hits world economic development, promote scientific and technological innovation and share the fruits of innovation. Innovation-driven development is the key to the indicator of openness and cooperation in the process of building an economic community, reflects to a certain extent the degree of tolerance and reciprocity among countries, and determines the degree of economic development and prosperity of various countries. Therefore, the weight of innovation-driven development should be set at 25% using the above method for determining indicator weight.

3."包容互惠"指标

包容互惠体现了最新的人类命运共同体思想,是构建人类命运共同体的初衷。"一花独放不是春,百花齐放春满园"。随着经济全球化的日益深化,包容普惠、互利共赢才是越走越宽的人间正道。"包容互惠"指标承认各国的差异,主张超越国家差异,推动包容发展、互惠发展,让各国人民共享经济全球化和世界经济增长的成果。它反映了中国推动全球治理和构建国际经济新秩序的新理念,提出了经济共同体的中国方案。因此,按照上述指标权重分配方法,将"包容互惠"指标权重设定为20%。

4."发展繁荣"指标

发展繁荣体现了前三个指标具体可操作性的指向,是人类命运共同体建设共同繁荣世界的最终体现。通过各国间加强开放合作、坚持创新引领、推动包容互惠,最终实现各国的共同繁荣发展。因此,"发展繁荣"指标可以看成是人类命运共同体的构建效果显现,按照上述指标权重分配方法,将其权重设定为25%。

"一带一路"倡议是推动构建人类命运共同体的重要实践平台。几年来,"一带一路"倡议从理念到行动,发展成为实实在在的国际合作,取得了令人瞩目的成就。在"一带一路"倡议国际合作框架内,各方能够秉持共商共建共享原则,携手应对世界经济面临的挑战,开创发展新机遇,谋求发展新

3. "Inclusiveness and reciprocity" indicator

Inclusiveness and reciprocity embody the latest thoughts on the Community with a Shared Future for Mankind. They are the ultimate purpose of building a Community with a Shared Future for Mankind. "A single flower does not make spring, while one hundred flowers in full blossom bring spring to the garden." With the deepening of economic globalization, inclusiveness, mutual benefit and win-win cooperation are the right, sustainable course of action. The indicator of inclusiveness and reciprocity recognizes the differences between countries and advocates transcending national differences and promoting inclusive and mutually beneficial development so thatpeople of all countries can share the fruits of economic globalization and world economic growth. It reflects China's new idea of promoting global governance and building a new international economic order and puts forward China's plan for an economic community. Therefore,the above method for determining indicator weightis used to set the weight of "inclusiveness and reciprocity" to 20%.

4. "Development and prosperity" indicator

Development and prosperity reflect the direction of the specific operability of the first three indicators, and are the ultimate purpose of the Community with Shared Future for Mankind. All countries can, through intensified openness and cooperation, continuing innovation-driven development and lasting inclusiveness and mutual benefit, can eventually achieve common prosperity and development. The indicator of development and prosperity can be seen as the fruits of Building a Community with a Shared Future for Mankind. Its weight is set to 25% using the above method for determining indicator weight.

The "Belt and Road Initiative" is an important, specific undertaking towards the building of a Community with a Shared Future for Mankind. Originally a concept, it materialized in recent years, becoming a platform for international cooperation that has racked up impressive achievements. Under

动力，拓展发展新空间，实现优势互补、互利共赢，不断朝着人类命运共同体方向迈进。因此，在对人类经济共同体构建进程指标体系进行测度时，将首先选择"一带一路"沿线国家作为样本。

the international cooperation framework of the "Belt and Road Initiative", all parties uphold the principle of consultation, co-building and sharing, work together to meet the challenges facing the world economy, create new opportunities for development, seek new impetus for development, expand the space for development, complement each other's advantages, achieve mutual benefit and win-win results, and make solid strides towards a Community with a Shared Future for Mankind. Countries along the "Belt and Road Initiative" are the first choice when selecting samples for the measurement of the building process indicator system for the Economic Community with a Shared Future for Mankind.

第三章
人类命运共同体构建进程文化维度指标体系

一、目的和意义

人类命运共同体构建进程文化维度指标体系的目的，是建立一套客观评价世界各国在增强文化自信、减少文化冲突、增进相互理解、实现价值观互相包容等方面的努力程度的评价标准。世界和平的阻力，很大程度上是由文化之间的互相不理解以及各国文化发展程度不平衡造成的。增进国家内部的理解和增进国家之间的互相理解，是解决文化冲突的主要手段。

人类命运共同体构建进程文化维度指标以和而不同、兼收并蓄、包容互鉴的文明交流为原则。政治、经济、安全、生态，都需要文化交流来加以实现。没有文化上的交流、相互的理解、价值观的趋同，其他几个方面的共同体的构建就会存在

Chapter III
An Indicator System for Measuring the Process of Building a Community with a Shared Future for Mankind: Cultural Dimension

I. Purpose and Significance

The purpose of the indicator system for measuring the building process of the Community with a Shared Future for Mankind Cultural Dimension is to lay down a set of objective criteria for evaluating the efforts of countries to bolster cultural self-confidence, reduce cultural conflicts, enhance mutual understanding and realize mutual tolerance of values. The obstacle to world peace is largely caused by the lack of mutual understanding between cultures and the imbalance in cultural development. The main means to solve cultural conflicts is to enhance understanding within and between countries.

The indicators for measuring the building process of the Cultural Community with a Shared Future for Mankind: Cultural Dimension are under the principle behind civilization communication that stresses harmony in diversity, inclusiveness and mutual learning. Cultural exchanges play a large part in building a political community, economic community, security community and ecological community. Without cultural exchanges, mutual understanding and

更多的阻力。只有加强文化交流、理解，加强文明与文明之间的相互包容、谅解，人类命运共同体才可能真正得以构建。

二、指导思想

本指标体系构建的指导思想来源有二：一是中国乃至世界从古至今人类的伟大理想，二是习近平总书记近年来的一系列讲话精神。

早在2 000多年前，中国孔子就提出了"和而不同"的社会和个人交往原则，强调文化的多元开放，倡导"中庸"的人生智慧。2 000多年以来，中国文化一直履行了这条原则，使中国文化成为一个具有巨大包容性和开放性的文化，最终将中华民族凝聚在一起。中国历史文化证明，只有倡导文化的交流与相互包容，才能加强文化凝聚力，才能使不同的社群成为具有合力的共同体。总结历史经验，费孝通先生提出"各美其美、美人之美、美美与共、天下大同"的设想，他强调的，正是文化的包容性。

西方世界的发展历史也证明，一个国家的文化越是具有包容性，这个国家的发展就会越好。越是不能达成文化上的相互谅解，就越有可能摧毁文明。九次十字军东征，起源于宗教和价值观的差异。基督教文化对犹太文化的误读以及犹太文化的内敛性，是犹太民族蒙受苦难的根源。因此，建设发展本国文化的程度、文化本身具有的包容性、文化沟通的畅通度、文化接纳他种文化的力度以及对外宣传本族文化的力

convergence of values, the building of other communities would face greater resistance. To build a Community with a Shared Future for Mankind, cultures must deepen exchanges and understanding, and civilizations must exercise mutual tolerance.

II. Guiding Ideology

The guiding ideology for this indicator system originated in the lofty ideal of China and the world which has spread wide and far and the spirit of the speeches made by General Secretary Xi Jinping in recent years.

Over 2,000 years ago, the Chinese philosopher Confucius formulated the principle of "harmony in diversity" for social and individual contacts. This concept advocates a free, open and pluralistic culture and the life wisdom of "moderation". Since that time, Chinese culture has been sticking to this principle. Today, it has developed into an all-inclusive and open culture that brings together the Chinese nation. Chinese history and culture have proved that cultural exchanges and mutual tolerance are essential to cultural cohesion and the building of a community where different social groups make concerted efforts to achieve their common goals. Fei Xiaotong said, "To achieve universal peace, one should value not only their own culture, but also the culture of others". This is his summary of historical experience, and what he emphasized was precisely cultural inclusiveness.

The development history of the Western world also proves that the more inclusive a country's culture is, the better it will develop. If we fail to promote mutual cultural understanding, we may run the risk of ruining civilization. The nine Crusades originated from differences in religion and value. The misreading of Jewish culture by Christian culture and the introverted nature of Jewish culture were the root cause of the suffering of the Jewish people. In this sense, the development of national culture, the inclusiveness of culture itself, the smoothness of cultural communication, the acceptance of other cultures

度，都是构建文化共同体的必需要素。

另一方面，如果文化仅仅强调"包容性"，强调对外来文化的吸收，又会使本民族文化精神丧失，从而使其他文化失去"借鉴"的对象。所以，各文化又必须增强文化自信，大力发展本民族文化。

习近平总书记在一系列讲话中都谈到了文化对于国家发展和人类发展的重要性，他一方面强调"文化自信"，另一方面强调文化"包容互鉴"。这些精辟论述，是在总结人类发展历史的基础上做出的，显示了高度概括的政治智慧和文化智慧，是顺应世界发展潮流的思想。2014年3月27日，习近平主席在联合国教科文组织总部发表题为《文明交流互鉴是推动人类文明进步和世界和平发展的重要动力》的演讲指出：第一，文明是多彩的，人类文明因多样才有交流互鉴的价值；第二，文明是平等的，人类文明因平等才有交流互鉴的前提；第三，文明是包容的，人类文明因包容才有交流互鉴的动力。强调文明的多彩和平等，就是要增强文化自信；强调文明的包容性，就是要增进文明之间的交流互鉴。

近年来，中国将"包容性发展"作为引领未来的重要理念，表明我们国家的改革与社会建设进入了一个新的历史阶段。中国肩负起大国的担当，力争促进世界和平，与世界人民一道走向人类历史的辉煌。在走向人类辉煌未来的进程中，凝聚世界各国人民的力量，在增强文化自信的同时减少文化差异和冲突，增进相互理解就显得至关重要。

and the efforts to introduce and promote national culture are all necessary for building a cultural community.

On the other hand, if a culture emphasizes "inclusiveness" only and stresses the need to assimilate foreign cultures, it may lose its own characteristics and fail to enlighten other cultures. So all countries must bolster their cultural self-confidence and vigorously develop their own national culture.

In his speeches, General Secretary Xi Jinping talked about the importance of culture to national development and human development, stressing "cultural self-confidence" as well as "cultural tolerance and mutual learning". These insights are based on his summary of human development. They embody incisive political wisdom and cultural wisdom and are consistent with the direction of world development. On March 27, 2014, President Xi Jinping delivered a speech at the headquarters of the UNESCO. In this speech titled *Exchanges and Mutual Learning Between Civilizations Drive Progress in Human Civilization and World Peace and Development*, he pointed out that the diversity, equality and inclusiveness in human civilization promotes exchanges and mutual learning. We emphasize the diversity and equality in civilization to explain why we should boost cultural self-confidence; we emphasize the inclusiveness of civilization to explain why we should promote exchanges and mutual learning among civilizations.

China introduced the concept of "inclusive development" in recent years to guide its future development — an indication that its reform and social development have entered a new historical stage. As a major power in the world, China is committed to shouldering its responsibilities, promoting world peace, and working with the people of the world towards mankind's moment of glory. In this process, it is very important to pool the strength of the people of the world, reduce cultural differences and conflicts while enhancing cultural self-confidence, and promote mutual understanding.

三、构建原则

构建文化共同体指标体系的基本原则是以习近平总书记有关文化发展的重要论述为指导,以文化交流基本规律和过程为框架建立起来的。指标体系的构建原则,就是以"文化自信"和"包容互鉴"为基本评价标准的原则。"文化自信"是就本国内部文化发展状况而言的,主要内涵是本国文化发展的总体水平,只有自身文化强大、沟通充分、国民之间相互理解,文化才能充满自信,才有与其他文化进行交流的基础。"包容互鉴"是就本国与他国文化交流而言的,是指文化对其他文化所采取的和而不同、美美与共、兼收并蓄、取长补短的文化态度和策略。"包容"就是"和而不同、美美与共"的态度,既指本国文化对其他文化的接受态度和程度,也指本国文化被其他文化接受的态度和程度;"互鉴"就是"兼收并蓄、取长补短"的文化策略,既指本国输入他国文化的力度,也指本国输出文化以供他国文化借鉴的力度。

因此,文化共同体的构建,总体上也应从这两个方面进行考虑。一级指标分别考量国家内部文化发展程度的"文化自信"和国家与国家之间的文化交流的"包容互鉴"。

四、指标体系框架

人类命运共同体构建进程文化维度指标体系包含两个一级指标。两个一级指标分别对应指导思想强调的两个方面,二

III. Guiding Principles

The basic principle behind the building of an indicator system for the cultural community is guided by General Secretary Xi Jinping's important remarks on cultural development and built within the framework of the fundamental laws and processes of cultural exchanges. The principle underlying the building of the indicator system is a principle which applies the basic assessment criteria of "cultural self-confidence" and "tolerance and mutual learning". "Cultural self-confidence" applies to national cultural development, and its main content is the overall level of national cultural development. A strong culture in which communication is effective and people fully understand each other constitutes the basis for cultural self-confidence and communication with other cultures. "Inclusiveness and mutual learning" applies to the cultural exchanges between one country and other countries. It is the attitude and strategy adopted by one culture towards other cultures which highlight harmony in diversity, equal treatment of cultures, inclusiveness and mutual learning. "Inclusiveness" is an attitude that values "harmony in diversity and equal treatment of cultures"; it is one culture's attitude of acceptance towards other cultures and the degree of acceptance as well as other cultures' attitude of acceptance towards one particular culture and the degree of acceptance. "Mutual learning" is a cultural strategy that values "inclusiveness and learning from each other"; it is the culture import intensity of one country as well as its culture export intensity.

Overall, these two aspects should be taken into account when building a cultural community. The Tier 1 indicators measure the "self-confidence" of a national culture and the "tolerance and mutual learning" of cultural exchanges between countries.

IV. Framework of Indicator System

The indicator system for measuring the building process of the Cultural Community with a Shared Future for Mankind is a concrete set of assessment

级指标是对一级指标不同对应方面的细化。在两个一级指标之下，分别设置4个二级指标。

"文化自信"这个一级指标下设立4个二级指标。

1. 国民受教育程度。该指标主要反映获得文化自信的国民素质基础和政府在提高国民素质方面所做出的贡献。没有良好的教育以提高国民素质，文化自信是不可能的。

2. 国民科技和文化发展。该指标主要反映政府在丰富国民文化生活方面可能采取的相关举措的力度和国民在文化生活方面的参与度。没有足够的人员、时间和国民的参与，文化自信也就是苍白无力的。

3. 国民内部文化交流。该指标主要考察政府为促进国民内部交流方面所做出的努力。文化发展的核心在于交流，没有充分的内部文化交流，就无法消除内部的文化误解，内部文化共同体建设也就成空中楼阁。

4. 国家内部文化共同体建设成效。该指标主要反映国家内部文化发展的实际效果，包括共同价值观被宣传和认同的程度、教育成效、文化产品及文化产业的数量等。

"包容互鉴"一级指标下设立3个二级指标。

1. 输入文化力度。该指标是"互鉴"的第一个方面，主要

includes two Tier 1 indicators. The two Tier 1 indicators correspond the two aspects emphasized by the guiding ideology, and the Tier 2 indicators are the breakdown of the different aspects of the Tier 1 indicators. Each of the two Tier 1 indicators provides four Tier 2 indicators.

Four Tier 2 indicators are developed under the Tier 1 indicator of "cultural self-confidence".

1. Education level of the population. This indicator mainly shows the population's education qualification for gaining cultural self-confidence and the government's contribution to improving the population's education qualification. Cultural self-confidence would be out of the question if the population lacked a good education.

2. National scientific, technological and cultural development. This indicator mainly shows the intensity of the measures that the government may take to enrich the cultural life of the population and the population's participation in cultural activity. Cultural self-confidence would be rootless if cultural organizations are understaffed, time is limited or participation is inadequate.

3. Cultural exchanges within the population. This indicator mainly shows the efforts made by the government to promote cultural exchanges within the population. The core of cultural development lies in communication. Without sufficient internal cultural communication, there would be no way of removing internal cultural misunderstanding, and the building of an internal cultural community would be a "castle in the air".

4. Achievements in the building of a national cultural community. This indicator mainly shows the actual status of cultural development within a country, covering the extent to which common values are publicized and recognized, education achievements, and the number of cultural products and cultural industries.

Three Tier 2 indicators are developed under the Tier 1 indicator of "inclusiveness and mutual learning".

1. Culture import intensity. This indicator is the first aspect of "mutual

考察一个国家在对他国文化吸收、借鉴方面做出的努力程度。

2. 输出文化力度。该指标是"互鉴"的第二个方面，主要考察一个国家在把本国文化输出到其他国家以供他国文化吸收、借鉴方面做出的努力程度。

3. 文化包容性。该指标主要考察"包容互鉴"中的"包容"。具体而言，主要考察一个国家的文化对异国文化的宽容态度，以及对建立"文化共同体"的总体态度。

权重说明："文化自信"反映的是本国内部文化建设的努力和成效，对"人类文化共同体"起到奠基作用，相对于国家之间的文化交流而言，贡献略小，因此权重为40%，其中40个三级指标分别赋值1%。人类文化共同体建设，更应看重各国在国际文化交流方面所做出的贡献，因此"包容互鉴"权重为60%，其中30个三级指标分别赋值2%。

本指标体系考量的时间，以一年为一个单位，数据均以被考察一年以内的数据为准。整个人类命运共同体构建进程文化维度指标体系如下：

（一）文化自信指标

1. 国民受教育程度（10个观测点）

1.1 初等教育毛入学率

1.2 中等教育毛入学率

1.3 高等教育毛入学率

learning". It mainly assesses the efforts made by a country to assimilate other cultures.

2. Culture export intensity. This indicator is the second aspect of "mutual learning". It mainly assesses the efforts made by a country to export its own culture to other countries.

3. Cultural inclusiveness. This indicator mainly assesses the aspect of "tolerance" in "tolerance and mutual learning". Specifically, it mainly assesses one culture's attitude of tolerance towards foreign cultures and its overall attitude towards the building of a "cultural community".

Note about indicator weight: "Cultural self-confidence" reflects the efforts towards and achievements in national cultural development. It plays a fundamental role in the "Cultural Community with a Shared Future for Mankind". It contributes less than international cultural exchanges, so its weight is set at 40%, and each of the 40 Tier 3 indicators under it is assigned a value of 1%. The contribution made by various countries in international cultural exchanges deserves a greater weight, so the weight of "inclusiveness and mutual learning" is set at 60%, and each of the 30 Tier 3 indicators under it is assigned a value of 2%.

This indicator system measures the building process of the cultural community yearly, and the data used is the data generated in the current year. The Indicator System for Measuring the Process of Building a Community with a Shared Future for Mankind: Cultural Dimension as follows:

(Ⅰ) Cultural self-confidence indicators

1. Education level of the population (10 observation points)

1.1 Gross enrollment rate of primary education

1.2 Gross enrollment rate of secondary education

1.3 Gross enrollment rate of higher education

1.4 每个学生教育支出占人均国内生产总值比重

1.5 国内公共教育经费支出占国内生产总值比重

1.6 人均纸质出版物数量

1.7 生师比

1.8 生均教学、科研仪器设备占有额

1.9 研究生人数占总人口比重

1.10 每百万人中研究人员和技术人员数

2. 国民科技和文化发展状况（9个观测点）

2.1 文化教育传媒投入占财政总支出比重

2.2 全国科技经费投入总量占 GDP 比重

2.3 法定节假日天数

2.4 文化遗产（包括非遗）数量

2.5 全国公共图书馆人均资源拥有率

2.6 人均文化单位机构数

2.7 全国文化单位从业人员数与总人口比例

2.8 人均文物保护科研机构数量

2.9 政府预算的文物保护、博物馆支出占 GDP 比重

3. 国民内部文化交流（10个观测点）

3.1 网民占国民比重

3.2 每年国内旅游人数占国民比重

3.3 国内旅游收入占 GDP 比重

3.4 客运量与人口的比例

1.4 Proportion of education expenditure per student in per capita GDP

1.5 Proportion of domestic public education expenditure in GDP

1.6 Number of paper publications per capita

1.7 Student-teacher ratio

1.8 Occupancy of teaching and research equipment per student

1.9 Proportion of graduate students in the total population

1.10 Number of researchers and technicians per million people

2. Status of national scientific, technological and cultural development (9 observation points)

2.1 Proportion of investment in culture, education and media in the total financial expenditure

2.2 Proportion of total national investment in science and technology in GDP

2.3 Number of legal holidays

2.4 Quantity of cultural heritage (including intangible cultural heritage)

2.5 Per capita ownership of public library resources

2.6 Number of cultural institutions per capita

2.7 Proportion of cultural staff in the total population

2.8 Number of research institutions for the protection of cultural relics per capita

2.9 Proportion of government budget for the protection of cultural relics and the management of museums in GDP

3. Cultural exchanges within the population (10 observation points)

3.1 Proportion of internet users in the population

3.2 Proportion of the yearly number of domestic tourists in the population

3.3 Proportion of domestic tourism revenue in GDP

3.4 Ratio of passenger volume to the population

3.5 传媒机构数量与人口比重

3.6 休闲场所数量

3.7 宣传文化发展专项支出预算额

3.8 每百万人拥有的互联网服务商

3.9 邮电通讯费用占 GDP 比重

3.10 政府预算的学术交流活动支出占 GDP 比重

4. 国家内部文化共同体建设成效（10 个观测点）

4.1 15 岁及以上成人识字率

4.2 语言保护投入资金

4.3 内部自主研发

4.4 高等学历人口比例

4.5 国内多元文化保护投入资金

4.6 人均拥有图书、期刊、报纸、音像制品和电子出版物总量

4.7 学术研究文章发表数量

4.8 艺术表演团体总收入占 GDP 比重

4.9 每万人群众文化设施建筑面积

4.10 全国文物机构接待观众人次与总人品比例

（二）包容互鉴指标

1. 输入文化力度（11 个观测点）

1.1 出国留学教育支出预算占财政总预算比例

3.5 Proportion of the number of media organizations in the population

3.6 Number of leisure facilities

3.7 Budget amount of special expenditure on publicity and cultural development

3.8 Number of Internet service providers per million people

3.9 Proportion of posts and telecommunications expenses in GDP

3.10 Proportion of government budget for academic exchanges in GDP

4. Achievements in the building of a national cultural community (10 observation points)

4.1 Literacy rate of adults aged 15 and above

4.2 Investment in language protection

4.3 In-house R&D

4.4 Proportion of college graduates in the population

4.5 National investment in language diversity protection

4.6 Total number of books, periodicals, newspapers, audio-visual products and electronic publications per capita

4.7 Number of academic research articles published

4.8 Proportion of the total income of art performing groups in GDP

4.9 Floorage of public cultural facilities per 10,000 people

4.10 Proportion of the number of visitors received by cultural institutions in the total population

(II) Inclusiveness and mutual learning indicators

1. Culture import intensity (11 observation points)

1.1 Proportion of budget for overseas studies in the total financial budget

1.2 官方列入可作为中小学第二语言学习的语种数量

1.3 外部知识获取（Acquisition of external knowledge）

1.4 入境旅游人次

1.5 译入电影种数

1.6 国际互联网用户数量

1.7 图书、报纸、期刊进口册数

1.8 版权引进项数

1.9 赴海外留学生人数及经费

1.10 免入境签证国家数

1.11 外籍教师数量

2. 输出文化力度（10个观测点）

2.1 来本国留学教育支出预算占财政总预算比例

2.2 出境旅游人次占国民比重

2.3 图书、报纸、期刊出口册数

2.4 版权输出项数

2.5 本国电影海外票房

2.6 接收外国留学生人数

2.7 国际科技交流与合作政府预算额

2.8 海外教育经费支出

2.9 国际航线数量

2.10 外派文教工作者人数

1.2 Number of languages officially listed as second languages in primary and secondary schools

1.3 Acquisition of external knowledge

1.4 Number of inbound tourists

1.5 Number of the types of films translated into the native language

1.6 Number of Internet users

1.7 Number of imported books, newspapers and periodicals

1.8 Number of copyright imports

1.9 Number of and expenditure for students studying overseas

1.10 Number of countries providing visa-free access

1.11 Number of foreign teachers

2. Culture export intensity (10 observation points)

2.1 Proportion of budget for incoming international students in the total financial budget

2.2 Proportion of the number of outbound tourists in the population

2.3 Number of exported books, newspapers and periodicals

2.4 Number of copyright exports

2.5 Overseas box office revenues of home-made films

2.6 Number of enrolled foreign students

2.7 Government budget for international scientific and technological exchanges and cooperation

2.8 Expenditure on overseas education

2.9 Number of international air routes

2.10 Number of cultural and educational workers deployed abroad

3. 文化包容性（8个观测点）

3.1 外国人文社科研究发文数量

3.2 学术著作外译数量

3.3 文化旅游体育交流与合作财政预算额

3.4 海外引进电影数量及票房

3.5 外国公民入境人次

3.6 来本国从事营业性演出参加总人次

3.7 举办大型国际体育赛事场数和参加人次

3.8 对外演出项数和参加人次

（三）指标体系框架附表

表3.1 人类命运共同体构建进程文化维度指标体系

一级指标	二级指标	三级指标
文化自信范畴	国民受教育程度测度	初等教育毛入学率观测点
		中等教育毛入学率观测点
		高等教育毛入学率观测点
		每个学生教育支出占人均国内生产总值比重观测点
		国内公共教育经费支出占国内生产总值比重观测点
		人均纸质出版物数量观测点
		生师比观测点
		生均教学、科研仪器设备占有额观测点
		研究生人数占总人口比重
		每百万人中研究人员和技术人员数观测点

3. Cultural inclusiveness (8 observation points)

3.1 Number of papers published on foreign cultures and social sciences

3.2 Number of academic works translated into foreign languages

3.3 Budget amount of cultural, tourism, and sports exchanges and cooperation

3.4 Number and box office revenues of imported foreign films

3.5 Number of entries of foreign nationals

3.6 Total attendance at commercial performances held domestically by foreign performers

3.7 Number of and attendance at large international sports events held

3.8 Number of performances held overseas and participants

(III) Schedule of Framework of Indicator System

Schedule 3.1 An Indicator System for Measuring the Process of Building a Community with a Shared Future for Mankind: Cultural Dimension

Tier 1 indicators	Tier 2 indicators	Tier 3 indicators
The sphere of cultural self-confidence	Measure of the education level of the population	Observation point for the gross enrollment rate of primary education
		Observation point for the gross enrollment rate of secondary education
		Observation point for the gross enrollment rate of higher education
		Observation point for the proportion of education expenditure per student in per capita GDP
		Observation point for the proportion of domestic public education expenditure in GDP
		Observation point for the number of paper publications per capita
		Observation point for the student-teacher ratio
		Observation point for the occupancy of teaching and research equipment per student
		Observation point for the proportion of graduate students in the total population

续表

一级指标	二级指标	三级指标
文化自信范畴	国民科技和文化发展测度	文化教育传媒投入占财政总支出比重观测点
		全国科技经费投入总量占GDP比重观测点
		法定节假日天数观测点
		文化遗产（包括非遗）数量观测点
		全国公共图书馆人均资源拥有率观测点
		人均文化单位机构数观测点
		全国文化单位从业人员数与总人口比例观测点
		人均文物保护科研机构数量观测点
		政府预算的文物保护、博物馆支出占GDP比重观测点
	国民内部文化交流测度	网民占国民比重观测点
		每年国内旅游人数占国民比重观测点
		国内旅游收入占GDP比重观测点
		客运量与人口的比例观测点
		传媒机构数量与人口比重观测点
		休闲场所数量观测点
		宣传文化发展专项支出预算额观测点
		每百万人拥有的互联网服务商观测点
		邮电通讯费用占GDP比重观测点
		政府预算的学术交流活动支出占GDP比重观测点

Continued Schedule

Tier 1 indicators	Tier 2 indicators	Tier 3 indicators
The sphere of cultural self-confidence	Measure of the status of national scientific, technological and cultural development	Observation point for the number of researchers and technicians per million people
		Observation point for the proportion of investment in culture, education and media in the total financial expenditure
		Observation point for the proportion of total national investment in science and technology in GDP
		Observation point for the number of legal holidays
		Observation point for the quantity of cultural heritage (including intangible cultural heritage)
		Observation point for per capita ownership of public library resources
		Observation point for the number of cultural institutions per capita
		Observation point for the proportion of cultural staff in the total population
		Observation point for the number of research institutions for the protection of cultural relics per capita
		Observation point for the proportion of government budget for the protection of cultural relics and the management of museums in GDP
	Measure of cultural exchanges within the population	Observation point for the proportion of Internet users in the population
		Observation point for the proportion of the yearly number of domestic tourists in the population
		Observation point for the proportion of domestic tourism revenue in GDP
		Observation point for the ratio of passenger volume to the population
		Observation point for the proportion of the number of media organizations in the population
		Observation point for the number of leisure facilities
		Observation point for for the budget amount of special expenditure on publicity and cultural development
		Observation point for the number of Internet service providers per million people
		Observation point for the proportion of posts and telecommunications expenses in GDP
		Observation point for the proportion of government budget for academic exchanges in GDP

续表

一级指标	二级指标	三级指标
包容互鉴范畴	国家内部文化共同体建设成效测度	15岁及以上成人识字率观测点
		语言保护投入资金观测点
		内部自主研发观测点
		高等学历人口比例观测点
		国内多元文化保护投入资金观测点
		人均拥有图书、期刊、报纸、音像制品和电子出版物总量观测点
		学术研究文章发表数量观测点
		艺术表演团体总收入占GDP比重观测点
		每万人群众文化设施建筑面积观测点
		全国文物机构接待观众人次与总人品比例观测点
	输入文化力度测度	出国留学教育支出预算占财政总预算比例观测点
		官方列入可作为中小学第二语言学习的语种数量观测点
		外部知识获取观测点
		入境旅游人次观测点
		译入电影种数观测点
		国际互联网用户数量观测点
		图书、报纸、期刊进口册数观测点
		版权引进项数观测点
		赴海外留学生人数及经费观测点
		免入境签证国家数观测点
		外籍教师数量观测点

Continued Schedule

Tier 1 indicators	Tier 2 indicators	Tier 3 indicators
The sphere of inclusiveness and mutual learning	Measure of the achievements in the building of a national cultural community	Observation point for the literacy rate of adults aged 15 and above
		Observation point for the investment in language protection
		Observation point for in-house R&D
		Observation point for the proportion of college graduates in the population
		Observation point for national investment in language diversity protection
		Observation point for the total number of books, periodicals, newspapers, audio-visual products and electronic publications per capita
		Observation point for the number of academic research articles published
		Observation point for the proportion of the total income of art performing groups in GDP
		Observation point for the floorage of public cultural facilities per 10,000 people
		Observation point for the proportion of the number of visitors received by cultural institutions in the total population
	Measure of culture import intensity	Observation point for the proportion of budget for overseas studies in the total financial budget
		Observation point for the number of languages officially listed as second languages in primary and secondary schools
		Observation point for the acquisition of external knowledge
		Observation point for the number of inbound tourists
		Observation point for the number of the types of films translated into the native language
		Observation point for the number of internet users
		Observation point for the number of imported books, newspapers and periodicals
		Observation point for the number of copyright imports
		Observation point for the number of and expenditure for students studying overseas
		Observation point for the number of countries providing visa-free access
		Observation point for the number of foreign teachers

续表

一级指标	二级指标	三级指标
包容互鉴范畴	输出文化力度测度	来本国留学教育支出预算占财政总预算比例观测点
		出境旅游人次占国民比重观测点
		图书、报纸、期刊出口册数观测点
		版权输出项数观测点
		本国电影海外票房观测点
		接收外国留学生人数观测点
		国际科技交流与合作政府预算额观测点
		海外教育经费支出观测点
		国际航线数量观测点
		外派文教工作者人数观测点
	文化包容性测度	外国人文社科研究发文数量观测点
		学术著作外译数量观测点
		文化旅游体育交流与合作财政预算额观测点
		海外引进电影数量及票房观测点
		外国公民入境人次观测点
		来本国从事营业性演出参加总人次观测点
		举办大型国际体育赛事场数和参加人次观测点
		对外演出项数和参加人次观测点

Continued Schedule

Tier 1 indicators	Tier 2 indicators	Tier 3 indicators
The sphere of inclusiveness and mutual learning	Measure of culture export intensity	Observation point for the proportion of budget for incoming international students in the total financial budget
		Observation point for the proportion of the number of outbound tourists in the population
		Observation point for the number of exported books, newspapers and periodicals
		Observation point for the number of copyright exports
		Observation point for the overseas box office revenues of home-made films
		Observation point for the number of enrolled foreign students
		Observation point for government budget for international scientific and technological exchanges and cooperation
		Observation point for the expenditure on overseas education
		Observation point for the number of international air routes
		Observation point for the number of cultural and educational workers deployed abroad
	Measure of cultural inclusiveness	Observation point for the number of papers published on foreign cultures and social sciences
		Observation point for the number of academic works translated into foreign languages
		Observation point for the budget amount of cultural, tourism, and sports exchanges and cooperation
		Observation point for the number and box office revenues of imported foreign films
		Observation point for the number of entries of foreign nationals
		Observation point for the total attendance at commercial performances held domestically by foreign performers
		Observation point for the number of and attendance at large international sports events held
		Observation point for the number of performances held overseas and participants

五、指标赋权方法

（一）文化自信指标

该一级指标主要考察一个国家内部文化发展状况和交流状况。只有当一个文化自身充分发展充分交流，形成一个具有一致认同性的文化之时，才具备与其他文化进行沟通和交流的能力，其他文化也才会觉得这个文化有学习借鉴之必要。一个国家，如果自己内部文化建设做得不好，对其他文化而言也就不具备交流之价值；如果自己内部文化交流做得不好，则意味着该文化本身不具备可交流的品质。打铁还需自身硬。构建人类文化共同体，对每个国家而言都需要该文化自身过硬，强调自身文化内涵建设，才具备构建人类文化共同体的基础。

1. 国民受教育程度

本观测点主要考察一个国家内部国民普遍受教育的程度。受教育程度越高，则其接受文化共同体的观念越有可能，且其在内部建立文化共同体的机会越大。只有当全民文化文化水平有一定高度时，才能说这个国家的文化建设是有成效的。因此，国民受教育程度是文化共同体建设成效的重要参考指标。

1.1 初等教育毛入学率

该指标数据来源于《国际统计年鉴》，反映国民接受初等教育人口比例。初等教育毛入学率反映了一个国家的总体受教育程度的状况，能反映该国扫盲工作的工作力度。人类文明共同体的理想，不是指一部分人能够享受人类文明成果，而是指全体人类都能享受人类文明成果。如果一个国家文盲

V. Indicator Weighting

(I) Cultural self-confidence indicators

These Tier 1 indicators mainly investigate the national cultural development and communication. Only when a culture is developed and communicated to such an extent as to have a uniform identity, can it acquire the ability to communicate with other cultures. And other cultures will feel that it is necessary to learn from this culture. An underdeveloped national culture will not likely provide a useful frame of reference for other cultures; and a poorly communicated national culture will not likely inspire other cultures. "It takes a good blacksmith to make steel". To build a Cultural Community with a Shared Future for Mankind, all countries need to have an excellent culture. A solid and strong culture is the basis for building a Cultural Community with a Shared Future for Mankind.

1. Education level of the population

This observation point mainly investigates the general education level of a country's population. The higher the level of education of a population, the more likely it is to accept the concept of cultural community and establish an internal cultural community. Only when the literacy level of the whole population has reached a certain height, can we say the national cultural development is fruitful. Therefore, the national education level is an important indicator of the achievements made in the building of a cultural community.

1.1 Gross enrollment rate of primary education

This indicator is based on data collected in the *International Statistical Yearbook*. It shows the proportion of people who have received primary education in the total population. The gross enrollment rate of primary education reflects the overall education level of a country and the intensity of its work to eliminate illiteracy. The ideal of a Civilization Community with a Shared Future for Mankind is that all mankind, not some people, have access to the fruits

率过高，则反映了该国内部在建立文化共同体方面工作做得不够。如果一个国家内部出现太大的教育程度差异，则说明该国本身在文化共同体建构方面观念不到位，或整体文明发展水平太低，不利于全人类文化共同体的形成。只有全人类都受到教育，那么人类命运共同体的教育也才能够有落实的基础。

1.2 中等教育毛入学率

该指标数据来源于《国际统计年鉴》，反映国民接受中等教育人口比例。中等教育毛入学率反映的是国家教育程度的另一重要指标。这一指标越高，说明该国国民受教育程度越高。联合国教科文组织对世界各国的中等教育毛入学率做了统计，以反映该国教育发展程度。例如，1997年的数据反映，中国的中等教育毛入学率为70.1%，而欧洲、亚洲/太平洋和北美发达国家以及转型国家的毛入学率分别为113.2%、102.4%、98.2%和87%[1]。这说明，越是发达的国家，这个指标一般会越高。受教育程度越高，则该国国民整体上认为人类命运共同体理念的可能性越大。文化程度越高，也意味着文化传承工作做得越好。

1.3 高等教育毛入学率

该指标数据来源于《国际统计年鉴》，反映国民接受高等教育人口比例。高等教育毛入学率指的是高等教育在学人数

---

[1] 杨成铭. 受教育权的促进和保护：国际标准与中国的实践 [M]. 北京：中国法制出版社，2004: 246.

of human civilization. A high illiteracy rate suggests that the country has not done enough in building an internal cultural community. An uneven national education level suggests that the country is not fully aware of the importance of building a cultural community, or that its overall level of civilization is so low that it is not possible to build a cultural community for mankind. Only when all mankind are educated, can the education about the Community with a Shared Future for Mankind be a feasible initiative.

1.2 Gross enrollment rate of secondary education

This indicator is based on data collected in the *International Statistical Yearbook*. It shows the proportion of people who have received secondary education in the total population. The gross enrollment rate of secondary education is another important indicator of the national educational level. A high gross enrollment rate of secondary education suggests a high national educational level. The UNESCO produces statistics on the gross enrollment rate of secondary education in various countries to show the level of their respective educational development. For example, according to the data collected in 1997, the gross enrollment rate of secondary education in China was 70.1%, while that in Europe, Asia / Pacific, North America and countries in transition were 113.2%, 102.4%, 98.2% and 87%[1], respectively. This shows that the more developed a country is, the higher this indicator will be. The higher the level of education, the more likely the concept of a Community with a Shared Future for Mankind is to materialize in the overall opinion of the people of the country. And a high literacy level suggests good work in the inheritance of cultural heritage.

1.3 Gross enrollment rate of higher education

This indicator is based on data collected in the *International Statistical Yearbook*. It shows the proportion of people who have received higher education in

---

[1] Yang Chengming. Promotion and Protection of the Right to Education: International Standards and China's Practice[M]. Beijing: China Legal Publishing House, 2004: 246.

与适龄人口之比率。国际上的通行标准认为"高等教育毛入学率15%以下属于精英教育阶段,15%—50%为高等教育大众化阶段,50%以上为高等教育普及化阶段"①。高等教育普及化,是各国文化发展的目标。联合国教科文组织非常重视这个比率,且将适龄人口设定在20—24岁之间。这个指标不但反映了国家的发展程度,也反映了一个国家的文化发展水平。高等教育毛入学率是一个国家综合实力的表现,也是一个文化的包容性得以实现的重要依托,还是一个国家文化创新性得以实现的根基。

1.4 每个学生教育支出占人均国内生产总值比重

该指标数据来源于《国际统计年鉴》和财政部官网,反映国内学生实际享受到的教育资源。这一指标主要反映该国国民对教育的重视程度。有的国家,虽然经济欠发达,但是国民愿意将有限的资源尽可能多地用于教育,在总体开支中比重较高,这就能够说明该国国民有重视教育的觉悟和意识。这一指标有利于平衡单纯以国家经济发展程度来反映其在文化共同体建构中的作用这一偏颇。即使经济欠发达,但是教育支出比重大,仍然可以认为他们愿意为文化共同体做贡献,因此应予以鼓励。

---

① 全国高等教育毛入学率51.6% 高等教育毛入学率怎么算?2020高等教育行业规模趋势预测.[EB/OL].[2020-05-21].http://www.chinairn.com/hyzx/ 20200521/144545717.shtml the total population. The gross enrollment rate of higher education refers to the ratio of the number of students receiving higher education to the college-age population. By conventional international standards, "A country is at the stage of elite education if the gross enrollment rate of higher education is below 15%, it is at the stage of higher education popularization if the rate is between 15% and 50%, and it is at the stage of universal higher education if the rate is above 50%".[①] Higher education popularization is the goal of national cultural development. The UNESCO attaches great importance to this ratio, and it sets the age range of college-age population at 20-24. This indicator reflects not only the level of national development, but also that of national cultural development. The gross enrollment rate of higher education is not only an indicator of national comprehensive strength, but also an important medium for achieving cultural inclusiveness and the foundation for national cultural innovativeness.

1.4 Proportion of education expenditure per student in per capita GDP

This indicator is based on data collected in the *International Statistical Yearbook* and the official website of the Ministry of Finance. It shows the amount of educational resources that domestic students actually have available. This indicator mainly reflects the importance that a country's citizens attach to education. In some underdeveloped countries, people are willing to spend as much of their limited resources on education as possible, and the proportion of expenditure on education is high in the total national expenses. This shows that they are conscious of the importance of education. This indicator can overcome the problem of overstating the role of national economic development in the building of a cultural community. Underdeveloped countries with a high education expenditure are obviously willing to contribute to the cultural community. Their efforts in this regard deserve encouragement.

---

① The national gross enrollment rate of higher education is 51.6%. How was this gross enrollment rate of higher education worked out? 2020 Forecast of the Scale of Higher Education[EB/OL]. [2020-05-21]. http://www.chinairn.com/hyzx/ 20200521/144545717.shtml

1.5 国内公共教育经费支出占国内生产总值比重

该指标数据来源于《国际统计年鉴》和财政部官网,反映国家对国民教育的财政投入水平和重视程度。这一指标主要反映国家层面对教育的重视程度。人类文化共同体的建构,不但需要人民群众的努力,更需要得到政府的支持和重视。一个国家愿意将更多的经费用于教育,则反映了该国政府在此方面做出的努力。这一指标也有利于平衡个别国家盲目发展教育的问题。如果盲目扩大招生规模,增加毛入学率指数,而在教育经费方面投入不足,则不能真实反映其对教育的重视度。

1.6 人均纸质出版物数量

该指标数据来源于《中国文化及相关产业统计年鉴》,反映国民可供购买的出版物数量和国民的阅读量。人均纸质出版物出版数量反映政府和国民对书籍的热爱程度。虽然现在的阅读普遍从纸本阅读转向了电子阅读,但是总体而言,纸本阅读和电子阅读的比例始终是趋于一致的。电子阅读的统计口径需要进一步完善,而纸质出版物的数量则有比较固定的数据来源。出版物数量反映了一个国家整体上对文化的重视程度,既包括国家层面对出版物的推广度,也包括国民对出版物的热爱度。

1.7 生师比

该指标数据来源于教育部官网《中国教育概况》,反映学生实际教师拥有率。生师比直接反映了教育的有效性和效果。

1.5 Proportion of domestic public education expenditure in GDP

This indicator is based on data collected in the *International Statistical Yearbook* and the official website of the Ministry of Finance. It shows the level of financial input into national education and the importance a country attaches to education. This indicator mainly reflects the importance that a country attaches to education. The building of a Cultural Community with a Shared Future for Mankind requires the efforts of the people as well as the support and attention of the government. A country's willingness to spend huge amounts of money on education reflects the efforts of the government in this regard. This indicator can overcome the problem of random educational development in some countries. Random enrollment expansion without sufficient financial support can increase the gross enrollment rate, but this does not truly reflect the importance attached to education.

1.6 Number of paper publications per capita

This indicator is based on data collected in the *Statistical Yearbook of Chinese Culture and Related Industries*. It shows the number of publications available for purchase in a country and how much is read. The number of paper publications per capita reflects the love of the government and the people for books. Although electronic publications are taking the place of paper publications, generally speaking, the ratio of paper publications to electronic publications tends to be the same. The statistical caliber of E-reading needs to be further improved, while the number of paper publications has a relatively fixed data source. The number of publications reflects the attention a country attaches to culture as a whole, including the promotion of publications at the national level and the population's love for publications.

1.7 Student-teacher ratio

This indicator is based on data collected in the *Overview of Chinese Education* on the official website of the Ministry of Education. It reflects the actual student-teacher ratio, which represents the effectiveness of and achievements in

生师比越高，则每个学生接受的个别辅导和因材施教式教育的机会越少。生师比是考察一个国家的教师配置、使用效益的重要指标，通常说越发达的国家生师比越低，越欠发达的国家生师比越高。在经济发展水平同等的情况下，生师比过高表明教育资源比较短缺，生师比过低表明使用效益低下。"生师比反映了学校的师资力量状况，是否能满足人才培养的需要。从评估标准来看，生师比相对越低，说明学校师资力量配备越充足，人才培养就越有保证。"[①] 因此，生师比实际反映了教育效果得以实现的保障。

1.8 生均教学、科研仪器设备占有额

该指标数据来源于教育部官网《中国教育概况》，反映学生实际享有的教学资源情况，与生师比指标具有相似的功能。学生占有的教育资源，既包括老师，也包括硬件设施。教学设施、科研仪器占有量越高，则教育的效果越能得到保障。另一方面，这也能够反映国家教育经费到底是否真正用到了学生身上，而不是单纯的投入。因此，这个指标能够反映出国民受教育的实际效益。

1.9 研究生人数占全国总人口比例

反映国家高等教育办学水平。本指标能够反映一个国家具备最高学历的人口比例，能够反映该国人口的总体素质，因而可以反映该国在教育方面取得的实际成果。

---

① 梁绿琦. 高等教育教学评估研究 [M]. 上海：上海交通大学出版社，2015:135.

education. The higher the student-teacher ratio, the fewer opportunities each student receives face-to-face tutoring and individualized education. The student-teacher ratio is an important indicator of the allocation and use efficiency of teachers in a country. Generally speaking, the more developed a country is, the lower the ratio of students to teachers, and the more underdeveloped a country is, the higher the ratio of students to teachers. In countries where the level of economic development is similar, an extra high student-teacher ratio indicates a shortage of educational resources, and a super low student-teacher ratio indicates low use efficiency. "The student-teacher ratio" shows the number of teachers available for use in a school and whether it can meet the needs of education. Judging from the evaluation criteria, the lower the student-teacher ratio is, the more sufficient the faculty is and the more guaranteed education is."[1] Therefore, the student-teacher ratio is an indicator of the guarantee for achieving education goals.

1.8 Occupancy of teaching and research equipment per student

This indicator is based on data collected in the *Overview of Chinese Education* on the official website of the Ministry of Education. It reflects the actual amount of educational resources available to students and is similar to the student-teacher ratio in terms of function. The educational resources available to students include both teachers and facilities. The higher the availability of teaching facilities and scientific research instruments, the better the effect of education. It can also reflect whether the national education funds are really used on students. Therefore, this indicator can show the actual benefits of national education.

1.9 Proportion of graduate students in the total population

This indicator reflects the level of higher education. It can show the proportion of the population which have received higher education, the overall quality of the population, and the actual achievements in education.

---

[1] Liang Lvqi. Research on Higher Education Evaluation[M]. Shanghai: Shanghai Jiaotong University Press, 2015, P. 135.

1.10 每百万人中研究人员和技术人员数

本项指标数据来源于《国际统计年鉴》，反映教育取得的实际效果和在国民生活中的重要程度，用于考察国民内部人员的分工结构。研究人员和技术人员越多，则说明该国对科学技术和文化研究的重视程度越高，"大学毛入学率、每百万人中研究人员和技术人员数、研究与开发经费支出和公共教育经费支出占国内生产总值比重、专利申请数量等是判断一个国家高等教育的重要指标。"据统计，以 2000 年、2004 年、2005 年的数据来看，我国的水平达到中等收入国家的水平。[①] 这项指标跟经济发达程度有关，也跟国家和国民的重视程度有关。

2. 国民科技和文化发展状况

2.1 文化教育传媒投入占财政总支出比重

该指标数据来源于《文化发展统计分析报告》、财政部官网与文化和旅游部官网，反映国家对文化建设的重视程度。除了对教育和科学技术发展的支持力度，一个国家是否重视发展文化教育是另一个重要参考因素。本项指标不以单纯的财政投入总额计算，也是考虑到各国发展经济不平衡，不能以总财政投入加以考察，而应以文化教育投入在财政支出中的比重来考察。即使是经济欠发达国家，如果他们在文化教

---

① 张婕. 地方高校发展：现实与理想 [M]. 武汉：华中师范大学出版社，2010:321-322.

1.10 Number of researchers and technicians per million people

This indicator is based on data collected in the *International Statistical Yearbook*. It reflects the actual effect of education and its importance in national life, and is used to investigate the division of labor among the people. The more researchers and technicians there are, the more attention a country attaches to science, technology and cultural research. "The gross enrollment rate of higher education, the number of researchers and technicians per million people, the proportion of R&D expenditure and public education expenditure in GDP, and the number of patent applications are important indicators of a country's higher education." According to data released in 2000, 2004 and 2005, China has reached the level of middle-income countries.[①] This indicator is related to the level of economic development, as well as the importance attached by a country and its people.

2. Status of national scientific, technological and cultural development

2.1 Proportion of investment in culture, education and media in the total financial expenditure

This indicator is based on data collected in the *Statistical Analysis Report on Cultural Development*, the official website of the Ministry of Finance, and the official website of the Ministry of Culture and Tourism. It shows the importance a country attaches to cultural development. In addition to the support for the development of education and science and technology, whether a country attaches importance to the development of culture and education is another important factor. Considering that economic development is uneven across countries, this indicator does not measure the total amount of financial investment. The total financial investment should not be a consideration; the proportion of cultural and educational investment in financial expenditure is

---

① Zhang Jie. Development of Sub-national Universities: Reality and Ideal[M]. Wuhan: Central China Normal University Press, 2010: 321-322.

育传媒方面的投入力度很大，也是有利于保护文化的。人类文化共同体的理念，就是要保护文化多样性，而在此方面给予的支持力度，则显示了该国在文化保护和发展方面做出的努力程度。

2.2 全国科技经费投入总量占 GDP 比重

本项指标数据来源于科学技术部官网《全国科技经费投入统计公报》，反映国家对科技的重视程度，与上一个指标是平行关系。文化与科技是人类文明的两个重要支柱，既不能重文化轻科技，也不能重科技轻文化。

2.3 法定节假日天数

本项指标数据来源于各国法律规定假期数和工作时长，反映国民法定享有的文化、节假日时间。只有有了充足的节假日时间，国民才有时间从事文化交流活动，才更有利于人们从事文化活动和与其他人进行沟通。法定节假日时间过少，则意味着人民整天忙于工作而无时间思考关于文化的问题。只有有了充足的时间，包括旅游业在内的休闲产业才能得到充足的发展。"国家法定休闲时间的进一步增加，也为流行品市场的繁荣增加了助力。"[1] 不仅如此，法定休闲时间增加之后，"形成了多种多样的潮流化社会互动"[2]。所以，节假日的增加，不仅改变了人们的生活方式，而且也为文化交流提供了条件。

---

[1] 王国荣. 信息化与文化产业 [M]. 上海：上海文化出版社，2004:140.
[2] 胡小武. 城市张力：咖啡馆与生活方式的转型 [M]. 南京：东南大学出版社，2011:110.

one important consideration. Economically underdeveloped countries which invest heavily in culture, education and media can effectively protect their cultures. The Cultural Community with a Shared Future for Mankind aims to protect cultural diversity, and the support in this regard shows the efforts made by a country in cultural protection and development.

2.2 Proportion of total national investment in science and technology in GDP

This indicator is based on data collected in the *Statistical Bulletin on National Funds for Science and Technology* issued by the Ministry of Science and Technology on its official website. It reflects the importance attached by the state to science and technology, and is parallel to the previous indicator. Culture and science and technology are the two important pillars of human civilization. Culture does not take precedence over science and technology, and the latter does not take precedence over the former.

2.3 Number of legal holidays

This indicator is based on the number of holidays and working hours stipulated by laws of various countries, and reflects the culture and holiday time legally enjoyed by citizens. With sufficient holidays, people will have time to engage in cultural exchanges, cultural activities and communication with others. Few legal holidays mean that people are busy working all day and have no time to think about culture. With enough time, leisure industries including tourism can achieve full development. "The further increase in legal leisure time has also given a boost to the popular goods market."[1] Moreover, after the increase in legal leisure time, "a variety of trendy social interactions have appeared".[2] Therefore, the increase in holidays not only changes people's way of life, but also provides conditions for cultural exchanges.

---

[1] Wang Guorong. Informatization and the Cultural Industry[M]. Shanghai: Shanghai Cultural Publishing House, 2004: 140.

[2] Hu Xiaowu. Urban Vibrancy: Coffee Shop and Lifestyle Transformation[M]. Nanjing: Southeast University Press, 2011: 110.

2.4 文化遗产（包括非遗）数量

反映该国历史上为人类文明做出的贡献和保护成效。本指标既能反映该国在人类文明史上做出了多少贡献，也能反映该国对这些贡献遗存的保护效果。文化遗产越多，说明该国曾经对人类文明做出的贡献越大，而且该国历朝历代均重视对这些遗产的传承和保护。

2.5 全国公共图书馆人均资源拥有率

该指标数据来源于《中国图书馆年鉴》和文化和旅游部《文化和旅游发展统计公报》，反映国家对图书馆文化建设的投入力度。公共图书馆人均拥有率反映国家对人民文化生活的重视度。文化发展，需要各种文化交流平台的搭建，既包括文化产业的发展，也包括公共文化事业的发展，包括博物馆、公共图书馆、展览厅、科技馆，等等。图书馆拥有率可以从一个方面反映国家在文化建设方面的投入力度和重视程度。

2.6 人均文化单位机构数

该指标数据来源于《文化发展统计分析报告》，反映国家对文化发展的重视程度，亦即反映了政府在文化机构建设和管理方面的深入程度。文化机构包括艺术表演团体、艺术表演场馆、文化站、公共图书馆、博物馆等。专设指标考察人均图书馆资源，表示了对图书馆权重的加强，为避免重复，这里的指标在计算的时候可将图书馆数扣除。

2.4 Quantity of cultural heritage (including intangible cultural heritage)

The quantity of cultural heritage reflects the contributions a country has made to human civilization and the achievements it has made in protection. This indicator can not only demonstrate the contributions a country has made in the history of human civilization, but also reflect the achievements the country made in the protection of these contributions. The more cultural heritage sites there are in a country, the greater contribution the country has made to human civilization. This is also an indicator of the country's past and present efforts to inherit and protect these heritage sites.

2.5 Per capita ownership of public library resources

This indicator is based on data collected in the *Library Yearbook* and the *Statistical Bulletin on Cultural and Tourism Development* released by the Ministry of Culture and Tourism. It shows a country's investment in the development of library culture. The per capita ownership of public libraries reflects a state's emphasis on cultural life. Cultural development requires the building of various cultural exchange platforms, including the development of the cultural industry and public cultural undertakings such as museums, public libraries, exhibition halls, and science and technology museums. The per capita ownership of public libraries can reflect the investment and attention of a country in cultural development.

2.6 Number of cultural institutions per capita

This indicator is based on data collected in the *Statistical Analysis Report on Cultural Development*. It reflects the importance attached by a state to cultural development as well as government involvement in the establishment and management of cultural institutions. Cultural institutions include art performing groups, art performing venues, cultural centers, public libraries, museums, etc. This indicator is specifically developed to investigate per capita library resources — an indication that the weight of libraries has increased. To avoid repetition, the number of libraries can be deducted in the calculation of this indicator.

2.7 全国文化单位从业人员数与总人口比例

本指标与上一指标具有接续性，数据来源于《文化发展统计分析报告》，反映国家和国民对文化建设的兴趣和参与度。一个国家的文化繁荣程度，不仅要看文化机构的数量，还要看国家在这方面投入的人力资源。投入人力资源越多，说明该国对文化事业的重视程度越高，也就越有利于文化共同体的形成。

2.8 人均文物保护科研机构数量

本指标数据来源于《文化发展统计分析报告》，反映国家对传统文化的保护力度。传统文化保护科研机构的数量，主要是反映一个国家在保护文化多样性方面做出的贡献。各国只有保护好自己的传统文化，才能真正有利于多彩文化的形成。如果这一指标统计有难度，可以用"人均物质文化遗产和非物质文化遗产数"来取代，这一指标反映了该国历史上对传统文化保护的成效，而不是仅仅反映现在政府对传统文化保护的投入。

2.9 政府预算的文物保护、博物馆支出占GDP比重

本指标数据来源于财政部官网，反映国家对传统文化的保护力度，是从国家经济投入方面衡量政府对于传统文化保护做出的贡献。人类文化共同体的建设不仅要有世界范围内的沟通与合作，也有赖于传统文化多样性的存在。从这个指标也可以看出该国对本国传统文化的重视程度。

2.7 Proportion of cultural staff in the total population

This indicator is derived from the previous indicator. The data comes from the *Statistical Analysis Report on Cultural Development*. It reflects the interest and participation of a country and its people in cultural development. The degree of national cultural prosperity depends not only on the number of cultural institutions, but also on the human resources invested by the country. The more human resources invested, the more attention the country attaches to cultural undertakings, and the more conducive it is to the formation of a cultural community.

2.8 Number of research institutions for the protection of cultural relics per capita

This indicator is based on data collected in the *Statistical Analysis Report on Cultural Development*. It demonstrates the efforts made by a country to protect traditional culture. The number of research institutions for the protection of traditional culture mainly reflects a country's contribution to the protection of cultural diversity. Only by protecting their own traditional culture can countries really maintain cultural diversity. If this indicator runs into statistical difficulties, it can be replaced by "the number of tangible and intangible cultural heritage per capita". This indicator reflects the achievements a country has made in the protection of traditional culture, rather than the government's investment in the protection of traditional culture.

2.9 Proportion of government budget for the protection of cultural relics and the management of museums to GDP

This indicator is based on data released on the official website of the Ministry of Finance. It reflects a country's protection of traditional culture and measures the government's contribution to the protection of traditional culture in terms of national economic input. To build a Cultural Community with a Shared Future for Mankind, the world needs to communicate and cooperate, and traditional culture needs to preserves its diversity. This indicator also shows the importance a country attaches to its traditional culture.

3. 国民内部文化交流

本观测点主要观察一个国家内部文化交流的活跃程度。如果一个国家内部文化交流不活跃，则该国不可能在国际文化交流方面活跃。内部文化交流不活跃，也不利于该国内部文化的保护与相互理解和尊重。因此，内部文化交流活跃度是文化共同体形成的重要参考指标。

3.1 网民占国民比重

该指标数据来源于《互联网研究报告》，反映国民文化交流的总体参与度。现代社会的文化沟通与交流更多依靠网络，网络交流打破了地域之间的距离屏障，因此对于文化交流而言具有无可比拟的快捷性和广泛性。网民的人数反映了该国人民沟通活跃程度，也能反映该国人民对于文化交流与沟通的实际参与度。"网民占城市人口的比例，反映居民信息获取和学习的水平。"[①] 因此，一个国家的网民比例，则反映了该国信息获取和学习的水平，同时也能反映其沟通水平。

3.2 每年国内旅游人数占国民比重

该指标数据来源于《中国统计摘要》，反映国民对国内不同地域文化的兴趣和参与度。不同于网络沟通的是，旅游是一种亲历性的文化体验和参与，是更为真实的文化交流活动。"旅游作为一种社会文化活动，在促进社会经济发展的同时，

---

① 中国智能城市建设与推进战略研究项目组. 智能城市评价指标体系研究 [M]. 杭州：浙江大学出版社，2016:124.

3. Cultural exchanges within the population

This observation point mainly observes the vitality of internal cultural exchanges. If a country lacks in active internal cultural exchanges, it will not be able to play an active role in international cultural exchanges. The lack of active internal cultural exchanges is not conducive to the protection, understanding, and respect for the internal culture. Therefore, the liveness of internal cultural exchange is an important indicator of the formation of a cultural community.

3.1 Proportion of Internet users in the population

This indicator is based on data collected in the *Research Report on the Internet*. It reflects the overall participation in cultural exchanges. The cultural communication and exchange in modern society rely more on the Internet, which shortens distance and makes communication convenient. It has incomparable rapidity and universality for cultural exchange. The number of internet users reflects not only the communication activity of the people of a country, but also the people's actual participation in cultural exchanges and communication. "The proportion of internet users in the urban population reflects the residents' capacity for information acquisition and learning."[1] Therefore, the proportion of internet users in a country reflects not only the capacity for information acquisition and learning, but also that for communication.

3.2 Proportion of the yearly number of domestic tourists in the population

This indicator is based on data collected in *China Statistical Digest*. It reflects people's interest and participation in different regional cultures. Unlike online communication, travel is a personal cultural experience and participation and a more real cultural exchange. "As a sociocultural activity, travel not only promotes social and economic development, but also shoulders the

---

[1] China Smart City Construction and Promotion Strategy Research Project Group. Research on Smart City Evaluation Indicator System [M].Hangzhou: Zhejiang University Press, 2016:124.

也肩负着如何使传统文化得以保护、传承的重任。"[①] 国内旅游人数比重反映了该国国民对文化交流感兴趣的人口比例和文化交流的实际参与人数比例。旅游越活跃的国家，地区之间的互相信任和理解程度越高。因为旅游，各地的文化也才更加具有保护的价值，所以能够促成文化保护的行动。

3.3 国内旅游收入占GDP比重

该指标数据来源于《中国统计摘要》和文化旅游部《文化和旅游发展统计公报》，是上一指标的延续和补充，反映国民文化交流和流动性的实际状况。旅游人数的统计只能反映国民参与比例，但不能反映参与程度，因此本指标就是必要的补充。本指标可以反映居民在旅游方面的花费情况，因而可以反映参与度，同时，由于旅游收入的增长也可以反过来刺激旅游项目的开发，增加旅游地文化保护的投入资金。因此，本指标是一个国家内部文化与交流活跃程度的重要衡量指标。

3.4 客运量与人口的比例

该指标数据来源于《中国统计摘要》，反映人口流动性水平，也可以反映一个国家的人口流动的活跃程度。固步自封永远不利于文化交流，文化交流首先需要依赖人口流动。由于发达国家很多人选择私家车出行，且不便于统计，若用此指标则对于不发达国家显得不公平。而长途旅行，不论是发达国家还是不发达国家，都会在客运量上反映出来。因此，

[①] 李金早. 当代旅游学（上）[M]. 北京：中国旅游出版社，2018：77.

responsibility of how to protect and inherit traditional culture."[1] The proportion of domestic tourists reflects the proportion of people who are interested in cultural exchanges and the proportion of people who actually participate in cultural exchanges. The more active a country is in tourism, the higher the degree of mutual trust and understanding between regions. Because of tourism, local culture becomes valuable and can stimulate cultural protection.

3.3 Proportion of domestic tourism revenue in GDP

This indicator is derived from *China Statistical Digest* and *Statistical Bulletin on Cultural and Tourism Development* released by the Ministry of Culture and Tourism. It is the continuation and supplement of the previous indicator and reflects the actual situation of national cultural exchange and mobility. The statistics on the number of tourists can only reflect the proportion of national participation. It can not reflect the degree of participation, so this indicator is a necessary supplement. This indicator can reflect residents' spending on tourism, so it can reflect the degree of participation. At the same time, the growth of tourism income can also stimulate the development of tourism projects in turn and increase the investment funds for cultural protection in tourist destinations. Therefore, this indicator is an important measure of the level of cultural and exchange activity within a country.

3.4 Ratio of passenger volume to the population

This indicator is derived from *China Statistical Digest*. It reflects the level of population mobility and the intensity of population mobility in a country. Resting complacently on one's laurels does no good to cultural exchange, which relies on population mobility in the first place. Because many people in developed countries choose private car tours, which is difficult to count. So it is unfair to apply this indicator to underdeveloped countries. Long distance travel, whether in developed or underdeveloped countries, will be reflected

---

[1] Li Jinzao. Contemporary Tourism (I) [M]. Beijing: China Tourism Press, 2018: 77.

此指标能够反映一个国家内部长途客运发生的数量比重，能够反映国家内部人口流动性情况。

3.5 传媒机构数量与人口比重

反映网络普及程度、文化交流硬件设施建设情况。传媒机构是文化交流的专门机构，传媒机构数量和从业人员越多，说明该国越重视文化交流和沟通，文化交流也越活跃。该指标可较好地反映文化交流的频率和国家投入及人民群众的时间投入。

3.6 休闲场所数量

反映国民文化交流硬件发展水平。休闲场所也是社交场所，是国民内部文化交流的重要平台和依托。休闲场所也是文化展示的窗口。休闲场所多，说明该国国民投放在文化生活方面的时间比投放在生产方面的时间多，有利于文化的交流和传承。

3.7 宣传文化发展专项支出预算额

该指标数据来源于财政部官网，反映政府对文化宣传、交流的重视程度。换言之，反映了政府在文化交流和宣传方面的意愿。文化宣传意愿越强，则越愿意在文化共同体建设方面做出贡献，该国也才具备构建文化共同体的资金来源。

3.8 每百万人拥有的互联网服务商

该指标数据来源于《世界统计年鉴》，反映国家实现文化多样性的条件。互联网服务商越多，表示该国对不同理念、

in the passenger volume. Therefore, this indicator can reflect the proportion of the quantity of long-distance passenger transport within a country and the population mobility within a country.

3.5 Proportion of the number of media organizations in the population

This reflects the popularity level of the Internet and the development of cultural exchange facilities. Media organizations are specialized in cultural exchanges. The more media organizations and media personnel there are, the more important cultural exchanges and communication are considered, and the more active cultural exchanges are. This indicator can well reflect the frequency of cultural exchanges and the national investment and people's investment of time.

3.6 Number of leisure facilities

This reflects the development of cultural exchange hardware. Leisure facilities are also social places. They are important places and media for internal cultural exchange. Leisure facilities are also the window to culture. The more leisure places there are, the more time people spend on cultural life. This is conducive to cultural exchange and inheritance.

3.7 Budget amount of special expenditure on publicity and cultural development

This indicator is based on data collected on the official website of the Ministry of Finance. It shows the importance a country attaches to cultural publicity and exchange. In other words, it shows how strong the government will is in cultural exchange and publicity. The stronger the will to do cultural publicity, the more willing it is to contribute to the building of a cultural community. Only in this way can a country get the funds it needs to build a cultural community.

3.8 Number of internet service providers per million people

This indicator is derived from the *World Statistical Yearbook*. It reflects the conditions for a country to maintain cultural diversity. The more internet

不同文化、不同观点的包容度越强。文化方面加强竞争，鼓励多家服务商发展，是文化包容性的体现。越是把宣传媒介掌握在少数集团手中，则代表该国家包容性越差。因此，本指标对于衡量国家内部文化包容性具有重要参考意义。

3.9 邮电通讯费用占GDP比重

本指标数据来源于《中国统计摘要》，反映国民交流在生活中实际占有的花费和时间比重，可以客观衡量国民在沟通交流方面的实际情况。邮电、快递、物流等都应纳入考察范围。这个指标既能反映物质流通度，也能反映文化交流活跃度。邮电不活跃的地方，往往是封闭的地区和人员太多，不利于文化共同体的建设

3.10 政府预算的学术交流活动支出占GDP比重

本指标数据来源于财政部官网，反映政府对文化学术交流活动的重视程度，亦即反映了高层文化交流的活跃程度和政府的重视程度。文化沟通和交流不仅要反映大众层面的参与度，也要反映高层次的文化交流与沟通。学术交流活动是高层次文化交流的重要方面，因此这一指标对于前述指标而言是一个重要的补充。

4. 国家内部文化共同体建设成效

本观测点是从实际效果方面考察一个国家内部文化共同体取得的实际效果。仅仅有政府的努力和国民的参与，并不能完全客观地反映文化共同体建设的实际效果，本观测点的各项指标与前述指标形成了照应关系。

service providers there are, the more tolerant a country is towards different ideas, cultures and views. Strengthening cultural competition and encouraging multiple service providers to develop are the indicator of cultural inclusiveness. If media outlets are controlled by the few, cultural inclusiveness will drop. Therefore, this indicator is of great significance for measuring internal cultural inclusiveness.

3.9 Proportion of posts and telecommunications expenses in GDP

This indicator is derived from *China Statistical Digest*. It reflects the actual cost and time people spend on communication and can objectively measure actual communication. Posts and telecommunications, express delivery, logistics, etc. should be included in the scope of investigation. This indicator can reflect not only the circulation of supplies, but also the activity of cultural exchanges. Where posts and telecommunications are not active, it is often closed, crowded areas. This is not conducive to the building of a cultural community.

3.10 Proportion of government budget for academic exchanges to GDP

This indicator is based on data collected on the official website of the Ministry of Finance. It shows the importance a country attaches to cultural exchanges and the activity of high-level cultural exchanges and government support. Cultural exchange and communication should not only reflect the participation of the public, but also reflect high-level cultural exchange and communication. Academic exchanges are an important aspect of high-level cultural exchange, so this indicator is an important supplement to the above indicators.

4. Achievements in the building of a national cultural community

This observation point investigates the actual effect of a country's internal cultural community. The efforts of the government and mass participation alone can not fully and objectively reflect the actual effect of the building of a cultural community. The indicators under this observation point correspond with the above indicators.

4.1 15 岁及以上成人识字率

该指标数据来源于《国际统计年鉴》,反映国民整体的实际基础教育水平。一个国家如果成人文盲过多,则不利于文化传承、沟通和文化共同体的形成。国民教育的毛入学率等教育指标,只能反映数年来的政府和国民投入,不能反映一个更长历史时期的教育水平,因此本指标对国民受教育程度的考察具有补充作用。

4.2 语言保护投入资金

该指标来源于《中国语言文字事业发展报告》和教育部官网《中国语言文字概况》,反映国家内部多语种保护措施及资金投入。语言保护是文化保护的核心,语言的消失往往意味着一种文化的消失。因此,对语言的保护就是文化保护最重要的举措之一。本项指标可以反映一个国家对文化保护的重视程度和实施力度。

4.3 内部自主研发

该指标数据来源于联合国教科文组织统计研究所报告(UIS Information Paper),反映国内研究和发展取得的实际成效。该指标的含义是国内研发,指国内研发取得的数量和成效。研发越多,则表示该国在科学技术方面取得的成就越高,为世界科技发展做出的贡献越大。各国内部自主研发实际上是为世界和全人类做出智力贡献,客观上起到了为文化共同体建构服务的作用。

4.1 Literacy rate of adults aged 15 and above

This indicator is based on data collected in the *International Statistical Yearbook*. It shows the actual level of basic education in a country. Widespread illiteracy is not conducive to cultural inheritance, cultural communication and the building of a cultural community. The gross enrollment rate of national education and other education indicators can only reflect the government and its people's investment in the past few years. It can not reflect the education level over a long historical period. Therefore, this indicator plays a complementary role in the investigation of national education level.

4.2 Investment in language protection

This indicator is based on *Report on the Development of the Chinese Language Undertaking,* and *Overview of Chinese Language and Characters* on the official website of the Ministry of Education, this reflects a country's measures for protecting multiple languages and its capital investment. Language protection is the core of cultural protection. The disappearance of language often means the disappearance of a culture. Therefore, the protection of language is one of the most important measures for cultural protection. This indicator can reflect a country's emphasis on cultural protection and its efforts in this aspect.

4.3 In-house R&D

This indicator is derived from the UNESCO report *UIS Information Paper*. It reflects the actual achievements made in domestic research and development. This indicator demonstrates the achievements made in domestic R&D. The more R&D activities, the greater a country's achievements in science and technology, and the greater its contribution to the development of science and technology in the world. In fact, independent R&D in various countries makes intellectual contribution to the world and the whole mankind, and objectively serves the building of a cultural community.

4.4 高等学历人口比例

该指标数据来源于《全国教育事业发展统计公报》和教育部官网,反映国内高等教育取得的实际成效。本指标也是高等教育毛入学率的补充指标,涉及一个比较长的历史时期的高等教育实际成效。高等教育人口比例越大,则该国国民总体高素质高学历人才越多,则越有利于文化共同体的形成。

4.5 国内多元文化保护投入资金

反映国内多元文化保护投入力度。本项指标可以反映一个国家在文化保护方面的态度,同时也可反映该国文化本身的多元化状态。

4.6 人均拥有图书、期刊、报纸、音像制品和电子出版物总量

该指标数据来源于《中国出版年鉴》和新闻出版广电部官网《全国新闻出版业基本情况》,反映国家在图书文化建设方面做出的实际成效,与上一指标形成互补关系。前者从实际消费角度考察,本指标从生产的角度考察。本指标可以客观反映一个国家在文化产品生产方面的兴趣和意愿,因而可以衡量这个国家在文化生产方面付出的努力。

4.7 学术研究文章发表数量

该指标数据来源于中国知网和其他国家类似学术搜索统计,有关国民在文化研究和建设方面的实际参与度和贡献,用以反映该国在高层次成果产出方面取得的实际成效。对于文化而言,普及和提高两方面都要重视。上述各指标主要反

4.4 Proportion of college graduates in the population

This indicator is derived from the *Statistical Bulletin on Education Development* and the official website of the Ministry of education, reflecting the actual fruits of China's higher education. This indicator is also a supplementary indicator of the gross enrollment rate of higher education, involving the actual effect of higher education in a relatively long historical period. The larger the proportion of people who have received higher education, the more high-quality talent there are in a country. This is conducive to the formation of a cultural community.

4.5 National investment in language diversity protection

This reflects national investment in language diversity protection. This indicator can reflect a country's attitude towards cultural protection, as well as the diversity of the national culture.

4.6 Total number of books, periodicals, newspapers, audio-visual products and electronic publications per capita

This indicator is derived from *China Publication Yearbook* and *Basics about the National Press and Publication Industry* on the official website of the Ministry of Press, Publication, Radio, Film and Television. It reflects the actual achievements the country made in the publication industry and forms a complementary relationship with the previous index. The former carries out investigation from the perspective of actual consumption, while this index carries out investigation from the perspective of production. This indicator can objectively reflect a country's interest and willingness in the production of cultural products, so it can measure a country's efforts in cultural production.

4.7 Number of academic research articles published

This indicator is derived from CNKI and similar academic search platforms in other countries. The actual participation and contribution of citizens in cultural research and development can reflect the actual achievements of a

映文化的大众普及方面取得的实际成效,而本指标则反映国家在文化、科技方面取得的高级别成果。

4.8 艺术表演团体总收入占 GDP 比重

该指标数据来源于文化旅游部《文化和旅游发展统计公报》,反映国民在艺术方面的参与度。本指标也是从消费角度考察人民文化艺术生活的实际参与度与热情度,与前述文化机构数量等指标形成补充关系。本指标亦不单纯用总量反映,而是考虑到各国经济发展不均衡的问题,用占 GDP 比重的形式考察。

4.9 每万人群众文化设施建筑面积

该指标数据来源于文化旅游部《文化和旅游发展统计公报》,反映政府在群众文化建设方面做出的实际成绩。与前述文化设施投入等指标形成照应关系,从另一个角度补充说明国家在文化建设方面做出的实际成绩,而且涉及一个更长历史时期的建设成果。

4.10 全国文物机构接待观众人次与全国总人口比例

该指标数据来源于文化旅游部《文化和旅游发展统计公报》,反映国民对传统文化继承的实际参与度,与文物保护机构数形成照应关系。前者只反映国家在文物和文化保护方面的投入,而本指标则反映国民对此投入的参与度,以及这个投入在国民中产生的实际效果。

country in high-level output. The popularization and improvement of culture are both important. The above indicators mainly reflect the actual achievements in the popularization of culture, while this indicator reflects the high-level achievements in culture, science and technology.

4.8 Proportion of the total income of art performing groups in GDP

This indicator is based on data collected in the *Statistical Bulletin on Cultural and Tourism Development* released by the Ministry of Culture and Tourism. It shows a country's participation in the development of arts. This indicator also investigates the actual participation in and enthusiasm for cultural and artistic life from the perspective of consumption, and forms a complementary relationship with the above indicators such as the number of cultural institutions. This indicator does not use the total amount alone. It takes the form of the proportion in GDP in consideration of the unbalanced economic development of various countries.

4.9 Floorage of public cultural facilities per 10,000 people

This indicator is based on data collected in the *Statistical Bulletin on Cultural and Tourism Development* released by the Ministry of Culture and Tourism. It shows a country's achievements in the development of mass culture. It corresponds with the above-mentioned indicators such as investment in cultural facilities, illustrates the actual achievements made by China in cultural development from another perspective, and involves the achievements made over a longer historical period.

4.10 Proportion of the number of visitors received by cultural institutions in the total population

This indicator is based on data collected in the *Statistical Bulletin on Cultural and Tourism Development* released by the Ministry of Culture and Tourism. It shows a country's actual inheritance of traditional culture and corresponds with the number of institutions for the protection of cultural relics. The former only reflects the state's investment in cultural relics and cultural protection, while this indicator reflects the participation of the people in this

（二）包容互鉴指标

"包容互鉴"是指一个国家除了自己国内文化建设之外，对于他国文化的接纳程度和宽容程度。人类文化共同体的建设，不是某一个国家的事，而是全世界所有国家的事。只重内部文化建设而不重与其他国家的文化交流与沟通理解，也就谈不上人类文化共同体。因此，在注重本国文化建设的同时，要以更多的精力关注国际文化交流与建设。本指标下属各级指标，均指向一个国家在国际文化交流方面做出的贡献。主要包括文化输入和文化输出两个方面，另加文化交流取得的实际效果，一共3个观测点。

1. 输入文化力度

国家与国家之间的文化交流，包括文化输入和文化输出两个方面。输入文化是指本国引入其他国家文化，向他国文化学习。本观测点包括输入文化的各个主要渠道。

1.1 出国留学教育支出预算占财政总预算比例

该指标数据来源于财政部官网，反映国家对接受外国文化的重视程度，亦即主要反映一个国家对出国留学向外国文化学习方面的重视程度。任何文化的真正发展，不能建立在仅仅重视本国国内文化发展与传承之上，而是要建立在向全世界不同文化学习的之上。派出本国国民，走向世界，向他国文化学习就是增强对他国文化了解的重要渠道。出国留学是文化输入的重要渠道，因此，本指标是反映一个国家文化输入力度的重要参考。

investment and the actual effect of this investment among the people.

(II) Inclusiveness and mutual learning indicators

"Inclusiveness and mutual learning" refers to a country's acceptance and tolerance of other cultures in addition to developing its own culture. The building of a Cultural Community with a Shared Future for Mankind is not the responsibility of one country; it is the responsibility of all countries in the world. If we only focus on internal cultural development and overlook the cultural exchanges with other countries, we will fail to build a cultural community for mankind. Therefore, we should highlight international cultural exchanges and development while ensuring internal cultural development. The various indicators under this one measure the contribution of a country to international cultural exchanges. It includes cultural import and cultural export, as well as the practical effects of cultural exchange.

1. Culture import intensity

Cultural exchanges between countries include cultural import and cultural export. Cultural import refers to introducing and learning from other cultures. This observation point covers the main channels of cultural input.

1.1 Proportion of budget for overseas studies in the total financial budget

This indicator is derived from the official website of the Ministry of finance. It reflects the importance a country attaches to accepting foreign cultures and to studying abroad and learning from foreign cultures. A culture can achieve real development only when it highlights the learning of foreign cultures and at the same time gives priority to the development and inheritance of the domestic culture. Sending citizens out to the world and learning from other cultures is an important channel to enhance our understanding of other cultures. Study-

1.2 官方列入可作为中小学第二语言学习的语种数量

反映国家对外国文化接受的开放程度。官方列入的第二语言学习语种，反映了该国接受他国文化的意愿，是文化开放性的表现。语种越多，表明该国的文化越具有开放的姿态，越容易接受外国文化。

1.3 外部知识获取

该指标数据来源于联合国教科文组织统计研究所报告（UIS Information Paper），反映国家对外国知识和文化的实际接受程度。本指标的含义是外部知识获取，也就是一个国家对外国创造的知识、文化的引入。联合国教科文组织将这个指标作为考察一个国家在对外文化交流方面的重要参考指数。本指标能够反映一个国家输入他国知识和文化的水平。只有不断积极努力向外部学习的国家，才是重视人类文化的国家，从而不会固步自封，而是向外国文化借鉴学习。

1.4 入境旅游人次

该指标数据来源于《入境旅游发展年度报告》、联合国世界旅游组织（UNWTO）公布数据和文化和旅游部官网，反映本国文化的吸引力和对外国游客的开放度。国家之间的旅游，是国与国之间文化交流的有效方式。接纳外国游客越多，说明该国对其他国家公民的接纳程度越高，也越是有利于文化输入，这个国家的文化就越是显得开放。同时，本指标越高，也说明该国文化具有更大的吸引力。比如戴斌就认为，中国对外国游客越来越具有吸引力，来华旅游人次大幅增加，原

ing abroad is an important channel of cultural import. Therefore, this indicator is an important tool to measure a country's cultural import intensity.

1.2 Number of languages officially listed as second languages in primary and secondary schools

This reflects the openness of a country to foreign cultures. The officially listed second language reflects a country's willingness to accept other cultures. It is the manifestation of cultural openness. The more languages there are, the more open the national culture is and the easier it is to accept foreign cultures.

1.3 Acquisition of external knowledge

This indicator is derived from the UNESCO report *UIS Information Paper*. It reflects the actual acceptance of external knowledge and cultures. This indicator measures the introduction of foreign knowledge and cultures. The UNESCO takes this indicator as an important indicator to study a country's cultural exchanges with foreign countries. This indicator can reflect the level of knowledge and culture import. Countries that constantly learn from the outside world are those that attach importance to a culture for mankind. They will never be complacent and keep learning from foreign cultures.

1.4 Number of inbound tourists

This indicator is derived from the *Annual Report on the Development of Inbound Tourism*, the data released by the United Nations World Tourism Organization (UNWTO) and the official website of the Ministry of Culture and Tourism, reflecting the attraction of domestic culture and the openness to foreign tourists. Tourism between countries is an effective way of cultural exchange. The more foreign tourists are received, the higher the degree of acceptance of other countries, the more conducive to cultural import, and the more open a culture is. At the same time, the higher the indicator is, the more attractive the culture is. Dai Bin, for example, believes that China is becoming more and more attractive to foreign tourists, and the number of tourists to

因就是"既有美丽的自然资源，又有将要实现全面小康社会；既有国家富强、人民幸福的内聚力，又有人类命运共同体的理念与行动能力的中国，构成了新时期国际游客到访的核心引力和关键动力"。①这一指标与国内旅游人数比形成呼应关系，但这里反映的是国家与国家之间的文化交流状况。

1.5 译入电影种数

该指标数据来源于《中国电影年鉴》，反映国家对外国电影文化的接纳力度。译入电影可以大大增加本国国民对国外文化的了解，也能培养他们不敌对世界其他国家文化的意识。电影交流是国家之间文化共同体形成的有效手段。文化输入不是仅仅体现在电影译入方面，包括在这个指标之中的，还有电视剧、网络剧等其他艺术形式的引入，选取电影译入，是将具有代表性的一个品种，作为艺术输入的衡量指标，减小了统计的口径难度。

1.6 国际互联网用户数量比重

该指标数据来源于《国际统计年鉴》，反映国家对外国文化信息的许可度和本国国民对外国文化的接纳度。本指标也主要反映了本国居民对国外文化的兴趣。只有当一个国家的居民有与世界接轨、交流沟通的意识，沟通才是可能的。如果本国网民上网都只是查看国内网站，那么他们的文化知识就永远是狭隘的、封闭的。本指标能够反映一个国家国民文化意识的开放程度，因此可以反映国民对文化输入的许可度。

---

① 戴斌. 旅游 & 中国 [M]. 北京：旅游教育出版社，2018:145.

China has increased significantly. The reason is that "there are both beautiful natural resources and the need to build a well-off society in an all-round way"; China is a country of strength and happiness, as well as the willpower to build a common cultural community. It constitutes the center of gravity and key driving force behind international visits to China in the new era."[1] This indicator corresponds with the ratio of domestic tourists, yet it reflects the cultural exchanges between countries.

1.5 Number of the types of films translated into the native language

This indicator is derived from *China Film Yearbook*, reflecting a country's acceptance of foreign films. Films translated into the native language can greatly increase a nation's understanding of foreign cultures and cultivate their friendlinesses towards other cultures in the world. Film exchange is an effective means to form a cultural community between countries. Cultural import is not limited to film translation. It also includes the introduction of other art forms such as TV series and Internet dramas. Translated films are a representative variety and as a measure of art import, they reduce the difficulty of statistical work.

1.6 Number of internet users

This indicator is derived from the *International Statistical Yearbook*. It reflects a country's recognition of foreign cultural information and the nation's acceptance of foreign cultures. This indicator also mainly reflects the interest of local residents in foreign culture. Only when the people of a country have the awareness of connecting with the world and communicating, can communication be possible. If domestic internet users only browse domestic websites, their cultural knowledge will always be narrow and limited. This indicator can reflect the openness of the national cultural awareness, so it can reflect the people's recognition of cultural import.

---

[1] Dai Bin. Tourism & China [M]. Beijing: Tourism Education Press, 2018:145.

1.7 图书、报纸、期刊进口册数

该指标数据来源于《中国出版年鉴》和新闻出版广电部官网《全国新闻出版业基本情况》，反映国家引进外国文化成果的力度。本指标与电影引进指标一样，反映的是纸本文化产品的输入数量。互联网沟通是一个渠道，电影是一个渠道，纸本图书、报纸、期刊也是重要的渠道，反映的是传统文化交流形式上的文化输入。国家每年都有对图书、报纸、期刊进口的统计口径，数据获取也比较方便。

1.8 版权引进项数

该指标数据来源于新闻出版广电部官网《全国新闻出版业基本情况》，反映国家引进外国文化成果的力度。与上一指标的区别在于，上一指标反映的是原版图书引入情况，而本项指标反映的是版权引进项数，即获取国外文化产品在本国出版的数量。这一指标显示了一个国家对外国文化的主动接纳、学习、宣传的力度。

1.9 赴海外留学生人数及经费

该指标数据来源于教育部官网、《中国出国留学发展趋势报告》和美国《门户开放报告》等，反映国家和国民深入学习外国文化的力度。海外留学生是亲自深入世界其他国家学习他国文化的行动者。在海外留学的人数越多，说明本国居民对其他国家文化的兴趣越高。由于留学生大都最终会回到本国工作生活，因此他们也将把其他国家的文化信息带回祖国。比如晚清时期，中国派出海外学习归国的留学生，深深

1.7 Number of imported books, newspapers and periodicals

This indicator is derived from *China Publication Yearbook* and *Basics about the National Press and Publication Industry* on the official website of the Ministry of Press, Publication, Radio, Film and Television. It reflects the efforts of a country to import foreign cultural achievements. This indicator, like the indicator for film introduction, reflects the quantity of imported paper cultural products. Internet communication is a channel, films are a channel, and paper books, newspapers and periodicals are also important channels, reflecting the cultural import in the form of traditional cultural exchange. China has a yearly statistical caliber for the import of books, newspapers and periodicals, and data acquisition is convenient.

1.8 Number of copyright imports

This indicator is derived from *Basics about the National Press and Publication Industry* on the official website of the Ministry of Press, Publication, Radio, Film and Television. It reflects the efforts of a country to import foreign cultural achievements. The difference from the previous indicator is that the previous indicator reflects the introduction of original books, while this indicator reflects the number of copyright imports, that is, the number of foreign cultural products published in China. This indicator shows the strength of a country's active acceptance, learning and publicity of foreign cultures.

1.9 Number of and expenditure for students studying overseas

This indicator is derived from the official website of the Ministry of Education, *Report on the Development of Overseas Studies* and *Open Door Report*, reflecting the intensity of a country and its citizens to learn foreign cultures in depth. Overseas students are the ones who personally go to other countries to learn other cultures. The bigger the number of students studying abroad, the higher the interest of local residents in the culture of other countries. Because most of the international students will eventually return to work and live in their own country, they will also bring the cultural information of other countries back to their motherland. For example, in the late Qing Dynasty, China

地改变了中国现代文化和科技，使中国迅速结束了数千年的封建统治，从而改变了国家的政治文化形态。

1.10 免入境签证国家数

该指标数据来源于公开信息，反映国家的整体性开放程度。免入境签证是一个对国家之间往来壁垒的取消，免入境签证国家越多，越是有利于国外文化的输入。上述各项指标基本上都是反映一个国家文化输入的实际情况，而本指标能够反映对于文化输入的国家态度。

1.11 外籍教师数量

反映引入外籍教师在本国传播文化的情况。外籍教师是指到本国传播外国文化的教师群体，这个群体越大，说明本国接受外国文化越多，因此可以反映文化输入的力度。

2. 输出文化力度

每个国家，不但要向他国学习，还要主动提供本国文化供其他国家学习和了解。输出文化力度，既要体现本国文化的吸引力和价值，又要有向外输出文化的行为和举措。任何交流都是双向的，所以本观测点与文化输入观测点是一种对应的关系。

2.1 来本国留学教育支出预算占财政总预算比例

该指标数据来源于财政部官网，反映国家输出本国文明的政府投入力度。吸引国外留学生来本国学习，是向外输出文化的重要手段。政府在这方面的投入资金多少，则反映了政

sent students overseas to study. These students returned home and profoundly changed China's modern culture and science and technology, and quickly ended the feudal rule of China which had lasted for thousands of years, changing the political and cultural landscape.

1.10 Number of countries providing visa-free access

This indicator is derived from disclosed information. It reflects the overall openness of a country. Visa-free access removes the barriers between countries. The more countries there are to provide visa-free access, the more this is conducive to the import of foreign cultures. The above indicators basically reflect a country's actual cultural import, and this indicator can reflect a country's attitude towards cultural import.

1.11 Number of foreign teachers

This reflects the introduction of foreign teachers to spread foreign cultures. Foreign teachers refer to the group of teachers who spread foreign cultures in a particular country. The larger the group, the more foreign culture is spread. Therefore, it can reflect the intensity of cultural import.

2. Culture export intensity

Each country should not only learn from other countries, but also actively provide its own culture for other countries to learn and understand. The intensity of culture export should reflect not only the attractiveness and value of the domestic culture, but also relevant measures. All communication is two-way, so this observation point and observation point for cultural import correspond with each other.

2.1 Proportion of budget for incoming international students in the total financial budget

This indicator is based on data collected on the official website of the Ministry of Finance. It shows the level of government input into culture export. Attracting foreign students is an important means to export culture. The amount of government investment in this area reflects the government's overall

府对文化输出的总体态度。胡刚认为"来华留学教育，尤其是学历教育的发展，对于国内高校教育对外开放和适应国际化竞争，对于'双一流'和'一带一路'建设，对于服务国家大外交战略具有重大意义"。[1] 因此，本指标是构建人类文化共同体的重要指标。

2.2 出境旅游人次占国民比重

该指标数据来源于《中国出境旅游发展年度报告》、联合国世界旅游组织公布数据，反映国民对外国文明的兴趣和参与度。出境旅游者，可以给其他国家带去关于本国的文化信息。出境人数越多，则别的国家了解本国的机会越多。2013年，习近平主席在俄罗斯中国旅游年开幕式致词中指出"旅游是人民生活水平提高的一个重要指标，出国旅游更为广大民众所向往"。中国旅游研究院《中国出境旅游发展年度报告2018》指出：改革开放40年来，"出境旅游市场规模逐步增长，产业发展日益开放，综合功能正在显现，已经成为'以人民为中心'发展的生动体现，中国对外开放扩大的直接见证与打造人类命运共同体的主要渠道"。[2] 因此，本指标具有重要参考价值。

---

[1] 胡刚. 论互联网＋教育［M］. 南京：江苏教育出版社，2017：343.
[2] 中国旅游研究院. 中国出境旅游发展年度报告2018［M］. 北京：旅游教育出版社，2018：2.

attitude towards cultural export. Hu Gang believes that "the development of international studies programs in China, especially academic education, is of great significance for the opening up of China's higher education and the adaptation to international competition, for the development of 'double first-class' universities and 'Belt and Road', and for serving the country's grand diplomatic strategy."[1] Therefore, this indicator is an important indicator for the building of a cultural community for mankind.

2.2 Proportion of the number of outbound tourists in the population

This indicator is derived from the *Annual Report on the Development of Inbound Tourism* and the data released by the United Nations World Tourism Organization, reflecting a nation's interest and participation in foreign cultures. Outbound tourists can take cultural information about their own country to other countries. The more people who leave the country, the more opportunities other countries will have to learn about this country. In 2013, President Xi Jinping delivered a speech in the opening ceremony of the China Tourism Year in Russia, pointing out that "tourism is an important indicator for the improvement of people's living standards, and that the masses look forward to traveling abroad." The *2018 Annual Report on China's Outbound Tourism* released by China Academy of Tourism Studies points out that in the 40 years since the reform and opening up, "the scale of the outbound tourism market has been on the rise, the industry has become more open, and comprehensive functions are emerging. It has become a vivid embodiment of 'people-centered' development, a direct witness of the expansion of China's opening-up, and a main channel for building a Community with a Shared Future for Mankind."[2] Therefore, this indicator is of great significance.

---

[1] Hu Gang. On Internet-based Education [M]. Nanjing: Jiangsu Education Press, 2017: 343.
[2] China Academy of Tourism. Annual Report on China's Outbound Tourism 2018 [M]. Beijing: Tourism Education Press, 2018: 2.

2.3 图书、报纸、期刊出口册数

该指标数据来源于《全国新闻出版业基本情况》，反映本国文化向外国的传播力度。本指标与图书、报纸、期刊进口数形成呼应关系，是其反向考察指标，显示了本国文化在传统载体和渠道方面对外国文化的影响力，能够反映本国文化输出的实际效果。

2.4 版权输出项数

该指标数据来源于《全国新闻出版业基本情况》，反映本国文化向外国的传播力度。本指标与版权输入项指标形成呼应关系，是其反向考察指标，显示了本国文化被外国文化接纳的程度和实际效果。

2.5 本国电影海外票房

该指标数据来源于《中国电影年鉴》和《中国电影智库》，反映本国电影文化在外国的影响力。本指标与输入电影指标遥相呼应，是其反向考察指标，显示了本国电影在国外被接纳的实际效果。

2.6 接收外国留学生人数

该指标数据来源于《中国留学发展报告》，反映本国对外国文化深入的影响力。本指标则反映外国留学生来本国的实际人数，人数越多，则本国输出文化的实际效果越好。

2.7 国际科技交流与合作政府预算额

该指标数据来源于财政部官网，反映政府对国际科技交流与合作的重视度。本指标是国家对国际科技交流与合作的实

2.3 Number of exported books, newspapers and periodicals

This indicator is derived from *Basics about the National Press and Publication Industry*. It reflects the efforts of a country to export its own culture. This indicator, as a reverse investigation indicator, corresponds with the number of books, newspapers and periodicals imported. It shows the influence of the domestic culture on foreign culture in terms of traditional medium and channels, and can reflect the actual effect of cultural export.

2.4 Number of copyright exports

This indicator is derived from *Basics about the National Press and Publication Industry*. It reflects the efforts of a country to export its own culture. This indicator, as a reverse investigation indicator, corresponds with the copyright export indicator. It shows the degree and actual effect of domestic culture being accepted by foreign cultures.

2.5 Overseas box office revenues of home-made films

This indicator is derived from *China Film Yearbook* and *China Film Think Tank*, reflecting the influence of domestic film culture in foreign countries.. This indicator corresponds with the indicator of imported films, which shows the actual acceptance of domestic films by foreign cultures.

2.6 Number of enrolled foreign students

This indicator is derived from the *Report on the Development of Overseas Studies*, reflecting a country's profound influence on foreign cultures. It shows the actual number of foreign students coming to China in pursuit of higher education. The more the number is, the better the actual effect of culture export.

2.7 Government budget for international scientific and technological exchanges and cooperation

This indicator is based on data collected on the official website of the Ministry of Finance, reflecting the government's attention to international scientific and technological exchanges and cooperation. This indicator measures

际投入，反映了政府对国际交流与合作的意愿和态度。全球文化共同体的形成，必有赖于各个国家在文化交流方面的具体支持力度，因而本指标可以反映出这一态度。

2.8 海外教育经费支出

该指标反映本国在本国之外传播本国语言、文化、科技等方面的投入力度。海外教育不是指对外国留学生的花销，而是指本国在海外从事文化教育的花销，比如中国在海外建立孔子学院的花销，这一指标从实际经济花销方面衡量所有用于海外教育的国家投资，反映了政府对文化输出的实际贡献。

2.9 国际航线数量

该指标数据来源于交通运输部官网《民航业发展统计公报》，反映国民在国际文化传播和交流方面的参与度。国际航线旅客运输人次，是来往于本国与外国之间的实际人流量。旅客越多，则说明往来于本国与他国之间的人员越多，则交流越是趋于活跃。本指标是文化交流的重要参考，可以考虑适当增加赋值。

2.10 外派文教工作者人数

本指标数据来源于教育部中外语言交流合作中心官网，其他国家类似机构官网，反映对外深入介绍和传播文明的实际参与度。本指标是从人力资源投入方面考察。外派文教工作者意味着文化输出的举措的落实。

the actual investment of a country in international scientific and technological exchanges and cooperation, reflecting the government's willingness and attitude towards international exchanges and cooperation. The formation of a global cultural community depends on the specific support of each country in cultural exchanges, so this indicator can reflect this attitude.

2.8 Expenditure on overseas education

This indicator reflects the investment intensity of a country in spreading its language, culture, science and technology outside the country. Overseas education does not refer to the expenditure on foreign students. It refers to the expenditure on overseas cultural education, such as the expenditure on the establishment of Confucius Institutes. This indicator measures all national investment in overseas education, reflecting the actual contribution of the government to cultural export.

2.9 Number of international air routes

This indicator is based on data collected in the *Statistical Bulletin on Civil Aviation Development* released by the Ministry of Transport on its official website, showing a country's participation in international cultural communication and exchange.. Passenger volume on international routes is the actual flow of people between home and abroad. The more tourists there are, the more people there are to commute between their home country and other countries, and the more active communication is. This indicator is an important reference for cultural exchange, so its weight can be increased.

2.10 Number of cultural and educational workersdeployed abroad

This indicator is derived from the official website of Center for Language Education and Cooperation and similar institutions in other countries, reflecting the in-depth introduction and promotion of civilization. This indicator carries out investigation from the perspective of human resource investment. The deployment of cultural and educational workers overseas means the implementation of cultural export measures.

3. 文化包容性

本观测点主要观测本国文化对外来文化的吸收和本国文化对外国文化的影响力。前两个观测点重点考察举措，本观测点重点考察效果。文化是否具有包容性是文化共同体能否构建成功的关键性因素。如果一个文化不具有包容性，再多的举措也不会带来最后的成功。文化包容性主要有两个维度，一是本国文化到底对外国文化有多宽容，二是本国文化是否容易被其他文化接纳。一个不具包容性的文化，既不愿意接纳其他文化和观念，自己也不容易被其他文化接受，具有排他性。而具有包容性的文化则与之相反。

3.1 外国人文社科研究发文数量

该指标数据来源于学术归类统计，反映国家和国民对外国文学和文化的接纳度、认同度、包容度。一个国家，只是简单接触外国文化，并不能说明对外国文化有深入的理解，而外国文学和文化研究，则是深入理解外国文化的表现。因此，对外国文学和文化研究文章的发表，就能够从较深的层次观察本国文化对他国文化的接纳度。

3.2 学术著作外译数量

反映本国学术研究被国外接受程度。学术著作外译，可以反映本国文化思想被国外接受的情况。一方面可以说明本国文化在外国的可接受程度，可接受度越高，该文化越具包容性；另一方面也可以反映出本国文化的输出情况。

3. Cultural inclusiveness

This observation point mainly investigates the assimilation of foreign cultures and the influence of the domestic culture on foreign cultures. The previous two observation points focus on the measures, and this observation point focuses on the effect. Cultural inclusiveness is the key to the building of a cultural community. If a culture is not inclusive, no amount of measures will lead to final success. There are two dimensions to cultural inclusiveness: how tolerant the national culture is towards foreign cultures, and can the national culture be easily accepted by other cultures? A culture that is not inclusive is neither willing to accept other cultures and concepts, nor easy to be accepted by other cultures. An inclusive culture is the opposite.

3.1 Number of papers published on foreign cultures and social sciences

This indicator is derived from academic statistics. It reflects the acceptance, recognition and tolerance of foreign literature and culture. Brief contacts with foreign cultures do not equal to a deep understanding of foreign cultures. Research on foreign literature and cultural is the manifestation of a deep understanding of foreign cultures. Therefore, the publication of research articles on foreign literature and cultural can reveal the degree of acceptance of other cultures.

3.2 Number of academic works translated into foreign languages

This reflects the degree of acceptance of domestic academic research by foreign countries. The translation of academic works into other languages can reflect the extent to which national culture and ideology are accepted by foreign countries. On the one hand, it can show the acceptability of domestic culture in foreign countries. The higher the acceptability, the more inclusive the culture is; on the other hand, it can also reflect the output of the national culture.

3.3 文化旅游体育交流与合作财政预算额

该指标数据来源于财政部官网，反映政府在文化合作方面做出的努力程度。它可以显示政府对于文化合作、文化交流的总倾向和态度。预算越高，表示这个国家越趋开放，越愿意为人类文化合作和交流做出贡献。

3.4 海外引进电影数量及票房

该指标数据来源于《中国电影年鉴》和《中国电影智库》，反映国民对外国电影的接受度和包容度。本指标反映的是国民对外国文化的整体心态。海外引进电影数量及票房越高，说明本国国民越愿意接受世界文化潮流，越关心别国文化动态，因而也可以显示本国居民对外国文化的包容程度。

3.5 外国公民入境人次

该指标数据来源于移民管理局官网数据统计，反映国家和国民对外国人的接纳程度。它可以从另一个角度考察一个国家的开放程度。外国公民入境越多，则说明本国对外开放力度越大。同时，入境人次多，也说明本国在文化、商业、旅游、政治等各方面的交流越活跃。一个开放的国家，其文化包容性当然也就是高的。闭关锁国的国家，入境人数肯定不高。

3.6 来本国从事营业性演出参加总人次

该指标数据来源于文化部官网《全国文化发展基本情况》，反映国家和国民对外国艺术的认同度和接纳程度。它与电影

3.3 Budget amount of cultural, tourism, and sports exchanges and cooperation

This indicator is based on data collected on the official website of the Ministry of Finance. It shows the efforts made by the government in cultural cooperation. It can show the general tendency and attitude of the government towards cultural cooperation and cultural exchange. The higher the budget, the more open the country is and the more willing it is to contribute to cultural cooperation and exchanges.

3.4 Number and box office revenues of imported foreign films

This indicator is derived from *China Film Yearbook* and *China Film Think Tank*, reflecting the national acceptance and tolerance of foreign films. This indicator reflects the overall national attitude towards foreign cultures. The higher the number and box office revenues of films imported from abroad, the more willing the citizens are to embrace new developments in world culture. They will follow the cultural development of other countries more and reveal the degree of tolerance of foreign cultures.

3.5 Number of entries of foreign nationals

This indicator is derived from statistics on the official website of the immigration administration. It reflects the acceptance of foreigners by the state and its citizens. It can examine the openness of a country from another angle. The more foreign citizens who enter the country, the greater the opening-up of the country. At the same time, large numbers of inbound visitors indicate that exchanges on culture, commerce, tourism and politics are very active. An open country is culturally inclusive. Few people travel to countries that shut their doors to communication and contacts.

3.6 Total attendance at commercial performances held domestically by foreign performers

This indicator is derived from *Basics About National Cultural Development* on the official website of the Ministry of Culture. It reflects a country's recog-

输入指标有类似性，但本指标反映的是现实生活中的交流情况，而电影输入的指标反映的是国民对虚构艺术的接受情况。来本国从事营业性演出人数越多，越能说明本国政府和国民在对外文化接受方面工作做得越好，国民的心态越具有包容性。

3.7 举办大型国际体育赛事场数和参加人次

该指标数据来源于《中国体育年鉴》，反映国家对世界各国文明的包容心态和参与度。大型国际体育赛事是人类文化交流的重要方式和渠道。体育赛事往往能够产生全世界影响，全世界各国对其关注度都很高，各国运动员和观众纷纷前来，全世界直播，因此能够产生巨大的文化影响。体育赛事转播往往能够带动一国的经济发展，让本国文化在世界范围内得到宣传。因此，举办国际性大型体育赛事越多，越能说明该国在世界文化交流方面做出了更多的努力。

3.8 对外演出项数和参加人次

该指标数据来源于文化和旅游部官网《全国文化发展基本情况》，反映本国国民对他国文化的包容心态和参与度。对外演出是文化输出的重要措施。对外演出不仅可以反映文化输出的情况，而且可以反映本国文艺演出在国外被接受的情况，因此可以反映本国文艺演出的包容性。

nition and acceptance of foreign arts. It is similar to the indicator of imported films, but this indicator reflects communication in real life, while the indicator of imported films reflects the acceptance of fictional art. The greater the number of people who come to a country to give commercial performances, the better the work of the government and the people in accepting foreign cultures, and the more inclusive the national mentality is.

3.7 Number of and attendance at large international sports events held

This indicator is derived from *China Sports Yearbook*, reflecting the state's mentality of inclusiveness and participation in the civilizations of the world. Large-scale international sports events are an important way and channel of human cultural exchanges. Sports events often have a worldwide impact, and countries all over the world show a great interest in them. The athletes and audiences who swarm to the venues, together with the worldwide live telecast, exert a huge cultural impact. The broadcasting of sports events can often promote the economic development of a country and its culture across the world. Therefore, the more international sports events that are held, the more efforts a country has made to world cultural exchanges.

3.8 Number of performances held overseas and participants

This indicator is based on *Basics about National Cultural Development* on the official website of the Ministry of Culture and Tourism, This reflects the tolerance of and participation in other cultures. Overseas performances are an important measure for cultural export. Overseas performances can not only reflect the export of cultural products, but also show the acceptance of Chinese performance among foreign audiences. It can reflect the inclusiveness of domestic artistic performance.

第四章
人类命运共同体构建进程安全维度指标体系

一、目的和意义

在人类命运共同体的建构中，普遍的安全是核心关键。构建普遍安全的世界，其要义就是树立命运与共的共识，坚持以对话解决争端、以协商化解分歧，统筹应对传统和非传统安全威胁，反对一切形式的恐怖主义与战争，最终形成国际环境的和谐安定。这既是人类命运共同体思想的外在要求，也是人类命运共同体其他构成部分的建设之盾。当今世界，安全形势错综复杂，霸权主义和强权政治依旧逞强，地区冲突、领土争端时有发生，恐怖主义、难民危机、重大传染性疾病、气候变化等安全问题日益多元，任何一个国家都不能脱离世界安全谈自身安全，也不能在其他国家不安全的基础上谈自己的安全。世界各国只有命运与共、共商共建、消弭

Chapter IV

An Indicator System for Measuring the Process of Building a Community with a Shared Future for Mankind: Security Dimension

I. Purpose and Significance

Universal security is a core concept in the Community with a Shared Future for Mankind. A universally secure world is ultimately one in which countries share the bound of a common destiny, settle disputes through dialog, resolve differences through consultation, face traditional and non-traditional security threats together, oppose all forms of terrorism and war, and create a harmonious, stable international environment. This is the requirement of the thought of the Community with a Shared Future for Mankind for countries around the world, as well as the goal of its constituents. The security situation in the world today is complicated, hegemonism and power politics are prevalent, regional conflicts and territorial disputes surface from time to time, and security issues such as terrorism, refugee crisis, major infectious diseases and climate change are becoming increasingly diverse. No country can talk about its own security out of the context of world security or in disregard of the insecurity of other countries. Only when countries of the world share weal and woe,

战争，实现全球普遍安全，才能保证世界的共同发展获得秩序与安定。

二、指导思想

以习近平总书记关于"营造公道正义、共建共享的安全格局"的讲话为原则，针对在全球化导致国际行为主体多元化的背景，观测构建合作、创新、法治、共赢的安全共同体构建的进程，从该系列讲话提出的"公道、正义、共同、综合、合作、可持续"六个方面，将内部指标与外部指标相结合。通过剖析翔实有力的基础资料，为安全共同体构建提供相应的数据支撑和理论指导。

可持续安全观和中国的传统"和"文化一脉相承。"和"文化既是天人合一的宇宙观、协和万邦的国际观、"和而不同"的社会观、人心和善的道德观，也是构建"新安全观"的奠基石，有利于勾画全球安全新蓝图，推动世界走向可持续发展的合作安全格局。因此，可持续安全观是世界安全观的革故鼎新，需聚焦发展主题，不断夯实安全根基。这不仅是和平发展观的具体表现，也是我国新时代扩大改革的时代要求，更是国际安全问题的现实需要，还是人类命运共同体构建的重要保障。

communicate and collaborate, avert war, and have universal security, can they ensure the orderly and stable development of the world.

II. Guiding Ideology

General Secretary Xi Jinping's speech "Creating a Security Framework Featuring Fairness, Justice, Collaboration and Sharing" is the principle which underlies this indicator system, which observes the process of building a security community of cooperation, innovation, rule of law and win-win results in an era when globalization is leading to the diversification of international behavioral agents, and combines internal and external indicators by the six standards of "fairness, justice, commonality, comprehensiveness, cooperation and sustainability". This indicator system analyzes detailed and reliable basic data to provide corresponding data support and theoretical guidance for the building of a security community.

The concept of sustainable security comes down in one continuous line with the traditional Chinese culture of "harmony". The culture of "harmony" is not only the world view of man-nature coexistence, the international view of peace among all nations, the social view of "harmony in diversity", and the moral view of inherent human kindness, but also the cornerstone of a "new security view", the guarantee for global security and the driving force behind sustainable world cooperative security. Therefore, the concept of sustainable security is an innovation in the concept of world security. It needs to focus on the theme of development and constantly consolidate the security foundation. This is a concrete manifestation of the concept of peaceful development, the requirement of deepening reform in the new era, the actual demand of international security, and an important guarantee for the building of the Community with a Shared Future for Mankind.

三、构建原则

系统逻辑性原则。各个一级指标是一个系统之内的子系统，彼此之间是平行关系且有一定的逻辑关系，不但要从不同的侧面反映出各个子系统的主要特征和状态，且要反映出这些子系统之间的内在联系。

时间动态性原则。公道—正义—共同—综合—合作—可持续六大一级指标内容的互动，需要通过一定时间尺度的指标才能反映出来，要延伸出二级指标，并为三级指标做出框定。

简明科学性原则。各指标体系的设计及评价指标的选择必须以科学性为原则，既能准确体现"营造公道正义、共建共享的安全格局"的内涵，又能客观全面反映"人类命运共同体构建进程指标体系"各指标之间的真实关系，最终能够测度出"构建安全共同体"的进程状况。

量化指向性原则。在指标选择上，须注意各个一级指标在总体范围内的一致性，指标体系的构建是为"人类命运共同体构建进程"这个主题而设立的，最终要反映的是指标选取在一级范畴上要符合习近平总书记已经明确表述过的关键词，以此为范畴，在二级延伸中要将习近平总书记讲话所涉及的下一级概念作为二级指标，并往下延伸包含可以计算的量度内容，各指标要尽量简单明了，便于量化的收集整理，为第三级的指标做出框定和导引。

多元综合性原则。尽可能囊括习近平总书记提出这个命

III. Guiding Principles

Principle of system logic. All Tier 1 indicators are parallel and logically coherent subsystems. They must portray the main characteristics and states of each subsystem from different perspectives and reveal their internal relations.

Principle of temporal dynamicity. The interaction between the six Tier 1 indicators of fairness, justice, commonality, comprehensiveness, cooperation and sustainability must be reflected by a time scale indicator, from which Tier 2 and 3 indicators are derived and framed.

Principle of conciseness and scientificity. The principle of scientificity must be established for the design of each indicator system and the selection of assessment indicators so that the content of "Creating a Security Framework Featuring Fairness, Justice, Collaboration and Sharing" is accurately reflected, the real relationships between the indicators of the "Indicator system of the Processes of Building the Community with a Shared Future for Mankind" are objectively and comprehensively mirrored, and the progress in "building a security community" is finally measured.

Principle of quantization directivity. Overall consistency must be ensured in the selection of Tier 1 indicators. The indicator system is built to measure "the process of building a Community with a Shared Future for Mankind". The selection of Tier 1 indicators should eventually incorporate the keywords that General Secretary Xi Jinping has come up with. Under this category, the next Tier of concepts involved in General Secretary Xi Jinping's speeches should be developed as Tier 2 indicators, which are extended to include computable measures. Individual indicators should be simple and easy to quantify so that they can frame and guide the development of Tier 3 indicators.

Principle of plural comprehensiveness. This indicator system should cover all the aspects of General Secretary Xi Jinping's proposition and avoid

题的全部内容，在不出现缺项的前提下，在一级指标中排除冗余，即所有一级指标不能少也不多余，同时在下一级指标中避免交叉，即所有二级指标都是能够单独观测，又能够分类处理好平行间的关系。在公道—正义—共同—综合—合作—可持续的 6 个范畴中，分别以二级指标具体测度互动"共赢"的程度，通过测度实现最终目的，这是能够依据本评价体系是否具有实际功能的重点。

四、指标体系框架

根据构建普遍安全世界的意义、人类命运共同体理论和指导思想，参考中国周边安全环境指标体系、"一带一路"大数据报告及习近平总书记在"安全格局"命题讲话内容，将内部指标与外部指标结合，从科学性、多元性、动态性、指向性、系统性五方面综合考虑，设计指标体系框架与各级指标：在目标层之下，以该系列讲话关键词分为 6 个一级指标，即公道的范畴、正义的范畴、共同的范畴、综合的范畴、合作的范畴及可持续的范畴，对应六大范畴下仍然以该系列讲话关键词设出二级指标，根据二级指标的内涵分解出三级指标，在实际测度运行时，以三级指标为观测点，收集数据后进行反推。

redundancy in Tier 1 indicators without missing any item. In other words, no Tier 1 indicator can be missing or superfluous, and the next Tier of indicators should avoid overlapping each other. All Tier 2 indicators can be observed singly, and the parallel relationships between them can be properly handled through classification. In the six categories of fairness, justice, commonality, comprehensiveness, cooperation and sustainability, the degree of "win-win" interaction is specifically measured by Tier 2 indicators to explain the purpose. This is the key to finding out whether this assessment system is practical.

IV. Framework of Indicator System

The framework of this indicator system is based on the significance of building a universally safe world, the theory and guiding ideology of the Community with a Shared Future for Mankind, the indicator system for China's external security environment, the "Belt and Road Initiative" big data report and General Secretary Xi Jinping's speeches on the proposition of "security environment". It is a combination of internal indicators and external indicators that considers security from five perspectives: scientificity, diversity dynamicity, directivity and systematicity. The target layer covers six Tier 1 indicators which correspond to the keywords of the speeches: fairness, justice, commonality, comprehensiveness, cooperation and sustainability. The Tier 2 indicators developed under this framework of six categories still correspond with the keywords of the speeches, and the Tier 3 indicators are developed according to the content of the Tier 2 indicators. In actual measurement, the Tier 3 indicators serve as observation points, and extrapolation is made after data is collected.

（一）指标体系框架附表

表 4.1 人类命运共同体构建进程安全维度指标体系

一级指标	二级指标	三级指标
公道的范畴	坚持正确义利观测度	领导人对国际事务善意表态次数观测点
		国家之间安全合作项目数量观测点
		涉及对他国人道援助的次数观测点
		非本国优先的外交政策文件数目观测点
		对外经援履责有利他国安全的条约数量观测点
		投资合作机制均衡乌海的联合声明观测点
		兼顾共同安全的协商会晤和谈判回合观测点
	维护国际法的权威测度	根据国际公法出台相关政策数目观测点
		参与有关传统安全条约的数量观测点
		缔结非传统安全条约的数量观测点
	维护正常的国际秩序测度	参加维护《联合国宪章》活动的次数观测点
		遵守联合国各个具体规定的政府表态次数观测点
		对国际争端不诉诸武力的政府文件数目观测点
	推动国际关系法制化测度	参与国际安全法规制定数量观测点
		制定国际安全的提议数目观测点
		遵守国际法的领导人表态数量观测点

(I) Schedule of Framework of Indicator System

Schedule 4.1   An Indicator System for Measuring the Process of Building a Community with a Shared Future for Mankind: Security Dimension

Tier 1 indicators	Tier 2 indicators	Tier 3 indicators
The sphere of fairness	Measure of compliance with the correct idea about moral and profit	Observation point for the number of positive attitudes expressed by state leaders on international affairs
		Observation point for the number of security cooperation projects between countries
		Observation point for the frequency of humanitarian assistance to other countries
		Observation point for the number of documents on the foreign policy of national interests first
		Observation point for the number of foreign economic assistance treaties that are beneficial to the security of other countries
		Observation point for joint statements on a balanced, unharmful investment cooperation mechanism
		Observation point for consultations and talks that give consideration to common security
	Measure of the respect for the authority of international laws	Observation point for the number of policies introduced according to international public laws
		Observation point for the number of ratified traditional security treaties
		Observation point for the number of ratified non-traditional security treaties
	Measure of maintaining normal international order	Observation point for the number of events participated to safeguard the *Charter of the United Nations*
		Observation point for the number of government statements on compliance with specific regulations of the United Nations
		Observation point for the number of government documents on not resorting to force in international disputes
	Measure of the legislation on international relations	Observation point for the number of international security regulations formulated in collaboration with other countries
		Observation point for the number of international security motions put forward
		Observation point for the number of statements made by state leaders on abiding by international law

续表

一级指标	二级指标	三级指标
正义的范畴	不干涉别国内政测度	不干涉别国内政的声明次数观测点
		签订双边或多边安全条约观测点
		不干涉他国内政的政策变动情况观测点
	尊重各国人民自主选择测度	奉行独立自主的和平外交政策观测点
		国家对他国领土完整的原则表述观测点
		不对他国输出意识形态的声明数量观测点
	反对以武力威胁他国测度	针对他国发动战争次数观测点
		针对他国军事演习次数观测点
		卷入战争或军事冲突风险次数观测点
		军费占国内生产总值观测点
		在国外军事基地数量观测点
	反对借口法治侵害他国测度	人道主义干涉行为的记录次数观测点
		对他国煽动群体性事件数量观测点
		介入他国民族宗教事件数量观测点
共同的范畴	体现各国人民命运与共测度	国家间政府层面外交友好的次数观测点
		国家消除战争的意愿声明数量观测点
		一国媒体舆论对人类命运关注度观测点
		达成面对全球性可能灾难的共识观测点
		在发生自然灾害时的互助情况观测点
		共同建立对生态环境治理的机制观测点
		缔结并实施影响各国命运的条约观测点

Continued Schedule

Tier 1 indicators	Tier 2 indicators	Tier 3 indicators
The sphere of justice	Measure of non-interference in other countries' internal affairs	Observation point for the number of statements on non-interference in other countries' internal affairs
		Observation point for bilateral or multilateral security treaties signed
		Observation point for changes in the policy of non-interference in other countries' internal affairs
	Measure of the respect for independent state choices	Observation point for pursuing an independent foreign policy of peace
		Observation point for government statements on the principle of maintaining the territorial integrity of other countries
		Observation point for the number of government statements on not exporting ideology to other countries
	Measure of opposition to threatening other countries with the use of force	Observation point for the number of military operations against other countries
		Observation point for the number of military exercises against other countries
		Observation point for the number of risks of getting involved in war or military conflicts
		Observation point for the proportion of military expenditure in GDP
		Observation point for the number of military bases abroad
	Measure of opposition to infringing on other countries under the pretext of rule of law	Observation point for recorded times of humanitarian intervention
		Observation point for the number of mass disturbances incited in other countries
		Observation point for the number of interventions in other countries' ethnic and religious affairs
The sphere of commonality	Measure of people of all countries sharing weal and woe	Observation point for friendly diplomatic visits at the governmental level
		Observation point for the number of statements made on the willingness to avert war
		Observation point for the attention a country's media and public opinion give to human destiny
		Observation point for reaching consensus on possible global disasters
		Observation point for mutual assistance in the event of natural disasters
		Observation point for jointly establishing a mechanism for eco-environment governance
		Observation point for concluding and implementing treaties that affect the destiny of all countries

续表

一级指标	二级指标	三级指标
共同的范畴	促进各国利益交融测度	经济贸易依存度观测点
		无害进口渗透率观测点
		对外开放高地增长率观测点
		对外贸易互补程度观测点
		对外经济技术合作程度观测点
	建立对话协商机制测度	两国元首互访次数观测点
		国际安全高峰会议召开次数观测点
		国际安全合作条约内协商测度观测点
	共同消除引发战争根源测度	双边或多边谈话、协商次数观测点
		双边友好和平的关系指数观测点
		符合五项基本原则的谈判次数观测点
		根据和平谈判达成的条约数目观测点
		世界主要国家接受该国军备程度观测点
		共享性海外经济利益的扩大速度观测点
		缔结消除战争的国际条约数目观测点
		控制进攻型武器的态势报告表述观测点
	建立国际安全保障测度	国家安全指数观测点
		地区安全指数观测点
		国际安全指数观测点
		建立国际安全保障机制观测点

Continued Schedule

Tier 1 indicators	Tier 2 indicators	Tier 3 indicators
The sphere of commonality	Measure of promoting interest convergence among all countries	Observation point for economic and trade dependence
		Observation point for harmless import permeability
		Observation point for the growth rate of major opening zones
		Observation point for foreign trade complementarity
		Observation point for the degree of economic and technological cooperation with foreign countries
	Measure of establishing mechanisms of dialog and consultation	Observation point for exchange visits by heads of state
		Observation point for the number of international security summits held
		Observation point for consultation under international security cooperation treaties
	Measure of jointly eliminating the root cause of war	Observation point for the number of bilateral or multilateral talks and consultations
		Observation point for the bilateral friendly and peaceful relationship indicator
		Observation point for the number of negotiations in line with the five basic principles
		Observation point for the number of treaties concluded through peaceful negotiations
		Observation point for major countries' acceptance of armament level
		Observation point for the expanding speed of shared overseas economic interests
		Observation point for the number of international treaties concluded to eliminate war
		Observation point for the preparation of a situation report on the control of offensive weapons
	Measure of providing an international security guarantee	Observation point for national security indicators
		Observation point for regional security indicators
		Observation point for international security indicators
		Observation point for providing an international security guarantee mechanism

续表

一级指标	二级指标	三级指标
综合的范畴	创新安全理念测度	提出符合时代要求的安全主张观测点
		在国际论坛提出的新观念观测点
		对全球安全的政策的倡议观测点
		对地区安全的实际行动观测点
	以人为本维护国家安全测度	公众安全感观测点
		国民失业率观测点
		公共场所滋事件数观测点
		国民幸福指数观测点
		报媒指数（舆论安全指数）观测点
	树立总体国家安全观测度	国情安全的指数观测点
		对新安全观的阐释文本数量观测点
		对11种安全概念的落实观测点
		经常性的安全观引导与教育观测点
	维护共同安全和世界和平，将政治、经济、文化、生态等安全综合考虑并统筹测度	联合国机制运转情况观测点
		世界经济景气指数观测点
		全球生态足迹指数观测点
		各国绿色GDP的指标观测点
		可持续性收入（SI）观测点
		真实进步指数（GPI）观测点
		人文发展指数（HDI）观测点
		城市发展指数（CDI）观测点

Continued Schedule

Tier 1 indicators	Tier 2 indicators	Tier 3 indicators
The sphere of comprehensiveness	Measure of an innovative concept of security	Observation point for a security proposition that meets the requirements of the era
		Observation point for new ideas put forward at international forums
		Observation point for initiatives on global security
		Observation point for actions taken to strengthen regional security
	Measure of strengthening people-first national security	Observation point for the public's sense of security
		Observation point for the unemployment rate of the population
		Observation point for the number of public disturbances
		Observation point for the gross national happiness indicator
		Observation point for the press and media indicator (public opinion security indicator)
	Measure of framing the concept of overall national security	Observation point for national conditions security indicators
		Observation point for the number of texts on the new concept of security
		Observation point for the implementation of 11 concepts of security
		Observation point for regular security guidance and education
	Measure of maintaining common security and world peace and of giving comprehensive consideration to and coordinating political, economic, cultural and ecological security	Observation point for the operation of United Nations mechanisms
		Observation point for the world economic prosperity indicator
		Observation point for the global ecological footprint indicator
		Observation point for the green GDP indicator
		Observation point for sustainable income (SI)
		Observation point for the genuine progress indicator (GPI)
		Observation point for the human development indicator (HDI)
		Observation point for the city development indicator (CDI)

续表

一级指标	二级指标	三级指标
合作的范畴	树立合作共赢理念测度	确立构建共建共商共享原则观测点
		联合发表国家间合作的声明观测点
		公布国际合作共赢的项目观测点
	推动和平建共享测度	反对推行单边主义的声明次数观测点
		主张多边和平发展的声明次数观测点
		达成共建共享意愿并实施的态势观测点
	建立多边合作机制测度	签署贸易自由化协定的数目观测点
		多方维护多边贸易体制的条目观测点
		关税削减幅度观测点
		非关税壁垒削减程度观测点
		参加联合国维和行动的次数观测点
	推动各个方面的合作共赢测度	建立相关国家的对话机制状况观测点
		各国对话的论坛情况（次数）观测点
		以国家无差别政策对待他国投资观测点
		建立地区安全合作机制的条约观测点
		以和平解决争端的组织形式进行合作的数量观测点
		合作国对世界GDP贡献的增长率观测点
		合作国对世界贸易贡献的增长率观测点
		合作国对国际直接投资贡献的变化率观测点

Continued Schedule

Tier 1 indicators	Tier 2 indicators	Tier 3 indicators
The sphere of cooperation efforts	Measure of framing the concept of win-win cooperation	Observation point for establishing the principle of consultation, collaboration, and sharing
		Observation point for issuing joint statements on inter-state cooperation
		Observation point for announcing international win-win cooperation projects
	Measure of promoting peaceful collaboration and sharing	Observation point for the number of statements against unilateralism
		Observation point for the number of statements on peaceful multilateral development
		Observation point for having the intention of collaboration, sharing and implementation
	Measure of establishing multilateral cooperation mechanisms	Observation point for the number of trade liberalization agreements signed
		Observation point for multi-party maintenance of multilateral trade framework clauses
		Observation point for tariff cuts
		Observation point for reduction in non-tariff barriers
		Observation point for the number of participations in UN peacekeeping operations
	Measure of promoting all-round win-win cooperation	Observation point for establishing mechanisms for dialogs between relevant countries
		Observation point for the number of dialog forums
		Observation point for non-discriminatory treatment of foreign investment
		Observation point for treaties signed to establish regional security cooperation mechanisms
		Observation point for the number of cooperations to settle disputes in peaceful ways
		Observation point for the growth rate of the contribution of cooperative countries to world GDP
		Observation point for the growth rate of the contribution of cooperative countries to world trade
		Observation point for the rate of change in the contribution of cooperative countries to foreign direct investment

续表

一级指标	二级指标	三级指标
	坚持互利共赢的开放战略测度	国家领导人互利的战略取向观测点
		国家之间共赢的基本方式观测点
		开放不封闭的国策变化测度观测点
	完全摒弃冷战思维测度	国家领导人国家关系讲话取向观测点
		以和平取代争执的行动次数观测点
		公开裁减军队的目标观测点
	推动建立新的国际秩序测度	国家领导人参加国际论坛的主张观测点
		遵守裁减军队和武器的条约观测点
		提出公平合理倡议的议案数目观测点
可持续的范畴	坚持走和平发展道路测度	对国际事务和平的承诺观测点
		制定本国和平发展政策观测点
		付诸于行动的有关法律法规观测点
	促成公正合理的国际规范测度	领导人提出国际公正规范的建议观测点
		在联合国提倡公正合理的秩序观测点
		以处理周边国家公正合理为示范观测点
	协调一致打击"三股势力"测度	缔结遏制三股势力的条约观测点
		联合打击恐怖袭击行动的次数观测点
		该国控制极端宗教思想发展速率观测点
		该国控制恐怖组织数量的成效观测点

Continued Schedule

Tier 1 indicators	Tier 2 indicators	Tier 3 indicators
The Sphere of sustainability	Measure of adhering to the opening strategy of mutual benefits and win-win results	Observation point for state leaders' strategic orientation towards mutual benefit
		Observation point for the basic way of inter-state win-win cooperation
		Observation point for the change in an open national policy
	Measure of doing away with the Cold War mentality	Observation point for state leaders' orientation regarding inter-state relations in their speeches
		Observation point for the number of actions to settle disputes peacefully
		Observation point for announcing disarmament goals
	Measure of keeping a new international order	Observation point for state leaders' propositions at international forums
		Observation point for ratifying disarmament treaties
		Observation point for the number of fair and reasonable initiatives introduced
	Measure of pursuit of peaceful development	Observation point for commitment to peace in handling international affairs
		Observation point for formulating peaceful national development policy
		Observation point for laws and regulations implemented
	Measure of establishing fair and reasonable international norms	Observation point for state leaders' proposal for fair international norms
		Observation point for advocating a fair and reasonable international order at the United Nations
		Observation point for demonstratively dealing with neighboring countries in a fair and rational way
	Measure of coordinated fight against the "three forces of terrorism, separatism, and extremism"	Observation point for conclusion of treaties on containing the "three forces of terrorism, separatism, and extremism"
		Observation point for the number of joint operations against terrorist attacks
		Observation point for controlling the development of extreme religious thoughts
		Observation point for the effective control of the number of terrorist organizations

续表

一级指标	二级指标	三级指标
可持续的范畴	丰富安全观的内涵外延测度	国家领导人提出新的安全理念观测点
		发布本国安全的白皮书数目观测点
		将传统安全与非传统安全结合的文献数量观测点
		按照新安全观制定的政策数目观测点
	建立普遍安全的世界测度	建立与保持各国之间的沟通观测点
		就安全事务建立协调机制观测点
		推动国家间的和平发展的联合宣言和行动观测点
		安全共商共建共享的项目数量观测点
		联合遏制核战争与大规模杀伤武器的条约数目观测点
		联合对网络主权与全球网络治理的声明次数观测点
		军事公开透明化的测度观测点
	建立卫生健康安全的世界测度	建立全球公共卫生安全合作治理框架
		建立公开透明的防控体系
		建立国际医疗卫生物资供应体系

注：权重赋值采用主观赋值法，即由评估者根据经验主观判断得到，系专家调查法和比较加权法。

五、指标赋权方法

1.公道作为安全共同体的第一原则，是建立安全共同体的需要。作为测度公道范畴的一级指标，既是人类共同体的

Continued Schedule

Tier 1 indicators	Tier 2 indicators	Tier 3 indicators
The Sphere of sustainability	Measure of enriching the connotations and extensions of the concept of security	Observation point for the new concepts of security put forward by state leaders
		Observation point for the number of white papers released on national security
		Observation point for the number of documents which combine traditional security and non-traditional security
		Observation point for the number of policies formulated according to new concepts of security
	Measure of creating a universally safe world	Observation point for establishing and maintaining inter-state communication
		Observation point for establishing mechanisms for coordinating security affairs
		Observation point for joint declarations and actions to promote peaceful inter-state relations
		Observation point for the number of projects of security consultation, collaboration and sharing
		Observation point for the number of treaties signed to jointly prevent nuclear war and the proliferation of weapons of mass destruction
		Observation point for the number of joint statements on cyber sovereignty and global cyber governance
		Observation point for military openness and transparency
	Measure of creating a world of health security	Establishment of a cooperative governance framework for global public health security
		Establishment of an open and transparent prevention and control system
		Establishment of an international medical and health supply system

Note: The assignment of weight is subjective. It is an expert survey method and comparative weight assignment method based on the evaluator's subjective empirical judgment.

V. Indicator Weighting

1. Fairness, as the No. 1 principle behind the security community, is necessary for the establishment of the latter. As a Tier 1 indicator to measure the

核心关键，又是亚洲共同体的核心关键。

2. 正义是由公道作为首要原则而派生出来的第二原则，这与公道具有紧密联系，是一体两面的关系。公道的原则要通过正义加以体现，否则没有正义也就无所谓公道。

3. 共同作为一级指标所体现的是最新的人类命运共同体的思想体现，没有共同的价值观，公道与正义只是单方或具有同盟性质的国家来体现这两者。一旦进入共同的范畴，将无差别的对待所有命运攸关的各方的框架之内。

4. 综合作为人类命运共同体的一项重要指标，反映了中国对于世界秩序重构的新理念，也就是说提出了一个关于安全共同体的中国方案，这与现在国际上所通行的诸多指标可以吻合起来。

5. 合作的指标体现了前四个方面具体可操作性指向，是中国方案推向合作方达成一致性的体现。

6. 可持续的指标主要在于以上五个范畴要有连续性，完全摒弃冷战思维、推动建立新的国际秩序、坚持走和平发展道路、促成公正合理的国际规范，协调一致打击"三股势力"、丰富安全观的内涵外延、建立普遍安全的世界。在可持续的范畴之中，对危害人类健康的重大传染病（疫情）如何进行防控，是一个重要的部分，对于命运安全共同体的构建不可或缺。

category of fairness, it is the core of both the human community and the Asian community.

2. Justice is the No. 2 principle derived from the No. 1 principle of fairness. It is closely related to fairness, and together with fairness, forms the two aspects of an integral whole. The principle of fairness is expressed by justice, without which there would be no fairness.

3. Commonality, as a Tier 1 indicator, represents the latest thought on the Community with a Shared Future for Mankind. Without shared values, fairness and justice would be unilateral, or what allies display. Under the category of commonality, all parties at stake will be treated without discrimination.

4. Comprehensiveness, as an important indicator of the Community with a Shared Future for Mankind, represents China's new vision to rebuild the world order. It is the Chinese plan for building the security community and is consistent with many general international indicators.

5. The indicator of cooperation points out the specific way of using the previous four indicators. It is the process of the Chinese plan being accepted by partners and of both sides reaching consensus.

6. The indicator of sustainability is developed to stress that the previous five categories should ensure continuity between doing away with the Cold War mentality, building a new international order, pursuing peaceful development, establishing fair and reasonable international norms to fight the "three forces of terrorism, separatism, and extremism" in a coordinated manner, enriching the connotations and extensions of the concept of security, and building a world of universal security. How to prevent and control major infectious diseases (epidemics) that endanger human health is an important part under the category of sustainability, and is indispensable for building a security community.

第五章
人类命运共同体构建进程
生态维度指标体系

一、目的和意义

新时代,"一带一路"架设起从中国西域为枢纽的陆地丝绸之路和南海为枢纽的海上丝绸之路到当代中国"丝绸之路经济带"和"21世纪海上丝绸之路"的桥梁通道,奠定国内和国际统筹的方略格局,推动中国进入新的全球化时代。因此,复兴中华民族、全面建成小康社会、实现现代化强国,需要超越历史研究的碎片化局限,创新中国历史"古今中西"叙事的话语体系,推动构建人类命运共同体。人类生活在同一个地球,同呼吸共命运,共同克服自然灾害,共同保护生态环境。2020年9月,习近平主席在第七十五届联合国大会一般性辩论会上郑重提出中国"二氧化碳排放力争于2030

Chapter V

An Indicator System for Measuring the Process of Building a Community with a Shared Future for Mankind: Ecological Dimension

I. Purpose and Significance

Under the "Belt and Road Initiative" for the new era, a network of passages comprising the Land Silk Road with western China as the hub, the Maritime Silk Road with the South China Sea as the hub, the Silk Road Economic Belt, and the 21st Century Maritime Silk Road has been completed. This has laid the groundwork for the strategic plan of domestic-international coordination and opened a new chapter in China's drive to go global. Therefore, to revive the Chinese nation, build a well-off society in an all-round way, and become modern and powerful, China needs to transcend the limitations of fragmented historical research, innovate the discourse system in which Chinese history is recounted in the order of "ancient times, modern times, China and the West", and strive to build a Community with a Shared Future for Mankind. We live on the same planet, are bound by a common destiny, and make concerted efforts to overcome natural disasters and protect the eco-environment. At the general debate of the 75th United Nations General Assembly held in September 2020, President Xi Jinping officially declared that China "pledges to bring its total carbon dioxide emissions

年前达到峰值，努力争取2060年前实现碳中和"。2021年1月，生态环境部印发《关于统筹和加强应对气候变化与生态环境保护相关工作的指导意见》，明确了统筹和加强应对气候变化和生态环境保护的工作思路。绿色低碳的生产生活方式，是实现碳达峰目标及碳中和愿景的基础支撑，而碳达峰目标及碳中和愿景的实现又是保证生态环境明显改善和根本性整体性好转的必要前提。因此，以生态安全作为切入点位，生态共同体作为物质和文化载体，在长期的发展变迁中既反映出人与自然交融博弈的烙印，也延续着古往今来"人化自然"的生态哲学，以共同的生态安全、共同的历史记忆、共同的价值观念为纽带，将世界各国福祸相依、荣辱与共凝聚在一起。

（一）构建目标

基于"生态文明建设"和"人类命运共同体"的时代背景，我们精准把握生态共同体对生态建设的现实要求，着力构建尊崇自然、绿色发展、科学合理的生态评价体系，探索生态共同体与人类命运共同体有机融合的内生途径，设计一套在高度上具有战略性、在视野上具有系统性、在操作上具有可行性的生态文明建设模式，为缔造互利共荣局面提供重要支撑。

人与自然的生态共同体是构建人类命运共同体的坚实基础。（1）构建"生态共同体"是马克思主义唯物史观的必然

to a peak by 2030 and achieve carbon neutrality by 2060". In January 2021, the Ministry of Ecology and Environment issued the *Guidelines on Coordinating and Strengthening the Work Related to Climate Change and Protection of the Ecological Environment*, which pointed out the direction for coordinating and strengthening the work related to climate change and protection of the ecological environment. Green and low-carbon production and life are the basis for bringing carbon dioxide emissions to a peak and achieving carbon neutrality, which in turn are the prerequisite for ensuring a notable, fundamental and overall improvement of the ecological environment. In this indicator system, ecological security serves as the ultimate goal and ecological community serves as the material and cultural medium. It reflects the integration of man into nature and the game going on between them in the long development and evolution process, and inherits the ecological philosophy of "humanized nature" that dates back to ancient times. In the framework of this indicator system, common ecological security, common historical memory and common values bring together all countries so they can depend on each other and share weal or woe in difficult times.

(I) Goal

In this era when China proposes to "create an ecological civilization" and build a "Community with a Shared Future for Mankind", we fully understand the actual requirements of the ecological community for ecological conservation, strive to build a scientific ecological assessment system that respects nature and green development, explore ways of integrating the ecological community into the Community with a Shared Future for Mankind, and design a model for creating an ecological civilization that is strategic, systematic and feasible so as to lend support to creating a mutually beneficial world of common prosperity.

The ecological community for man and nature provides a solid foundation for building a Community with a Shared Future for Mankind. (1) The building of the "ecological community" is the inevitable choice of Marxist historical

抉择，是在人的本质力量的对象化过程中所达到的人与自然、人与社会、人与人的和谐统一，是人的本质复归的真正表现；（2）构建"生态共同体"符合"天人合一"的思想，是历史生态文明的传承和见证；（3）"生态共同体"是人类命运共同体不可或缺的要素，区域内的经济体都是生态共同体。基于"生态共同体"的相互依赖关系，保障区域环境利益共享是可持续发展的根本，需要国家之间、区域之间和洲际之间在广度与深度上的通力合作，建立环境利益共享机制，加强全球人类命运共同体的紧密性和合作性。（4）"生态共同体"是生态全球化的时代要求，打破全球"零和博弈"局面，是全球面临的共同挑战和共同的责任。经济全球化带来的产业全球化，使发展中国家承受着发达国家产业转移的环境负担，生态评价体系能够精准分析环境污染，利用区域生态补偿作为调节机制，能够促进命运共同体的建设，从而推动国际上全球僵化局面。（5）构建"生态共同体"是全球范围内多边机制的要求，是国家之间的双边协商判准，是"一带一路"的国际价值诉求。寻求多边合作是解决人类共同生态问题的明智选择。"一带一路"倡议是构建责任、利益、生态和人类命运共同体的实践路径，应把握生态文明足迹的历史脉动，追

materialism, the harmonious unity between man and nature, man and society, and man and man brought about by the objectification of man's essential power, and the true expression of the return of man's essence; (2) The building of the "ecological community" conforms to the theory that "man is an integral part of nature" and is the inheritance and witness of the historical ecological civilization; (3) The "ecological community" is an indispensable element of the Community with a Shared Future for Mankind where all economies are ecological communities. Due to the interdependence of "ecological communities", ensuring the sharing of regional environmental benefits is the foundation of sustainable development. This requires the in-depth and extensive cooperation among countries, regions and continents, the establishment of the mechanism for sharing environmental benefits, and an increase in the tightness and cooperativeness of the global Community with a Shared Future for Mankind. (4) The "ecological community" is the requirement of ecological globalization, and the whole world faces the common challenge of bringing an end to "zero-sum games". Industrial globalization brought about by economic globalization has shifted the environmental burden of industrial transfer in developed countries to developing countries. The ecological assessment system can accurately analyze environmental pollution, and adopt regional ecological compensation as the adjustment mechanism to promote the building of the Community with a Shared Future for Mankind and break the global stalemate. (5) The building of the "ecological community" is the requirement of the global multilateral mechanism, the criterion for bilateral consultation, and the international value appeal of the "Belt and Road Initiative". Multilateral cooperation is a wise choice for solving the common ecological problems faced by all mankind. The "Belt and Road Initiative" provides a specific solution to building a responsibility community, an interest community, an ecological community and a Community with a Shared Future for Mankind. We should trace the footprints of ecological civilization, discover the value appeal of the Ecological Community with a Shared Future for Mankind, and promote its progress.

寻人类生态命运共同体建设的价值诉求，推进其进程。

构建生态共同体，应牢记为全人类谋福祉的初心，弘扬经世致用优良传统，清晰认识全球生态恶化的研究背景；围绕重大现实问题，牢牢把握人与自然和谐的时代要求，为全球治理提供借鉴，为全球绿色可持续发展提供对策建议，助推全球共享共赢、共生共荣、和谐发展。

（二）现实意义

从20世纪90年代开始，亚洲各国迅速崛起，被称为"世界工厂"。亚洲国家大量引入和发展劳动密集型产业，环境污染严重、资源消耗高，加上发展中国家缺乏治理环境的巨额资金和先进技术，致使"环境治理"明显落后于"经济发展"，生态安全岌岌可危。发达国家在过去的几十年内，以自然资源与生态环境为代价赢得了经济增长，尤其是工业耗损品的处理以及温室气体的排放，加大了全球环境承载力。2020年以来，全球多灾多难，这就要求各国人民同心协力、携手前行。诸如：新型冠状病毒肺炎、流感病毒、"登革热"、澳洲森林大火、南极冰川现"血雪"、蝗灾、大气污染、河流污染加剧、固体废物造成连锁灾害反应、森林滥伐等。

（三）人类生态共同体的理论基础

马克思在《1844年经济学哲学手稿》中首次提到"人化自然"，即客观的自然界不断进入人的活动的过程。"人化自

To build an ecological community, we should keep in mind our original intention of seeking benefits for all mankind, follow in the fine tradition of humanistic pragmatism, and outline the background to global ecological deterioration. We should work to address major realistic problems, fully comprehend the requirement of our era that harmony must be maintained between man and nature, provide a useful frame of reference for global governance, come up with suggestions for green and sustainable global development, and promote sharing, win-win cooperation, common prosperity and harmonious development on a global scale.

(II) Practical Significance

Asian countries have been rising at a rapid pace since the 1990s. They are called the "world factory". They rolled out labor-intensive industries on a massive scale, resulting in serious environmental pollution and high resource consumption. In addition, developing countries lack the huge funds and advanced technologies necessary for environmental governance, making "environmental governance" lag behind "economic development" and putting ecological security in jeopardy. In the past decades, developed countries achieved economic growth at the expense of natural resources and the eco-environment. The disposal of industrial consumables and the emission of greenhouse gases, in particular, have placed an extra burden on the global environment. The world has been plagued by disasters since 2020. This requires the people of all countries to work together to fight disasters like the novel coronavirus, influenza virus, "dengue fever", the forest fire in Australia, the "blood-snow" on Antarctic glaciers, locust plagues, air pollution, worsening river pollution, the chain reaction of solid waste, deforestation and etc.

(III) The Theoretical Basis for the Ecological Community with a Shared Future for Mankind

Marx was the first to come up with the concept of "humanized nature" in *The Economic and Philosophic Manuscripts of 1844*. It refers to the process of incor-

然"是马克思主义生态观,也是人类对"物化自然"的扬弃,是人类根据自身需要改造自然界的结果。

1. 马克思主义"人化自然"生态观的启迪

随着全球化扩张,亚洲各国之间紧密联系。面对生态安全问题,构建生态共同体,既是马克思"人化自然"思想的创新,也是人类发展的实践探索。从历史发展来看,人与自然经历了从"自在自然"到"人化自然"的转化过程;从人与物的"依赖关系"到"自由个性"的觉醒,再到"和谐共生",人与自然和解成为历史选择。因此,生态共同体是生态问题的最优解。从生态文明建设实践来看,人化自然是其发展核心,主张生态整体是主体,强调生态整体的合理性和生态内部的共生性,揭示了人与自然的一体性,为保护环境和加强生态共同体建设起到了指导作用,使从社会共同到生态共同成为可能。

2. 中国优秀传统文化的传承

2.1 "天人合一"历史观的传承

我国优秀的传统文化孕育了朴素的生态哲学。儒家将"天人合一"作为生态思想的理论基础与核心内容,认为不能离开人而谈天,也不能离开天而谈人,"天"与"人"是内外相通的一体。"天人合一"主张兼顾"尽人之性"与"尽物之性",即人与物都能各自发挥天性,自然生存;同时提倡坚守"中道",即兼顾天、地、人之间的和谐。因此,"天人合一"视

porating the objective nature into human activities. "Humanized nature" is the ecological view of Marxism, the sublation of "materialized nature" by mankind, and the result of mankind transforming nature according to their own needs.

1. Inspiration from "humanized nature", the ecological view of Marxism

Globalization is connecting Asian countries closer than ever before. The building of the ecological community is not only an innovation in Marx's concept of "humanized nature", but also a practical exploration for human development. Historically, man and nature underwent the transformation from "free nature" to "humanized nature", from the "dependence" between man and things to the awakening of "free personality" and "harmonious coexistence". The reconciliation between man and nature has become a historical choice. Therefore, the ecological community is the optimal solution to ecological issues. Humanized nature is the core of ecological civilization, and the proposition of ecological unity is the principal part. Ecological civilization emphasizes the rationality of ecological unity and the symbiosis of the ecosystem, reveals the unity of man and nature, plays a guiding role in protecting the environment and building the ecological community, and makes possible the transition from social community to ecological community.

2. Inheritance of excellent traditional Chinese culture

2.1 Inheritance of the historical view that "man is an integral part of nature"

Excellent traditional Chinese culture has fostered simple ecological philosophy. "The unity of man and nature" is the theoretical basis and core content of the ecological thought of Confucianism, which holds that neither nature nor man can be separated from each other because they form an integral whole. According to the theory that "man is an integral part of nature", man and nature should be given the opportunity to play to their full potential. At the same time, it advocates the "middle path" so that harmony is achieved between heaven, earth and people. "The unity of nature and man" regards nature as a

自然界为一个有机的生命体，认为自然是大天地，人是小天地，人和自然在本质上是相通的，要求生产生活皆应符合自然规律，逐渐演变成一系列道德原则、行为规范等社会契约，构成了早期自然状态下的生态共同体。生态安全观是"天人合一"历史观的传承，只有将"天人合一"的历史观与当代的制度、管理、科技相结合，才能实现人与自然和谐发展。

2.2 "人与自然和谐"历史观的传承

人与自然和谐是中国古代朴素生态思想的立足点。道家"人与自然和谐"观认为自然与人平等，一方面指自然界按本身法则运转，宇宙万物保持和谐共生、繁衍生息；另一方面强调人与自然的友好关系，人与自然融为一体。道家传统的"用养结合"生态思想就是最好的印证，它是现代生态建设的文化渊源。"用养结合"是道家的消费观，即从自然界获取资源时，不可一味单项索取，应顺应自然万物生长发育的规律，留下成长和发展的空间，给予他们休养生息的时间。新时期，我们既要节约和高效利用资源、倡导绿色发展，又要提倡人与自然和谐共生的思想，彰显出生态共同体的深刻内涵。

3. "绿色发展"观的时代要求

党的十九大报告强调"人与自然是生命共同体，人类必须尊重自然、顺应自然、保护自然"。习近平总书记在唯物主义

living organism and holds that nature, as the big world, is intrinsically related to man, the small world. It requires production and life to abide by the laws of nature, resulting in a series of social contracts, such as moral principles and behavioral norms, of the early natural ecological community. The concept of ecological security is the follow-up of the historical view that "man is an integral part of nature". To achieve harmony between man and nature, we must apply the historical view that "man is an integral part of nature" in a way that suits the systems, management and technology of today.

2.2 Inheritance of the historical view of "harmony between man and nature"

"Harmony between man and nature" was the foothold of the simple ecological thoughts in ancient China. The Taoist view of "harmony between man and nature" holds that nature and man are equal. This means that nature takes its course according to certain laws and everything in the universe thrives in a harmonious way. On the other hand, this Taoist view highlights the friendly relationship between man and nature and their integration. The traditional Taoist ecological thought of "combination of use and maintenance" is the best proof. It is the cultural origin of ecological conservation today. "Combination of use and maintenance" is the Taoist view on consumption. It means that we cannot be greedy when obtaining resources from nature, and should instead observe the laws of the growth of all natural beings by leaving room for their growth and time for their recuperation. In the new era, we should avoid wasting resources, make efficient use of them and pursue green development. In the meantime, we should promote the idea of harmonious coexistence between man and nature and highlight the profound connotations of the ecological community.

3. Requirements of "green development" for the new era

The report to the 19th National Congress of the Communist Party of China emphasizes that "man and nature form the community of life, and man must respect, conform to and protect nature". General Secretary Xi Jinping formulated concepts of "green development", such as "lucid waters and lush moun-

自然观、马克思唯物史观的基础上结合整体性原则提出了"绿水青山就是金山银山"等"绿色发展观"。它是马克思主义生态理论与当今时代发展特征相结合的发展理念，解决了和谐社会的生态发展问题。

二、指导思想

立足于全球生态利益共同体的视阈角度，在建立全球多元化的交流协作和发展机制背景下，旨在构建开放创新、包容互惠的生态共同体。构建生态共同体指标体系应遵循"人与自然和谐共生、生产生活绿色发展、全球生态共享共治"的原则，拟从载体、时间、空间三个维度，"山水林田湖草"六大方面，将过程性指标和结果性指标结合，积累翔实有力的基础资料，提供相应的技术路线和理论指导。

三、构建原则

人与自然和谐共生原则。人与自然的生命共同体是构建人类命运共同体的坚实基础。生态共同体指标体系基于马克思主义"人化自然的"的生态观、我国古代"天人合一"思想以及人类命运共同体思想而建立，具有坚实的理论基础以及现实意义，可用于指导全球生态共同体的建设和发展，是明确全球生态文明建设方向的依据。

tains are invaluable assets", based on the materialist view on nature and Marx's materialist view on history. It is an idea of development that combines Marx's ecological theory with the actual development of our era, and has addressed the ecological issues facing harmonious social development.

II. Guiding Ideology

This indicator system is developed from the perspective of the global ecological interest community and against the background of establishing a diversified global communication, cooperation and development mechanism. It aims to build an open, innovative, inclusive and mutually beneficial ecological community. The building of an indicator system for the ecological community should stick to the principle of "harmonious coexistence between man and nature, green production and life, and sharing and co-governance of the global ecosystem". It will cover the three dimensions of medium, time and space, include the six aspects of "mountains, rivers, forests, farms, lakes and grass", combine process indicators with result indicators, accumulate detailed and reliable basic data and provide corresponding technical routes and theoretical guidance.

III. Guiding Principles

Principle of harmonious coexistence between man and nature. The life community for man and nature provides a solid foundation for building a Community with a Shared Future for Mankind. The indicator system for the ecological community is based on the Marxist ecological view of "humanized nature", the ancient Chinese thought of "the unity of man and nature" and the concept of Community with a Shared Future for Mankind. It has a solid theoretical foundation and great practical significance, can guide the building and development of the global ecological community, and can point global ecological civilization in the right direction.

生产生活绿色发展原则。生态共同体指标体系的构建是一个较为长期过程，它是对过去不均衡以及毁灭式发展的一种摒弃及修正体系，通过结合生态文明建设的经验及人类命运共同体的理念，对未来全球的绿色发展以及可持续发展做出科学的指导。

全球生态共享共治原则。针对目前缺乏全球生态环境治理的制度体系的约束，各国使用人类共有的生态环境资源时，更多考虑的是短期经济利益，而导致的"公地悲剧"，以及部分霸权主义国家牺牲别国生态利益，作为自己发展前进的基础，而导致的"零和博弈"等问题。生态共同体指标体系的建立成为如今全球生态均衡发展的首要目标，从环境利益共享机制及生态补偿机制两方面，使全球各国生态环境得到可持续、平等、公平的发展。

四、指标体系框架

根据生态文明的内涵、人类共同体理论和指导思想，主动对标"十四五规划"和 2035 年美丽中国远景目标以及习近平总书记碳达峰和碳中和愿景，参考联合国 2030 年可持续发展目标（SDGs）评价指标体系，将过程型指标与结果型指标结合，从多维度、多层面、多综合三方面综合考虑，按照指标的易得性、易理解性、可测度、显著性、可获得性、可比性和指标通用性选取原则，设计如下指标体系，共分为 3 个一级指标，自然资源保护度、生态环境治理度、生态制度完备

Principle of green production and life. The building of an indicator system for the ecological community is a long-term process. It is a system for rejecting and correcting the unbalanced and destructive development of the past, and draws on the experience of creating an ecological civilization and the concept of Community with a Shared Future for Mankind to offer scientific guidance to future green global development and sustainable development.

Principle of sharing and co-governing the global ecosystem. Due to the lack of institutional constraints on global eco-environment governance, countries using the ecological resources shared by all mankind pursue short-term economic benefits, resulting in the "tragedy of the commons". Some hegemonic countries pursue their own development and progress at the expense of the economic benefits of other countries, resulting in problems such as "zero-sum games". The establishment of an indicator system for the ecological community has become the primary goal of balanced global ecological development. It provides the environmental benefit sharing mechanism and the ecological compensation mechanism for the sustainable, equal and fair development of the eco-environment of all countries.

IV. Framework of Indicator System

The framework of this indicator system is based on the connotations of ecological civilization and the theory and guiding ideology of the human community. It is an active response to the "14th Five-Year Plan", the 2035 Vision for Beautiful China and General Secretary Xi Jinping's vision for bringing carbon dioxide emissions to a peak and carbon neutrality. Drawing on the indicator system for the 2030 United Nations Sustainable Development Goals (SDGs), it combines process indicators with result indicators, and develops the following indicator system according to the principle of indicator accessibility, clarity, measurability, significance, availability, comparability and universality and from multiple perspectives. This indicator system comprises three Tier 1 indicators, which measure the protection of natural resources, the governance of the eco-environment and

度（数据来源：IMF/ 相关政府网站 / 白皮书、UN 开发计划署 /UN 环境规划署 /UN 工业发展组织等）。

（一）自然资源保护范畴

自然资源是指自然界中人类可以直接获得用于生产和生活的物质，包括气候资源、生物资源、水资源等。

1. 气候变化（3 个观测点）

1.1 平均气温的升高度数

1.2 拉尼娜现象的天数

1.3 厄尔尼诺现象的天数

2. 陆地生态（7 个观测点）

2.1 植被覆盖率

2.2 沙漠化治理增长贡献率（中国地球大数据）

2.3 湿地保护率

2.4 植被净初级生产力 (NPP)

2.5 陆地生物多样性指数

2.6 过境水体化学需氧量（COD）[①] 变化率

2.7 过境水体磷酸盐的浓度

3. 海洋环境（4 个观测点）

3.1 主要入海河流重金属砷的排放量

---

① 化学需氧量（COD），是在一定的条件下，采用一定的强氧化剂处理水样时，所消耗的氧化剂量。

the completeness of the eco-governance system. (Data source: IMF/ relevant government websites/white papers, UNDP/UNEP/UNIDO, etc.)

(Ⅰ) The sphere of natural resources protection

Natural resources refer to the substances that mankind can directly obtain from nature for production and life, including climate resources, biological resources, water resources, etc.

1. Climate change (3 observation points)

1.1 Rise in the average temperature

1.2 Number of days when La Nina phenomenon occurs

1.3 Number of days when El Nino phenomenon occurs

2. Terrestrial ecosystem (7 observation points)

2.1 Vegetation coverage

2.2 Contribution to desertification control (China Earth Big Data)

2.3 Rate of wetland protection

2.4 Vegetation net primary productivity (NPP)

2.5 Terrestrial biodiversity indicator

2.6 Change in COD[①] of cross-border water bodies

2.7 Concentration of phosphate in cross-border water bodies

3. Marine environment (4 observation points)

3.1 Discharge of the heavy metal arsenic from main seagoing rivers

---

① Chemical oxygen demand (COD) is the oxidation dose consumed when water samples are treated with a certain strong oxidant under certain conditions.

3.2 主要入海河流的 COD 变化率

3.3 海洋生物多样性指数

3.4 海岸垃圾的持续存量分布密度

（二）生态环境治理范畴

1. 绿色经济（9 个观测点）

1.1 单位 GDP 二氧化碳排放

1.2 工业废水排放达标比重

1.3 工业固体废物综合利用比重

1.4 单位耕地面积化肥使用量降低率

1.5 单位耕地面积农药使用量降低率

1.6 受污染耕地安全利用率

1.7 可再生资源占能源消费总量的比例

1.8 绿色基础设施建设量（绿道、国家公园、湿地、森林公园、雨水花园等）

1.9 退耕还林和天然林保护

2. 城乡宜居（8 个观测点）

2.1 城市空气质量年优良天数

2.2 城市绿地率

2.3 城市垃圾分类普及率

2.4 城镇每万人口公共交通出行量

2.5 农村卫生厕所普及率

3.2 Change in COD of main seagoing rivers

3.3 Marine biodiversity indicator

3.4 Distribution density of the continuous stock of coastal garbage

(II) The sphere of eco-environment governance

1. Creen economy (9 observation points)

1.1 Garbon dioxide emissions per unit of GDP

1.2 Proportion of up-to-standard discharged industrial wastewater

1.3 Rate of the comprehensive utilization of industrial solid waste

1.4 Rate of reduction in fertilizer use per unit cultivated land area

1.5 Rate of reduction in pesticide use per unit cultivated land area

1.6 Rate of safe utilization of contaminated farmland

1.7 Proportion of renewable resources in total energy consumption

1.8 Amount of green infrastructure facilities (greenways, national parks, wetlands, forest parks, rainwater gardens, etc.)

1.9 Conversion of farmland into forest and protection of natural forests

2. Urban and country livability (8 observation points)

2.1 Number of days of excellent urban air quality

2.2 Urban green coverage

2.3 Rate of urban garbage classification

2.4 Amount of trips made by every 10,000 urban residents on public transport

2.5 Toilet coverage in rural areas

2.6 农村自来水普及率

2.7 生活垃圾无害化处理率

2.8 污水集中处理率（污水处理率＝污水处理量÷污水排放总量×100%）

3. 灾害防治（4个观测点）

3.1 重大自然灾害的发生率

3.2 减灾投入额

3.3 重大自然灾害的监测和预警

3.4 重大自然灾害的灾后重建

（三）生态制度完备范畴

1. 跨国协作度（4个观测点）

1.1 《京都议定书》等全球生态框架参与数

1.2 《"一带一路"倡议》等多边生态框架参与数

1.3 《生物多样性公约》等国际环境条约参与数

1.4 《巴黎协定》等国际环境条约参与数

2. 政府参与度（3个观测点）

2.1 生态建设法律文书颁布数

2.2 生态违法违规事件查处率

2.3 生态专利申请受理数

2.6 Tap-water coverage in rural areas

2.7 Rate of harmless treatment of domestic waste

2.8 Rate of centralized sewage treatment (rate of sewage treatment = amount of sewage treated ÷ total sewage discharge × 100%)

3. Disaster prevention and control (4 observation points)

3.1 Incidence of major natural disasters

3.2 Amount of investment in disaster reduction

3.3 Monitoring and early warning of major natural disasters

3.4 Post-disaster reconstruction

(III) The sphere of eco-governance system completeness

1. Cross-border cooperation (4 observation points)

1.1 Ratification of global ecological frameworks such as the *Kyoto Protocol*

1.2 Ratification of multilateral ecological frameworks such as the "*Belt and Road Initiative*"

1.3 Ratification of international environmental treaties such as the *Convention on Biological Diversity*

1.4 Ratification of international environmental treaties such as the *Paris Agreement*

2. Government involvement (3 observation points)

2.1 Number of legal documents issued on ecological conservation

2.2 Investigation of infringements of ecological regulations

2.3 Number of ecological patents granted

3. 社会参与度（3个观测点）

3.1 环保办公设备采购率

3.2 生态文明学校教育普及率

3.3 生态研究成果转化率

（四）指标体系框架附表

表 5.1　人类命运共同体构建进程生态维度指标体系

一级指标	二级指标	三级指标
自然资源保护范畴	气候变化测度	平均气温升高的度数观测点
		拉尼娜现象的天数观测点
		厄尔尼诺现象的天数观测点
	陆地生态测度	植被覆盖变化率观测点
		沙漠化治理贡献率（中国地球大数据）观测点
		湿地保护率观测点
		植被净初级生产力（NPP）观测点
		陆地生物多样性指数观测点
		过境水体化学需氧量（COD）变化率观测点
		过境水体磷酸盐的浓度观测点
	海洋环境测度	主要入海河流重金属砷的排放量观测点
		主要入海河流的COD变化率观测点
		海洋生物多样性指数观测点
		海岸垃圾的持续存量分布密度观测点

3. Societal involvement (3 observation points)

3.1 Procurement of office equipment for environmental protection

3.2 Education about ecological civilization at schools

3.3 Utilization of ecological research results

(IV) Schedule of Framework of Indicator System

Schedule 5.1 An Indicator System for Measuring the Process of Building a Community with a Shared Future for Mankind: Ecological Dimension

Tier 1 indicators	Tier 2 indicators	Tier 3 indicators
The sphere of natural resource protection	Measure of climate change	Observation point for the rise in the average temperature
		Observation point for the number of days when La Nina phenomenon occurs
		Observation point for the number of days when El Nino phenomenon occurs
	Measure of the terrestrial ecosystem	Observation point for the rate of change in vegetation coverage
		Observation point for contribution to desertification control (China Earth Big Data)
		Observation point for the rate of wetland protection
		Observation point for vegetation net primary productivity (NPP)
		Observation point for the terrestrial biodiversity indicator
		Observation point for change in COD of cross-border water bodies
		Observation point for concentration of phosphate in cross-border water bodies
	Measure of the marine environment	Observation point for the discharge of the heavy metal arsenic from main seagoing rivers
		Observation point for change in COD of main seagoing rivers
		Observation point for the marine biodiversity indicator
		Observation point for distribution density of the continuous stock of coastal garbage

续表

一级指标	二级指标	三级指标
生态环境治理范畴	绿色经济测度	单位GDP二氧化碳排放观测点
		工业废水排放达标比重观测点
		工业固体废物综合利用比重观测点
		单位耕地面积化肥使用量降低率观测点
		单位耕地面积农药使用量降低率观测点
		受污染耕地安全利用率观测点
		可再生资源占能源消费总量的比例观测点
		绿色基础设施建设量观测点
		退耕还林和天然林保护观测点
	城乡宜居测度	城市空气质量年优良天数
		城市绿地率观测点
		城市垃圾分类普及率观测点
		城镇每万人口公共交通出行量观测点
		农村卫生厕所普及率观测点
		农村自来水普及率观测点
		生活垃圾无害化处理率观测点
		污水集中处理率观测点
	灾害防治测度	重大自然灾害的发生率观测点
		减灾投入额观测点
		重大自然灾害的监测和预警观测点
		重大自然灾害的灾后重建观测点

Continued Schedule

Tier 1 indicators	Tier 2 indicators	Tier 3 indicators
The sphere of ecoenvironment governance	Measure of the green economy	Observation point for carbon dioxide emissions per unit GDP
		Observation point for the proportion of up-to-standard discharged industrial wastewater
		Observation point for the rate of the comprehensive utilization of industrial solid waste
		Observation point for the rate of reduction in fertilizer use per unit cultivated land area
		Observation point for the rate of reduction in pesticide use per unit cultivated land area
		Observation point for the rate of safe utilization of contaminated farmland
		Observation point for the proportion of renewable resources in total energy consumption
		Observation point for the amount of green infrastructure facilities
		Observation point for the conversion of farmland into forest and protection of natural forests
	Measure of urban and country livability	Number of days of excellent urban air quality
		Observation point for urban green coverage
		Observation point for the rate of urban garbage classification
		Observation point for the amount of trips made by every 10,000 urban residents on public transport
		Observation point for toilet coverage in rural areas
		Observation point for tap-water coverage in rural areas
		Observation point for the rate of harmless treatment of domestic waste
		Observation point for the centralized treatment of sewage
	Measure of disaster prevention	Observation point for the incidence of major natural disasters
		Observation point for the amount of investment in disaster reduction
		Observation point for monitoring and early warning of major natural disasters
		Observation point for post-disaster reconstruction

续表

一级指标	二级指标	三级指标
生态制度完备范畴	跨国协作度测度	《京都议定书》等全球生态框架参与数观测点
		《"一带一路"倡议》等多边生态框架参与数观测点
		《生物多样性公约》等国际环境条约参与数观测点
		《巴黎协定》等国际环境条约参与数观测点
	政府参与度测度	生态建设法律文书颁布数观测点
		生态违法违规事件查处率观测点
		生态专利申请受理数观测点
	社会参与度测度	环保办公设备采购率观测点
		生态文明学校教育普及率观测点
		生态研究成果转化率观测点

五、指标赋权方法

1. 自然资源保护是以人与自然和谐为价值取向，以低碳循环发展为原则，从气候变化、陆地生态、海洋环境三方面入手，按照生态系统的整体性、系统性、内在规律，进行整体保护、系统修复、综合治理，像对待生命一样对待环境，实行严格的生态环境保护制度，从而达到对自然资源环境的统一保护。权重最重，占 36%。

2. 生态环境治理立足于共同的生态利益，构建开放创新、包容互惠的生态共同体须以生态文明建设为抓手，以效率、

Continued Schedule

Tier 1 indicators	Tier 2 indicators	Tier 3 indicators
The sphere of ecogovernance system completeness	Measure of cross-border cooperation	Observation point for the ratification of global ecological frameworks such as the *Kyoto Protocol*
		Observation point for the ratification of multilateral ecological frameworks such as the "*Belt and Road Initiative*"
		Observation point for the ratification of international environmental treaties such as the *Convention on Biological Diversity*
		Observation point for the ratification of international environmental treaties such as the *Paris Agreement*
	Measure of government involvement	Observation point for the number of legal documents issued on ecological conservation
		Observation point for the investigation of infringements of ecological regulations
		Observation point for the number of ecological patents granted
	Measure of societal involvement	Observation point for the procurement of office equipment for environmental protection
		Observation point for the education about ecological civilization at schools
		Observation point for the utilization of ecological research results

V. Indicator Weighting

1. The protection of natural resources is orientated towards the harmony between man and nature, sticks to the principle of low-carbon cyclic development, focuses on climate change, terrestrial ecosystem and marine environment, and carries out overall protection, systematic restoration and comprehensive treatment according to the integrity, systematicness and inherent laws of the ecosystem, treats the environment like its own life, and implements a rigorous eco-environment protection system to protect the natural environment. This indicator is assigned the greatest weight of 36%.

2. Eco-environment governance is based on common ecological interests. To build an open, innovative, inclusive and mutually beneficial ecological

可持续为目标的经济增长方式。在全球多元化的交流协作和发展机制背景下实现可持续生态经济，必然以积累绿色财富为目标，以"科学布局、合理消费、低碳循环"为特征，加强城乡环境建设，调整生态经济结构，注重灾害防治，实现绿色发展。权重次之，占34%。

3.生态制度完备按照推动构建人类命运共同体生态文明思想所体现的系统观、整体观、全局观，立足于从源头的自然资源产权制度到生产过程再到末端消费的全过程，从跨国协作度、政府参与度和社会参与度三方面，系统推进全面节约制度、资源有偿使用和生态补偿制度，权重占30%。

在完善法律法规方面，从生态文明与美丽中国建设的相关内容写入宪法，到建立生态环境领域各类法律，再到细化相关部门规章，逐步形成了生态文明制度体系法治框架；在加强组织力量方面，优化重组了从中央到地方的各级自然资源、生态环境等领域的行政管理机构，推进了省以下生态环境机构监测监察执法垂直管理；在提高机制效能方面，除夯实法治建设、规范行政监管外，还实施了中央生态环保督察制度，强化监督问责；同时，加快完善市场机制，赋权民众参与、强化社会约束机制。

community, we must first create an ecological civilization and adopt a growth model that highlights efficiency and sustainability. To build a sustainable ecological economy against the background of a diversified global communication, cooperation and development mechanism, we must accumulate green wealth and highlight "a scientific layout, rational consumption and low-carbon cyclic development", improve the urban and rural environments, restructure the ecological economy, prevent disasters and strive to achieve green development. This indicator is assigned the second greatest weight of 34%.

3. The indicator of ecological system completeness aims to display the systematicity, wholeness and comprehensiveness of Building a Community with a Shared Future for Mankind on ecological civilization. It covers the whole process from the natural resources property right system at the source end to the production process and consumption at the tail end, and systematically promotes comprehensive economizing, the paid use of resources and ecological compensation on the three dimensions of cross-border cooperation, government involvement and societal involvement. This indicator is assigned a weight of 30%.

With respect to the improvement of laws and regulations, the concept of ecological civilization and the building of a beautiful China have been written into the constitution, various laws relating to the eco-environment have been passed, and regulations at the departmental level have been set out — a legal framework for ecological civilization is in the making. With respect to organization, administrations at all levels for the management of natural resources and the protection of the eco-environment have been optimized and reorganized, and eco-environment authorities below the provincial level have ramped up vertical management such as monitoring, supervision and law enforcement. With respect to improving mechanism efficiency, in addition to strengthening the rule of law and standardizing administrative supervision, the central government has implemented the eco-environment protection supervision system to step up supervision and ensure accountability. At the same time, the market mechanism has been improved, people are encouraged to get involved and a social restraint mechanism has been provided.

附录

人类命运共同体构建进程安全维度指标体系排序案例

人类命运共同体构建进程安全维度指标体系排序案例,选取澳大利亚、加拿大、中国、印度、印度尼西亚、日本、南非、美国等 8 个国家作为比照开展研究。

一、研究对象与选择

A. 可参照的 8 个国家

1. 澳大利亚

澳大利亚,其领土面积 7 692 024 km^2,位于南太平洋和印度洋之间,四面环海,是世界上唯一国土覆盖一整个大陆的国家。有很多独特动植物和自然景观的澳大利亚,是一个多元文化的移民国家。作为南半球经济最发达的国家和全球第十二大经济体、全球第四大农产品出口国,其也是多种矿产出口量全球第一的国家,因此被称作"坐在矿车上的国家"。

Appendix

Ordering of the Indicator System for Measuring the Process of Building a Community with a Shared Future for Mankind: Security Dimension

The ordering of the indicator system for measuring the process of building a Community with a Shared Future for Mankind: Security Dimension is a case study involving the comparison of the eight representative countries of Australia, Canada, China, India, Indonesia, Japan, South Africa, and the United States.

I. Objects of Study and the Choice of Them

A. The eight representative countries

1. Australia

Australia, with a territorial area of 7,692,024 km^2, is located between the South Pacific Ocean and the Indian Ocean. It is surrounded by the sea on all four sides and is the only country in the world that occupies a whole continent. Australia is home to a diversity of unique animals, plants and natural landscapes. It is a multicultural country of immigrants. As the most developed country in the southern hemisphere, the world's 12th largest economy, and the world's fourth largest exporter of agricultural products, Australia ranks

同时，澳大利亚也是世界上放养绵羊数量和出口羊毛最多的国家，也被称为"骑在羊背的国家"。

2. 加拿大

加拿大，位于北美洲北部的北美海陆兼备国，东临大西洋，西濒太平洋，西北部邻美国阿拉斯加州，南接美国本土，北靠北冰洋。加拿大面积 9 980 000km^2，居世界第二位，其中淡水覆盖面积 890 000km^2。加拿大是世界工业大国和西方七大工业国之一，制造业和高科技产业较发达，资源工业、初级制造业和农业为国民经济的主要支柱。加拿大原油储量居世界第二位，森林覆盖率达 44%，淡水资源总量占世界 7%，是小麦出口国和最大的渔产品出口国。

3. 中国

中国，位于亚洲东部，太平洋西岸，陆地面积约 9 600 000km^2，东部和南部大陆海岸线超过 18 000km，内海和边海的水域面积约 4 700 000km^2。中国是世界上人口最多的发展中国家，国土面积居世界第三位，是世界第二大经济体，并持续成为世界经济增长最大的贡献者。中国坚持独立自主的和平外交政策，是联合国安全理事会常任理事国，也是许多国际组织的重要成员，被认为是潜在超级大国之一。

4. 印度

印度，位于南亚，是南亚次大陆最大的国家，东北部同孟加拉国、尼泊尔、不丹和中国接壤，东部与缅甸为邻，东南与斯里兰卡隔海相望，西北与巴基斯坦交界。东临孟加拉湾，

No. 1 for its mineral exports, hence the name "country sitting on minecarts". Australia also ranks No. 1 for the number of the sheep it rears and the wool it exports, hence the name "a country on the sheep's back".

2. Canada

Canada, a land and maritime country in North America, is bordered by the Atlantic Ocean to the east, the Pacific Ocean to the west, Alaska to the northwest, the United States to the south and the Arctic Ocean to the north. Canada covers an area of 9.98 million km^2, ranking second in the world, and 890,000 km^2 of its territory is covered with fresh water. It is an industrial power and one of the G7. Its manufacturing and high-tech industries are quite developed, and resource processing, primary manufacturing and agriculture are the pillars of its national economy. Canada ranks second in the world for its crude oil reserves, has a forest coverage rate of 44% and is in possession of 7% of the world's freshwater resources. It is a wheat exporter and the largest exporter of fishery products.

3. China

China lies in the east of Asia and on the west coast of the Pacific Ocean. China has a land area of about 9.6 million km^2, a coastline that stretches over 18,000 km from the east to the south, and about 4.7 million km^2 of enclosed seas and border seas. China is the most populous developing country in the world. It ranks third in terms of land area and second in terms of size of the economy and has been the largest contributor to world economic growth in recent years. China pursues an independent foreign policy of peace. It is a permanent member of the United Nations Security Council and an important member of many international organizations. China is considered a prospective superpower.

4. India

India in South Asia is the largest country on the South Asian subcontinent. It borders Bangladesh, Nepal, Bhutan and China to the northeast, Myanmar to the East, Sri Lanka to the southeast and Pakistan to the northwest. India borders the Bay of Bengal to the east and the Arabian Sea to the west, with a

西濒阿拉伯海，海岸线长 5 560 km。印度也是一个由 100 多个民族构成的统一多民族国家，主体民族为印度斯坦族，约占全国总人口的 46.3%。

5. 印度尼西亚

印度尼西亚，是东南亚国家，首都为雅加达。与巴布亚新几内亚、东帝汶和马来西亚等国家相接。由约 17 508 个岛屿组成，是全世界最大的群岛国家，疆域横跨亚洲及大洋洲，也是多火山多地震的国家。印度尼西亚是东南亚国家联盟创立国之一，也是东南亚最大经济体及 G20 成员，航空航天技术较强，石油资源可实现净出口。

6. 日本

日本，位于东亚，领土由北海道、本州、四国、九州四个大岛及 6 800 多个小岛组成，总面积 378 000 km^2。日本是一个高度发达的资本主义国家，世界第三大经济体，G7、G20 等成员。其资源匮乏并极端依赖进口，发达的制造业是国民经济的支柱。科研、航天、制造业、教育水平均居世界前列。此外，以动漫、游戏产业为首的文化产业和发达的旅游业也是其重要象征。日本在环境保护、资源利用等许多方面堪称世界典范，其国民普遍拥有良好的教育、生活水平和国民素质。

7. 南非

南非，地处南半球，有"彩虹之国"之美誉，位于非洲大陆的最南端，陆地面积为 1 219 090 km^2，是非洲的第二大经济体，国民拥有较高的生活水平，经济相比其他非洲国家

coastline of 5, 560 km. It is also a unified multi-ethnic country comprising 100 ethnic groups. Hindustanis are the main ethnic group, accounting for about 46.3% of the total population.

5. Indonesia

Indonesia is a Southeast Asian country; its capital is Jakarta. It borders Papua New Guinea, East Timor and Malaysia. Consisting of about 17,508 islands, it is the largest archipelagic country in the world that spans Asia and Oceania. Indonesia is also a country where volcanoes erupt, and earthquakes strike frequently. As one of the founders of the Association of Southeast Asian Nations, it is the largest economy in Southeast Asia and a member of the G20. Indonesia has some superiority in aerospace technology, and its petroleum exports produce a trade surplus.

6. Japan

Japan in East Asia consists of four large islands — Hokkaido, Honshu, Shikoku, Kyushu, and over 6,800 small islands. It has a total land area of 378,000 km^2. Japan is a highly developed capitalist country, the third largest economy in the world, and member of the G7 and G20. Japan has a severe shortage of resources; it is highly dependent on imports. Developed manufacturing is the pillar of its national economy. Japan's scientific research, aerospace technology, manufacturing and education are at the cutting edge of the world. Its cultural industry (chiefly animation and gaming) and developed tourism are important national images. Japan plays an exemplary role in environmental protection and resource utilization; Japanese citizens are well-educated and cultivated; they lead high-quality lives.

7. South Africa

South Africa in the southern hemisphere enjoys a reputation as the "rainbow nation". It is located in the southernmost part of the African continent, with a land area of 1,219,090 km^2. South Africa is the second largest economy in Africa. South African citizens live fairly wealthy lives, and eco-

相对稳定。南非财经、法律、通讯、能源、交通业较为发达，拥有完备的硬件基础设施和股票交易市场，黄金、钻石生产量均占世界首位。深井采矿等技术居于世界领先地位。

8. 美国

美国，是由华盛顿哥伦比亚特区、50个州和关岛等众多海外领土组成的联邦共和立宪制国家，总面积是 9 373 000 km^2，人口 3.3 亿。美国是一个高度发达的资本主义国家，在两次世界大战中，美国和其他盟国取得胜利，经历数十年的冷战，在苏联解体后，成为唯一的超级大国，在经济、文化、工业等领域都处于全世界的领先地位。美国的白宫、硅谷、华尔街、好莱坞、百老汇等等在全球范围内都享有声誉。

B. 作为特殊条件的两个国家的对比

特殊条件的含义是：世界上经济体量排名在前，对世界的生物安全与卫生安全举足轻重的国家，在世界性重大疫情发生期间所做出的决策以及实施决策过程中产生的影响。在当前，满足这个特殊条件能够进行对比测度的国家为美国和中国，特别是在2020年发生世界性新冠肺炎疫情时期，美国和中国医疗卫生体制的对比呈现出鲜明的差异，特别是因社会制度的不同，在对疫情的防控反馈与决策上，对比明显。这对人类命运共同体的建构以及在生物安全和人口健康上分别产生了不同的影响。

1. 美国

美国是世界上最发达的国家，其医疗卫生体系也常被认

nomic development is more stable than other African countries. In South Africa, finance, law, telecommunication, energy and transportation are the developed sectors. It has a full set of hardware infrastructure and stock exchange markets and ranks first in the world in terms of gold and diamond production. Its deep well mining technology is at the cutting edge of the world.

8. The United States

The United States is a federal constitutional republic composed of Washington D.C., 50 states, Guam and many overseas territories. It has a total land area of 9.373 million km^2 and a population of 330 million. The United States is a highly developed capitalist country that has, together with its allies, won the two world wars. After decades of Cold War, it became the only superpower in the world after the disintegration of the former Soviet Union. The US economy, culture and industries are at the cutting edge of the world. The White House, Silicon Valley, Wall Street, Hollywood, Broadway, etc. are household names.

B. Comparison of two countries that meet special conditions

Special conditions: top-ranking economic volume; crucial for world biosafety and health security; decisions made during major pandemics and the impact of the decisions implemented. The two comparable countries that meet these special conditions are the United States and China. During the spread of the COVID-19 pandemic in 2020, a distinct difference existed in the healthcare systems of the United States and China. Different social systems, in particular, have led to a stark contrast in feedback and decision-making regarding epidemic prevention and control. This has had different impacts on the building of a Community with a Shared Future for Mankind, biosafety and population health.

1. The United States

The United States, together with its healthcare system, is considered the

为是世界上最发达的。据2019年发布的全球健康安全指数，美国以83.5分位列第一。但是，在另外一些排名体系中，美国的医疗卫生水平又经常在发达国家群体中位居末位。排名虽然不能说明一切，但美国在医疗卫生方面的科技和资金优势，以及在医疗资源的可获得性和公平性等方面的劣势，却也是世界公认的。美国医疗系统是由许多个合法个体提供的医疗服务业。美国的医疗设施和医疗保险大部分都由私营部门经营，美国政府会通常提供辅助性质的公共医疗保险、医疗辅助计划、小童医疗保险计划和荣民（退伍军人）健康管理。欧盟和美国的药业组织认为美国是全球医学研究及推出新型医术和医疗产品的龙头国，他们又表示必须依靠美国高昂的医疗开支才能有效推动这些研发的进行。世界卫生组织在2000年的世界卫生报告中比较了191个成员国的医疗质素，美国的医疗消费与应变能力都在榜首、总体卫生系统表现排第37位、总体人口健康程度排第72位。2008年美国联邦基金比较19个已发展国家的医疗系统质量，美国排名榜尾。经济合作与发展组织2020年7月公布的数据显示，2019年美国人均医疗开支超过1.1万美元，远高于其他发达国家水平，而美国人均预期寿命却在发达国家中排名靠后。

美国医疗资源分布是市场为主、政府为辅的模式。美国的医疗资源非常分散、多元。独立医生是美国一个重要的医疗传统。2018年，美国医生中的47.4%为医疗机构的雇员，45.9%为独立医生。在医疗机构中，政府所占的比例也非常低。2020年初，美国共有6 146座医院，其中联邦政府医院

most developed in the world. According to the 2019 Global Health Security Index, the United States ranks first with a score of 83.5. However, it often ranks last among developed countries in terms of healthcare quality in other rankings. Rankings can't tell everything, but the United States' scientific and capital superiority in healthcare and its inferiority in medical resource availability and equity is also widely recognized. The US healthcare system comprises a huge number of legal medical practitioners. Most of the medical facilities and medical insurance in the United States are operated by the private sector. The US government provides auxiliary public health insurance, subsidiary medical plans, children healthcare insurance plans and veterans health management. Pharmaceutical organizations in the European Union and the United States believe that the United States is a leader in global medical research and new medical skills and products, and they also say that the high medical expenses in the United States promote these research and development. WHO compared the healthcare quality of 191 member states in the 2000 World Health Report. The United States ranked first for medical consumption and adaptability, 37th for overall health system performance and 72nd for overall population health. In 2008, the US Federal Fund compared the quality of the healthcare systems of 19 developed countries. The United States ranked last. According to the data released by the Organization for Economic Cooperation and Development in July 2020, the per capita medical expenditure of the United States in 2019 exceeded 11,000 US dollars, far higher than that of other developed countries, but its average life expectancy ranked low among developed countries.

In the United States, the market determines the allocation of medical resources; the government just plays a marginal role. Medical resources in the United States are scattered and diverse. "Independent doctor" is an important medical tradition of the United States. In 2018, 47.4% of American doctors were employees of medical institutions and 45.9% were independent doctors. And the proportion of government-funded medical institutions is also very

只有209座，占总数的3.4%；社区医院有5 198座，占总数的84.6%，支出额为1.01万亿美元，占美国医院支出总额的91%；州和地方政府医院只有965座，是社区医院总数的19%左右。

美国是一个资本主义国家，政府与社会之间是契约关系。政府与社会之间的互动、对社会力量的动员，也往往有高额的经济成本。这导致面对COVID-19疫情时，无论是联邦政府还是州政府，其实都不愿意、也不敢轻易下达停止经济运行的任何指令。经济一停摆，政府的收入会大幅减少，开支会迅速增加。为刺激经济，美国出台了总额为2万亿美元的财政刺激计划，相当于2008年金融危机美国刺激计划的近3倍。但是美国政府监管缺失、大公司垄断药品市场、商业保险公司游说力量强大等多重因素叠加，导致美国医疗投入大、效率低，美国低收入群体无法及时获得有效救治。美国有近3 000万人没有医疗保险，还有更多人因为医疗费太高而尽量不去看病。美国低收入人群患病后，"通常会延迟去看医生，不是因为他们不想康复，而是因为根本没有钱"。

美国对大规模爆发的疫情没有针对性的提出全国防控措施，在2020年最佳防控窗口期，无所作为，各个地方自行其是，难以形成合力，已成为全球新冠肺炎疫情累计确诊病例数最多的国家。根据约翰斯·霍普金斯冠状病毒资源中心的数据，到2021年1月这场疫情已经夺走了52.8万美国人的生命。在2020年，美国医疗体系碎片化问题凸显，2020年12

low. There were 6,146 hospitals in the United States in early 2020. Of these hospitals, only 209 were federal hospitals, accounting for 3.4%, and 5,198 were community hospitals, accounting for 84.6%. The expenditure of community hospitals was 1.01 trillion US dollars, accounting for 91% of the total hospital expenditure in the United States. Only 965 hospitals were run by state and local governments, accounting for about 19% of all community hospitals.

The United States is a capitalist country, and there exists a contractual relationship between the government and society. The interaction between the government and society and the mobilization of social resources often have high economic costs. As a result, neither the federal government nor the state government is willing or dares to impose an economic lockdown when faced with COVID-19 epidemics. This is because an economic lockdown will reduce government revenue and drive up expenditure drastically. To stimulate the economy, the United States introduced a fiscal stimulus plan totaling 2 trillion US dollars, nearly tripling the stimulus plan for coping with the financial crisis of 2008. However, the lack of government supervision, the monopoly of the drug market by large companies, and the huge lobbying efforts by insurance companies combined to drive up medical investment, cut efficiency and cause medical treatment unavailability for low-income Americans. Nearly 30 million people in the United States have no medical insurance, and more avoid seeing the doctor because of the high medical expenses. Sick low-income people in the United States usually delay seeing the doctor — not because they don't want to recover, but because they have no money for the treatment.

The United States didn't introduce national prevention and control measures against large-scale outbreaks and did nothing in the 2020 window period. Local governments acted separately. The lack of coordinated efforts turned the United States into a country with the largest number of confirmed COVID-19 cases. According to the Johns Hopkins Coronavirus Resource Center, by January 2021, the pandemic had claimed 528,000 American lives. The most prominent problem with the US healthcare system in 2020

月才启动大规模新冠疫苗接种，但两个月时间的接种进度远不及预期。疫苗发放缺乏全国统筹、分配不合理、有色人群被冷落等问题持续引发争议，也凸显美国医疗体系碎片化的问题。其中最主要的问题在于美国的社会制度以及国体政体决定了在大规模疫情流行期间，各自为政，松散应对，甚至将疫情的不可控状态归咎于他国的情形。2020年，特朗普政府并未认识到疫情防控的紧迫性，白宫已下令联邦卫生官员将最高级别的冠状病毒会议列为机密，这一不同寻常的举措限制了信息传播，并阻碍了美国社会以及医疗机构对疫情的应对，对世界的公共卫生安全形成严重危害。

2. 中国

中国是一个发展中的国家，至2020年已经建立了由医院、基层医疗卫生机构、专业公共卫生机构等组成的覆盖城乡的医疗卫生服务体系。中国政府在2015年明确提出，优化医疗卫生资源配置，构建与国民经济和社会发展水平相适应、与居民健康需求相匹配、体系完整、分工明确、功能互补、密切协作的整合型医疗卫生服务体系，为实现2020年基本建立覆盖城乡居民的基本医疗卫生制度和人民健康水平持续提升奠定坚实的医疗卫生资源基础。

中国的医疗卫生体系明确了坚持健康需求导向。以健康需求和解决人民群众主要健康问题为导向，以调整布局结构、提升能级为主线，适度有序发展，强化薄弱环节，科学合理确定各级各类医疗卫生机构的数量、规模及布局。坚持公平

lay in its fragmented structure. Large-scale COVID-19 vaccinations didn't get started until December 2020, but the progress made in two months fell short of expectations. Problems such as lack of national vaccine coordination, unreasonable distribution and neglect of colored people caused long-lasting controversies and highlighted the fragmented structure of the US healthcare system. The main problem lies in the social, national and political systems of the United States. The government didn't join hands with the general public, and shamelessly attributed the rampant spread of the disease to China. The Trump administration didn't realize the urgency of epidemic prevention and control in 2020, and the White House ordered federal health officials to keep the highest-level coronavirus conferences confidential. This unusual move restricted the spread of information, hindered the ability of the American society and medical institutions to respond to COVID-19, and seriously harmed global health security.

2. China

China is a developing country. By 2020, it has established a healthcare service system composed of hospitals, grass-roots medical institutions and professional public health institutions across the country. In 2015, the Chinese government proposed to optimize the allocation of medical resources and build an integrated healthcare service system that adapts to national economic and social development, matches the health needs of residents, and features completeness, clear division of labor, complementarity and close cooperation. The aim was to lay a solid foundation for basically establishing a basic healthcare system for both urban and rural residents and for continuing to improve people's health by 2020.

China's healthcare system is clearly oriented towards the demand for health. China's healthcare system is oriented towards the demand for health and providing solutions to the health issues facing the people, focuses on structural adjustment and energy level improvement, develops moderately and orderly, overcomes weaknesses, and scientifically and reasonably determines the number, scale and

与效率统一。优先保障基本医疗卫生服务的可及性，促进公平公正。同时，注重医疗卫生资源配置与使用的科学性与协调性，提高效率，降低成本，实现公平与效率的统一。坚持政府主导与市场机制相结合。切实落实政府在制度、规划、筹资、服务、监管等方面的责任，维护公共医疗卫生的公益性。大力发挥市场机制在配置资源方面的作用，充分调动社会力量的积极性和创造性，满足人民群众多层次、多元化医疗卫生服务需求。坚持系统整合。加强全行业监管与属地化管理，统筹城乡、区域资源配置，统筹当前与长远，统筹预防、医疗和康复，中西医并重，注重发挥医疗卫生服务体系的整体功能，促进均衡发展。坚持分级分类管理。充分考虑经济社会发展水平和医疗卫生资源现状，统筹不同区域、类型、层级的医疗卫生资源的数量和布局，分类制订配置标准。促进基层医疗卫生机构发展，着力提升服务能力和质量；合理控制公立医院资源规模，推动发展方式转变；提高专业公共卫生机构的服务能力和水平。

新冠肺炎疫情发生以来，中国始终把人民群众生命安全和身体健康放在第一位，充分发挥制度优势，付出巨大努力，为防止疫情在世界范围内扩散做出了重要贡献。国际人士普遍认为，中国秉持人类命运共同体理念，既对本国人民生命安全和身体健康负责，也对全球公共卫生事业尽责，展现出负责任大国的担当。国际舆论普遍认为，中国构建起全方位多层次的疫情防控体系，最大程度遏制疫情蔓延，值得各国

layout of all medical institutions. Unity between fairness and efficiency China works to ensure the accessibility of basic healthcare services as well as fairness and justice in medical work. China also works to ensure the scientificity and coordination of the allocation and use of medical resources, improve efficiency, reduce costs, and bring about the unity between fairness and efficiency. Unity between government guidance and market mechanism The Chinese government assumes its system, planning, financing, service and supervision responsibilities and makes sure its public healthcare services reach the people. China gives full play to the role of the market mechanism in resource allocation, fires the enthusiasm and creativity of social resources, and meets the people's multifaceted and diversified needs for healthcare services. Systematic integration China strengthens industry-wide supervision and localized management, coordinates urban, rural and regional resource allocation, aligns present needs with long-term needs, considers prevention, treatment and rehabilitation simultaneously, practices both Chinese and Western medicine, values the overall function of the healthcare system, and promotes development in a balanced way. Classified and tiered management China gives full consideration to the level of economic and social development and the quality and amount of medical resources, coordinates the quantity and allocation of medical resources across regions, types and levels, and sets allocation standards according to classification. China promotes the development of grassroots healthcare institutions, focuses on the improvement of service capabilities and quality, reasonably controls the amount of resources in public hospitals, promotes the transformation of the development pattern, and improves the service capacity and level of professional public health institutions.

Since the outbreak of COVID-19, China has always put people's life safety and health first, given full play to its institutional advantages and made great efforts to prevent the spread of the epidemic worldwide. The international community generally believes that China adheres to the concept of a Community with a Shared Future for Mankind, cares for not only the life safety and health of its people but also global public health, and has performed its duties as a responsible major power. International public opinion

借鉴。中国作为世界第二大经济体，在全球产业链供应链中占据重要地位，中国政府在加强疫情防控的同时，从财政、金融、税收等方面采取一系列措施，积极复工复产。经过艰苦卓绝的努力，中国付出巨大代价和牺牲，有力扭转了疫情局势，用一个多月的时间初步遏制了疫情蔓延势头，用两个月左右的时间将本土每日新增病例控制在个位数以内，用3个月左右的时间取得了武汉保卫战、湖北保卫战的决定性成果，疫情防控阻击战取得重大战略成果，维护了人民生命安全和身体健康，为维护地区和世界公共卫生安全做出了重要贡献。中国的抗疫分为五个阶段：

第一阶段：迅即应对突发疫情（2019年12月27日至2020年1月19日）湖北省武汉市监测发现不明原因肺炎病例，中国第一时间报告疫情，迅速采取行动，开展病因学和流行学调查。第二阶段：初步遏制疫情蔓延势头（2020年1月20日至2月20日）全国新增确诊病例快速增加，中国采取阻断病毒传播的关键一招，坚决果断关闭离汉离鄂通道，武汉保卫战、湖北保卫战全面打响。第三阶段：本土新增病例数逐步下降至个位数（2月21日至3月17日）中共中央做出统筹疫情防控和经济社会发展、有序复工复产重大决策。第四阶段：取得武汉保卫战、湖北保卫战决定性成果（3月18日至4月28日）以武汉市为主战场的全国本土疫情传播基本阻断，离汉离鄂通道管控措施解除，武汉市在院新冠肺炎患者清零。

generally holds that China has built an all-round and multi-level epidemic prevention and control system to maximally curb the spread of COVID-19. It is a role model on the international stage. As the world's second largest economy, China is crucial on the global supply chain. While doubling down on the prevention and control of COVID-19, the Chinese government has taken a series of financial, banking and taxation measures to resume production. Despite great losses in its all-out effort to contain COVID-19, China reversed the situation, curbing the spread of the virus in a little over one month, reducing the number of domestic daily new cases to single digits in about two months, and winning decisive victories in Wuhan and Hubei's battle against the virus in about three months. The major strategic achievements that China made safeguarded people's life safety and health and made important contributions to regional and world public health security. China's fight against COVID-19 is divided into five stages:

Stage 1: Quick response to the sudden outbreak of COVID-19 (from December 27, 2019 to January 19, 2020). After a pneumonia case of unknown cause was detected in Wuhan, Hubei province, China immediately announced the discovery and took prompt actions to carry out etiological and epidemiological investigations. Stage 2: Preliminary containment of the spread of COVID-19 (from January 20 to February 20, 2020). The number of newly confirmed cases in China increased rapidly. China took a decisive measure to block the spread of the virus and resolutely put Wuhan under lockdown. Wuhan and Hubei's war on COVID-19 began. Stage 3: The number of domestic new cases decreased to single digits (from February 21 to March 17, 2020). The Central Committee of the Communist Party of China made the major decision of coordinating epidemic prevention and socio-economic development and resuming production in an orderly way. Stage 4: A decisive victory in Wuhan and Hubei's war on COVID-19 (from March 18 to April 28, 2020). The spread of COVID-19 in the epicenter Wuhan was basically blocked, the control over the passages from and to Hubei and

第五阶段：全国疫情防控进入常态化(2020年4月29日以来)境内疫情总体呈零星散发状态，局部地区出现散发病例引起的聚集性疫情，境外输入病例基本得到控制。

世卫组织高级官员高度评价中国采取有力措施对新冠肺炎疫情进行科学有效防控，展现了勇气和担当。认为中国出现新冠肺炎疫情后，中国科学家快速甄别病原体、对病毒进行基因测序，并同世界卫生组织及相关国家和地区分享研究成果，为快速诊断做出独特贡献。中国卫生部门第一时间同相关国家和地区分享疫情信息，也为快速采取行动提供了宝贵时间。世卫组织总干事谭德塞说："我对中国应对疫情采取的有力措施印象十分深刻。中国采取的有力措施不仅对中国有利，对世界也有利"。他说，他对中国领导层和中国人民抗击疫情的决心感到十分震撼，对中方展现出的勇气和担当表示敬佩。

世界卫生组织高级官员在2020年11月16日举行新冠肺炎疫情例行发布会。世卫组织卫生紧急项目负责人迈克尔·瑞安表示：现有证据表明，新冠病毒在中国的传播水平极低。中国对任何的新冠病例激增都采取了非常积极的应对措施。比如采取大规模检测，这不是所有国家都能做到的，需要大量资源才能实现。在这种情况下，仅发现了极少数病例。假如有大量未被发现的病例存在本土传播，大规模检测就会发现一些病例。因此，并无任何证据表明中国面临显著的疫情问题。

Wuhan were lifted, and the number of COVID-19 patients in Wuhan was reduced to zero. Stage 5: Regular national epidemic prevention and control (after April 29, 2020). Cases erupted sporadically in China, isolated cases in some areas caused collective outbreaks, and imported cases were basically put under control.

Senior WHO officials spoke highly of China's scientific and effective prevention and control of COVID-19, as well as its courage and responsible attitude. After the outbreak of COVID-19 in China, Chinese scientists began immediately to search for the pathogen and sequenced the virus, and shared their research results with WHO and other countries and regions, making rapid diagnosis possible. Chinese health departments shared information with other countries and regions, saving time for quick action. WHO Director-General Tedros Adhanom Ghebreyesus said: "I am impressed by China's decisive measures to cope with the epidemic. The effective measures that China takes are not only beneficial to China, but also beneficial to the world." He said he was impressed by the resolve of the Chinese leadership and the Chinese people to fight COVID-19, and expressed his respect for China for its courage and responsible attitude.

On November 16, 2020, senior WHO officials held a regular press conference on COVID-19. Michael Ryan, director of WHO's Health Emergencies Program, said, "Existing evidence shows that COVID-19 is spreading in China at an extremely low level. China has taken very active measures to deal with any surge in COVID-19 cases. For example, China did testing on a large scale. Not all countries can manage to do such resource-consuming testing. Only a few cases were found in their massive testing. Some cases will be found in large-scale testing if large numbers of cases are spreading domestically. Therefore, there is no evidence that China is facing a serious epidemic situation.

中国社情普遍表示：病毒是人类共同的敌人，团结合作是战胜疫情最有力的武器。维护各国人民生命健康，维护全球公共卫生安全，离不开守望相助、同舟共济的坚定信念。任何人不走团结合作、统一行动的正道，都是对全球抗疫力量的削弱。

中国国家领导人明确指出："人类是命运共同体，团结合作是战胜疫情最有力的武器"。"中国始终秉持构建人类命运共同体理念，既对本国人民生命安全和身体健康负责，也对全球公共卫生事业尽责。""要针对这次疫情暴露出来的短板和不足，完善公共卫生安全治理体系，提高突发公共卫生事件应急响应速度，建立全球和地区防疫物资储备中心。"

二、可参照的 8 个国家指标数据描述

1. 指标分类概述

根据数据库归类和指标相近原则，选取了一共 18 个三级指标，并根据指标意义分类为国际安全、生态安全、经济安全和社会安全 4 个二级指标，最后将其作为人类安全共同体的近似指标体系。指标的选取与分类，见表 1：

Chinese people say that viruses are the common enemy of mankind, and unity and cooperation are the most powerful weapons to overcome them. It would be impossible to safeguard the lives and health of people around the world and ensure global public health security without the firm belief that we must help each other in the face of a common threat. Anyone who defies unity, cooperation and coordination will weaken the global power to fight COVID-19.

Chinese president Xi Jinping said, "We live in a Community with a Shared Future for Mankind. Unity and cooperation are the most powerful weapons to defeat COVID-19". "China adheres to the concept of a Community with a Shared Future for Mankind, and cares for not only the life safety and health of its people but also global public health". "In view of the shortcomings and deficiencies we exposed during the epidemic, we will improve the system for managing public health security, act promptly in the face of public health emergencies, and establish global and regional centers for the storage of epidemic prevention supplies".

II. Description of the Indicators of the Eight Representative Countries

1. Overview of indicator classification

A total of 18 Tier 3 indicators are selected according to the principle of database classification and indicator proximity, and the four Tier 2 indicators of international security, ecological security, economic security and social security are derived depending on their meaning. They are finally used as the approximate indicator system for measuring the process of building the Security Community with a Shared Future for Mankind. See Table 1 for the selection and classification of indicators:

表 1 指标分类情况

一级指标	二级指标	三级指标	序号
人类安全共同体	国际安全（3个）	安全峰会的召开次数	1
		军费	2
		驻联合国部队人数	3
	生态安全（8个）	属于生产中的二氧化碳排放量	1
		可持续竞争力	2
		经济自由度	3
		城市人口	4
		真实进步指数	5
		人类发展指数	6
		生态足迹指数	7
		对外经济贸易依存度	8
	经济安全（4个）	自由协定	1
		平均税率	2
		反倾销措施	3
		对外直接投资贡献变化率	4
	社会安全（3个）	和平指数	1
		失业率	2
		幸福指数	3

Table 1 Classification of Indicators

Tier 1 indicators	Tier 2 indicators	Tier 3 indicators	S/N
Community of security for mankind	International security (3)	Number of security summits held	1
		Military expenditure	2
		Number of troops sent on UN peace-keeping missions	3
	Ecological security (8)	Carbon dioxide emissions in production	1
		Sustainable competitiveness	2
		Economic freedom	3
		Urban population	4
		Genuine progress indicator (GPI)	5
		Human development index	6
		Ecological footprint indicator	7
		Degree of foreign trade dependence	8
	Economic security (4)	Free trade agreement	1
		Average tax rate	2
		Anti-dumping measures	3
		Rate of change in contribution of outward foreign direct investment (OFDI)	4
	Social security (3)	Global peace index	1
		Unemployment rate	2
		Gross national happiness indicator	3

2. 安全峰会召开次数（属国际安全）

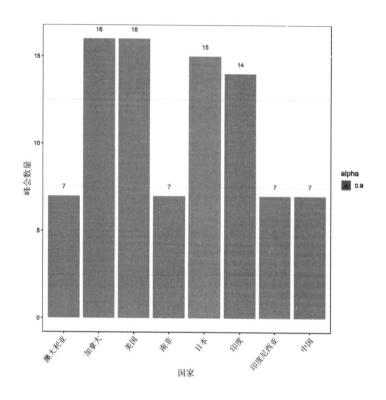

图1 各国安全峰会召开次数对比图

图1呈现了选取的8个标志性国家的安全峰会召开次数情况，依次序：加拿大是16次，美国是16次，日本是15次，印度是14次，澳大利亚是7次，中国是7次，印度尼西亚是7次，南非是7次，发现加拿大、美国、日本是选取国家中的前三名。

2. Number of security summits held (under the category of international security)

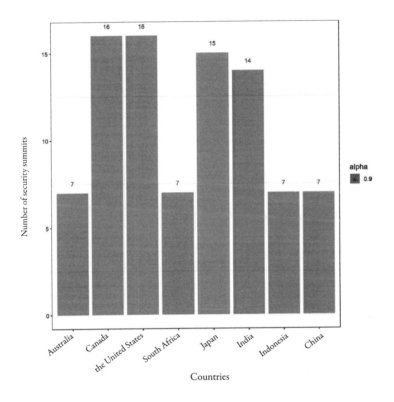

Figure 1 Comparison of Numbers of Security Summits Held

Figure 1 shows the number of security summits held in the eight representative countries selected for this study: Canada, 16; the United States, 16; Japan, 15; India, 14; Australia, 7; China, 7; Indonesia, 7; South Africa, 7. Canada, the United States and Japan top the list.

表2 峰会数量排名情况

国家	峰会数量							
	加拿大	美国	日本	印度	澳大利亚	中国	印度尼西亚	南非
排名	1	1	2	3	4	4	4	4
峰会	16	16	15	14	7	7	7	7

3.国民幸福指数（属社会安全）

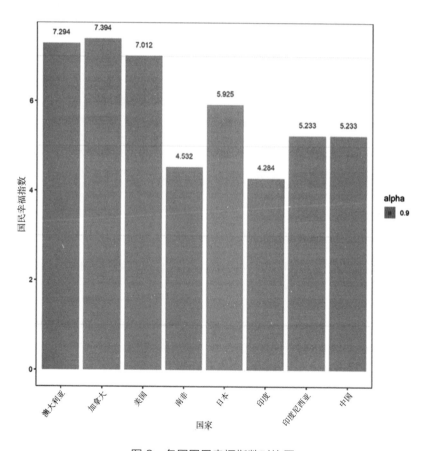

图2　各国国民幸福指数对比图

Table 2 Ranking of the Number of Security Summits Held

Number of security summits								
Country	Canada	the United States	Japan	India	Australia	China	Indonesia	South Africa
Ranking	1	1	2	3	4	4	4	4
Number of security summits held	16	16	15	14	7	7	7	7

3. Gross national happiness index (under the category of social security)

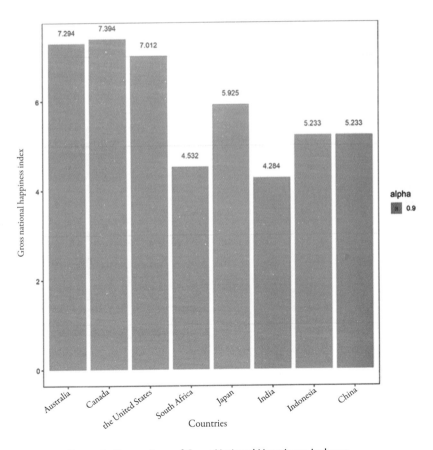

Figure 2 Comparison of Gross National Happiness Indexes

经过观察 2013—2017 年数据相差不大，取 2013—2017 年的平均值，图 2 呈现了选取的 8 个标志性国家的国民幸福指数情况，依次序：加拿大是 7.39，澳大利亚是 7.29，美国是 7.01，日本是 5.92，印度尼西亚是 5.23，中国是 5.23，南非是 4.53，印度是 4.28，发现加拿大、澳大利亚、美国是选取国家中的前三名。

表 3　国民幸福指数排名情况

国民幸福指数								
国家	加拿大	澳大利亚	美国	日本	印度尼西亚	中国	南非	印度
排名	1	2	3	4	5	6	7	8
均值	7.3941	7.2937	7.0119	5.9253	5.2334	5.2329	4.5319	4.2839

4. 二氧化碳排放指数（属生态安全）

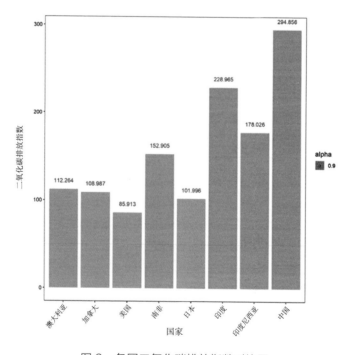

图 3　各国二氧化碳排放指数对比图

Relevant data does not differ much from 2013 to 2017, so the average value of this period is used in this study. Figure 2 shows the gross national happiness indexes of the eight representative countries selected for this study: Canada, 7.39; Australia, 7.29; the United States, 7.01; Japan, 5.92; Indonesia, 5.23; China, 5.23; South Africa, 4.53; India, 4.28. Canada, Australia, and the United States top the list.

Table 3 Ranking of Gross National Happiness Indexes

	Gross national happiness index							
Country	Canada	Australia	the United States	Japan	Indonesia	China	South Africa	India
Ranking	1	2	3	4	5	6	7	8
Average value	7.3941	7.2937	7.0119	5.9253	5.2334	5.2329	4.5319	4.2839

4. Carbon dioxide emission index (under the category of ecological security)

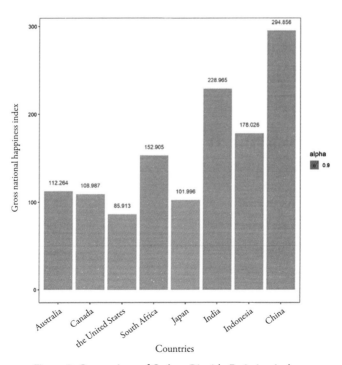

Figure 3 Comparison of Carbon Dioxide Emission Indexes

经过观察2013—2017年数据相差不大,取2013—2017年的平均值,图3呈现了选取的8个标志性国家的二氧化碳排放指数情况,依次序:中国是294.85,印度是228.96,印度尼西亚是178.02,南非是152.90,澳大利亚是112.26,加拿大是108.98,日本是101.99,美国是85.91。

表4 二氧化碳排量情况

二氧化碳								
国家	美国	日本	加拿大	澳大利亚	南非	印度尼西亚	印度	中国
排名	1	2	3	4	5	6	7	8
均值	85.912	101.99	108.98	112.26	152.90	178.02	228.96	294.85

5.税率均值(属经济安全)

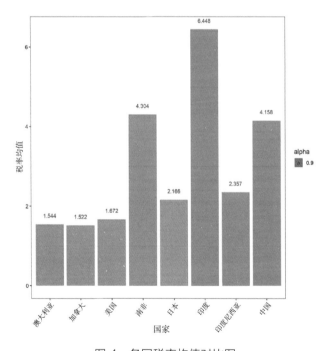

图4 各国税率均值对比图

Relevant data does not differ much from 2013 to 2017, so the average value of this period is used in this study. Figure 3 shows the carbon dioxide emission indexes of the eight representative countries selected for this study: China, 294.85; India, 228.96; Indonesia, 178.02; South Africa, 152.90; Australia, 112.26; Canada, 108.98.

Table 4 Carbon Dioxide Emissions

Country	\multicolumn{8}{c}{Carbon dioxide}
Country	the United States	Japan	Canada	Australia	South Africa	Indonesia	India	China
Ranking	1	2	3	4	5	6	7	8
Average value	85.912	101.99	108.98	112.26	152.90	178.02	228.96	294.85

5. Average tax rate (under the category of economic security)

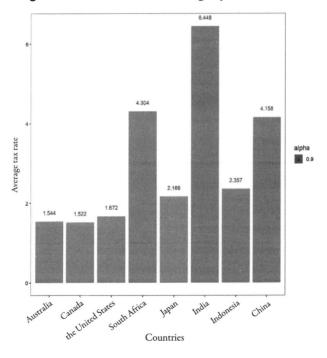

Figure 4 Comparison of Average Tax Rates

经过观察 2013—2017 年数据相差不大，取 2013—2017 年的平均值，图 4 呈现了选取的 8 个标志性国家的税率均值情况，依次序：印度是 6.44，南非是 4.30，中国是 4.15，印度尼西亚是 2.35，日本是 2.16，美国是 1.67，澳大利亚是 1.54，加拿大是 1.52。

表 5　税率均值排名

税率均值								
国家	加拿大	澳大利亚	美国	日本	印度尼西亚	中国	南非	印度
排名	1	2	3	4	5	6	7	8
均值	1.522	1.544	1.672	2.166	2.3566	4.1575	4.304	6.4475

三、建模及结果分析

1. 建模技术流程图

图 5　建模技术流程图

Relevant data does not differ much from 2013 to 2017, so the average value of this period is used in this study. Figure 4 shows the average tax rates of the eight representative countries selected for this study: India, 6.44; South Africa, 4.30; China, 4.15; Indonesia, 2.35; Japan, 2.16; the United States, 1.67; Australia, 1.54; Canada, 1.52.

Table 5 Ranking of Average Tax Rates

Average tax rate								
Country	Canada	Australia	the United States	Japan	Indonesia	China	South Africa	India
Ranking	1	2	3	4	5	6	7	8
Average value	1.522	1.544	1.672	2.166	2.3566	4.1575	4.304	6.4475

III. Modeling and Analysis of Results

1. Flow chart of modeling technology

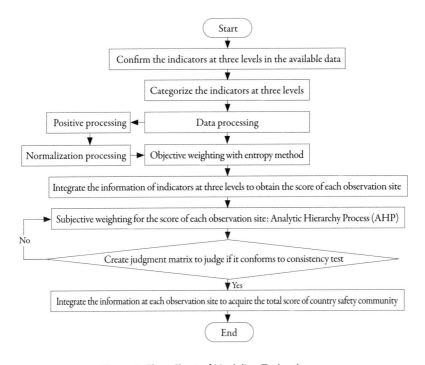

Figure 5 Flow Chart of Modeling Technology

由于数据获取较为困难且需要时间，本文选择能查找到数据较为完整的澳大利亚，加拿大，中国，印度，印度尼西亚，日本，南非，美国这些国家作为前期研究对象，对此开展相关研究。

首先，关于安全共同体研究的技术路线图，见图5。其中，三级指标已作为附录材料，请见附录表1。（1）三级指标归类原则：数据库归类和指标意义相近原则。（2）正向化处理：比如失业率，越大越不好，而真实进步指数越大越好。在这里本文需要做一个统一，将数据统一成同指标同趋势化，即越大越好（3）归一化处理：为了消除数据特征之间的量纲影响，本文需要对特征进行归一化处理，使得不同指标之间具有可比性。其中间过程用到了如下方法，如非负化处理，极值差处理，平移处理。（4）赋权原则：考虑指标的重要性，即主观赋权；考虑指标的离散程度，即客观赋权。我们不仅要考虑指标的重要性（主观），而且要考虑指标的离散程度（客观）。在指标效应相差不大时，指标客观离散程度成为赋权主要参考；在指标效应相差较大时，指标客观离散程度成为考虑的较小因素，应以主观重要性为主要参考。（5）一致性检验：为了使主观赋权的权重比例具有合理性，本文采取构造判断矩阵，当其 CR 小于 0.1 时，本文就认为设定的权重具有合理性。

2. 方法一：熵值法与层次分析法建模及结果分析

2.1 熵值法与层次分析法的赋权结果

熵值法的计算过程，见附录2熵值法。熵值法是一种成熟、

As data acquisition is difficult and time-consuming, Australia, Canada, China, India, Indonesia, Japan, South Africa, and the United States, the data about which are relatively complete, are selected as the objects of our preliminary research.

First, see Figure 5 for the technical roadmap of the research of the security community. See Appendix Table 1 for Tier 3 indicators. (1) Principle for the classification of Tier 3 indicators: principle of database classification and indicator proximity. (2) Positive processing: For example, a high unemployment rate is a bad indicator, and a high genuine progress indicator (GPI) is a good sign. Here, we need to convert all the data in such a way that the bigger the indicator, the better. (3) Normalization processing: To eliminate the dimensional influence between data features, this paper needs to normalize the features so that different indicators are comparable. The following methods are used in this process: nonnegative number processing, range processing and translation processing. (4) Weighting principle: Consider the significance of indicators (subjective weighting); consider the dispersion degree of indicators (objective weighting). The significance of indicators (subjective) and the dispersion degree of indicators (objective) should be considered on an equal basis. When indicator effects do not differ much, the objective dispersion degree of indicators provides the main framework of reference for weighting; when indicator effects differ much, the objective dispersion degree of indicators is a minor influencing factor, and subjective significance should provide the main framework of reference. (5) Consistency test: To make the ratio of subjective weighting reasonable, this paper constructs a judgment matrix. When its CR is less than 0.1, the weight placed will be considered reasonable.

2. Method 1: Entropy evaluation method and analytic hierarchy process modeling and analysis of results

2.1 Weights placed through the entropy evaluation method the analytic hierarchy process

See the appendix for the calculation process of the entropy evaluation method. The entropy evaluation method is a mature and widely used objective

应用广泛的客观赋权方法。通过熵值法，我们获得如下4个观测点的权重表格，见表6。

表6 安全人类命运共同体4个观测点熵值法的客观赋权结果

观测点	指标1	指标2	指标3	指标4	指标5	指标6	指标7	指标8	指标数量	平均权重
国际安全	0.605	0.047	0.348						3	0.333
生态安全	0.097	0.152	0.165	0.109	0.192	0.189	0.092	0.004	8	0.125
经济安全	0.311	0.144	0.496	0.049					4	0.250
社会安全	0.112	0.038	0.850						3	0.333

表6显示，安全命运共同体各观测点熵值法的客观赋权结果与平均赋权值相比合理。而每一个观测点的三级指标都是经过原指标体系的一级指标归类和指标意义相近原则进行指标归类，为此安全人类命运共同体可直接采用客观赋权方式进行信息集成。当客观赋权和主观赋权相差较大时，根据实际情况考虑，分别对客观赋权和主观赋权信息集成赋予不同的重要度权重。

表7 层次分析法的判断矩阵

安全共同体	观测点1 国际安全	观测点2 生态安全	观测点3 经济安全	观测点4 社会安全
重要性	5	1	3	2

method of weighting. Through the entropy evaluation method, we obtain the weights of the following four observation points, as shown in Table 6.

Table 6 Weights of the Four Measuring Points for the Security Community with a Shared Future for Mankind Placed through the Objective Entropy Evaluation Method

Measuring Points	Indicator 1	Indicator 2	Indicator 3	Indicator 4	Indicator 5	Indicator 6	Indicator 7	Indicator 8	Number of indicators	Average weight
International security	0.605	0.047	0.348						3	0.333
Ecological security	0.097	0.152	0.165	0.109	0.192	0.189	0.092	0.004	8	0.125
Economic security	0.311	0.144	0.496	0.049					4	0.250
Social security	0.112	0.038	0.850						3	0.333

Table 6 shows that the weights of the measuring points for the Security Community with a Shared Future for Mankind placed through the objective entropy evaluation method are reasonable compared to the average weight. The Tier 3 indicators for each observation point are classified according to the principle of classification and indicator proximity applied to the Tier 1 indicators of the original indicator system. Therefore, the Security Community with a Shared Future for Mankind can integrate information through objective weighting. When there is a large difference between objective weighting and subjective weighting, different weights can, on a case-by-case basis, be attached to information integration in objective weighting and subjective weighting.

Table 7 Judgment Matrix of the Analytic Hierarchy Process

Security community	Observation point 1	Observation point 2	Observation point 3	Observation point 4
	International security	Ecological security	Economic security	Social security
Significance	5	1	3	2

成对比较矩阵：

$$A = \begin{pmatrix} 1 & 5 & 3 & 2 \\ \frac{1}{5} & 1 & \frac{1}{2} & \frac{1}{3} \\ \frac{1}{3} & 2 & 1 & \frac{1}{2} \\ \frac{1}{2} & 3 & 2 & 1 \end{pmatrix}$$

一致性检验：$CI = 0.005$ 通过一致性检验。

随后，根据指标之间的重要性，给出判断矩阵，再通过R程序获得各观测点赋权权重，见表6。

最后，我们采用熵值法对国际安全、生态安全、经济安全、社会安全等4个观测点进行客观赋权，并参考主观赋权结果，分别对4个观测点的三级指标进行信息集成，得到安全共同体中国、加拿大、澳大利亚、美国、南非、日本、印度、印度尼西亚的各观测点得分情况，如图6所示。

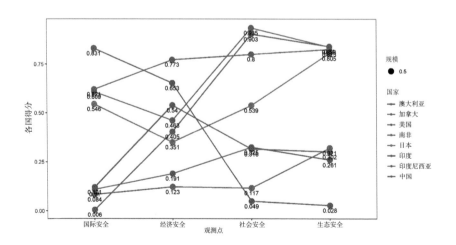

图6 安全共同体各国各观测点得分情况

Pairwise comparison matrix:

$$A = \begin{pmatrix} 1 & 5 & 3 & 2 \\ \dfrac{1}{5} & 1 & \dfrac{1}{2} & \dfrac{1}{3} \\ \dfrac{1}{3} & 2 & 1 & \dfrac{1}{2} \\ \dfrac{1}{2} & 3 & 2 & 1 \end{pmatrix}$$

Consistency check: $CI = 0.005$ consistency maintained.

A judgment matrix is then formed according to the relative importance of indicators, and the R program is run to work out the weights of each measuring point, as shown in Table 1.

The entropy evaluation method is finally adopted to objectively attach weights to the four measuring points of international security, ecological security, economic security and social security. And the weights placed subjectively are consulted to integrate the information about the Tier 3 indicators for the four measuring points. In this way, the scores of the measuring points for China, Canada, Australia, the United States, South Africa, Japan, India and Indonesia in the security community are obtained, as shown in Figure 6.

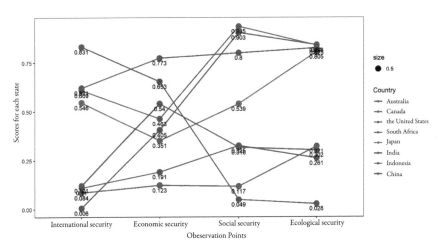

Figure 6 Scores on Observation Points for the Security Community

2.2 各国在 4 个二级指标下的排名

通过数据收集,以及初步对三级指标进行归类,以形成 4 个观测点(二级指标)。然后采用熵值法对国际安全、经济安全、社会安全、生态安全等 4 个观测点进行客观赋权,并参考主观赋权结果,分别对 4 个观测点的三级指标进行信息集成,得到安全共同体澳大利亚、加拿大、中国、印度、印度尼西亚、日本、南非、美国的各观测点得分情况(如图 6 所示)。结果显示:澳大利亚在 4 个观测点的依次得分分别为 0.006、0.840、0.405、0.903,排序分别为 8、5、2、1;加拿大在 4 个观测点的依次得分分别为 0.609、0.838、0.463、0.935,排序分别为 3、4、1、2;中国在 4 个观测点的依次得分分别为 0.121、0.302、0.540、0.316,排序分别为 5、3、6、6;印度在 4 个观测点的依次得分分别为 0.831、0.028、0.653、0.049,排序分别为 1、2、8、8;印度尼西亚在 4 个观测点的依次得分分别为 0.110、0.26、0.191、0.325,排序分别为 6、7、5、7;日本在 4 个观测点的依次得分分别为 0.546、0.805、0.351、0.539,排序分别为 4、6、4、4;南非在 4 个观测点的依次得分分别为 0.084、0.321、0.123、0.117,排序分别为 7、8、7、5;美国在 4 个观测点的依次得分分别为 0.621、0.825、0.773、0.800,排序分别为 2、1、3、3。排名总览见表 8。

优势初步归纳:澳大利亚、加拿大在生态安全、社会安全都排前二,这两个国家的环境让人感到更舒适,城市人口占比更少,国民感到更幸福;美国在经济安全排第一,国际安全、生态安全、社会安全都排前三,超级强国的经济领先,生态也不落下。

2.2 Ranking by the four Tier 2 indicators

Data is collected and Tier 3 indicators are preliminarily classified to derive four observation points (Tier 2 indicators). The entropy evaluation method is then adopted to objectively attach weights to the four observation points of international security, economic security, social security and ecological security. And the weights placed subjectively are consulted to integrate the information about the Tier 3 indicators for the four observation points. In this way, the scores on the observation points for Australia, Canada, China, India, Indonesia, Japan, South Africa and the United States in the security community are obtained, as shown in the Figure 6. Australia scores 0.006, 0.840, 0.405 and 0.903 on the four observation points, ranking 8th, 5th, 2nd and 1st, respectively; Canada scores 0.609, 0.838, 0.463 and 0.935 on the four observation points, ranking 3rd, 4th, 1st and 2nd, respectively; China scores 0.121, 0.302, 0.540 and 0.316 on the four observation points, ranking 5th, 3rd, 6th and 6th, respectively; India scores 0.831, 0.028, 0.653 and 0.049 on the four observation points, ranking 1st, 2nd, 8th and 8th, respectively; Indonesia scores 0.110, 0.26, 0.191 and 0.325 on the four observation points, ranking 6th, 7th, 5th and 7th, respectively; Japan scores 0.546, 0.805, 0.351 and 0.539 on the four observation points, ranking 4th, 6th, 4th and 4th, respectively; South Africa scores 0.084, 0.321, 0.123 and 0.117 on the four observation points, ranking 7th, 8th, 7th and 5th, respectively; the United States scores 0.621, 0.825, 0.773 and 0.800 on the four observation points, ranking 2nd, 1st, 3rd and 3rd, respectively. See the following table for the overall ranking.

Preliminary summary of advantages: Australia and Canada rank among the top two in terms of ecological security and social security. The natural environment of these two countries is comfortable, the proportion of the urban population is small, and the citizens feel happy; the United States ranks first in terms of economic security and among the top three in terms of international security, ecological security and social security — the ecological security situation in this superpower matches its world-leading economy.

表8 各国在4个二级指标下的排名情况

国家	国际安全排名	经济安全排名	社会安全排名	生态安全排名
澳大利亚	8	5	2	1
加拿大	3	4	1	2
中国	5	3	6	6
印度	1	2	8	8
印度尼西亚	6	7	5	7
日本	4	6	4	4
南非	7	8	7	5
美国	2	1	3	3

劣势初步归纳：澳大利亚在国际安全排第八，澳大利亚地广人稀，在军费上投入也较少；南非在经济安全排第八，说明南非整体经济情况很差；印度在社会安全排第八，可知印度需要为劳动力人口的增加创造相应的就业机会。

差距初步分析：

①国际安全、生态安全、经济安全、社会安全等4个观测点的全距（最大值与最小值之差）依次为0.825、0.811、0.649、0.885，其中国际安全、社会安全、生态安全全距都较大，只有经济安全全距相对较小。

②澳大利亚、加拿大、美国的社会安全和生态安全相差较小，均远超印度；

Table 8 Ranking by the Four Tier 2 Indicators

Country	Ranking by international security	Ranking by economic security	Ranking by social security	Ranking by ecological security
Australia	8	5	2	1
Canada	3	4	1	2
China	5	3	6	6
India	1	2	8	8
Indonesia	6	7	5	7
Japan	4	6	4	4
South Africa	7	8	7	5
the United States	2	1	3	3

Preliminary summary of disadvantages: Australia ranks eighth in terms of international security because it is a sparsely populated large country that invests sparingly in military equipment; South Africa ranks eighth in terms of economic security, an indication that the overall economic situation in South Africa is bad; India ranks eighth in terms of social security, an indication that India needs to create employment opportunities for its increasing labor force.

Preliminary analysis of the gap:

1) The range (the difference between the maximum value and the minimum value) of the four observation points of international security, ecological security, economic security and social security is 0.825, 0.811, 0.649 and 0.885, respectively; the range of international security, social security and ecological security is large, and that of economic security is small.

2) Australia, Canada and the United States don't differ much in terms of social security and ecological security; they far exceed India in these two respects;

③差距适中的观测点：加拿大、澳大利亚社会安全相差适中，且远超印度和印度尼西亚，说明加拿大、澳大利亚人民失业率比印度和印度尼西亚低，也自我感到更幸福；

④差距较小的观测点：澳大利亚、加拿大、美国、日本的生态安全相差适中，且依次递减，这几个国家的CO_2生产排量会更少，生态足迹等都更好。

⑤差距大的观测点印度、美国、加拿大在国际安全位居前三的位置，且遥遥领先与后三位。同时加拿大、美国在社会安全也位居前三，在国际安全、经济安全也靠前。而南非与印度尼西亚在国际安全、社会安全、生态安全、经济安全4个观测点都靠后，应引起重视。

2.3 安全共同体各国总得分

通过层次分析法对国际安全、经济安全、社会安全、生态安全等4个观测点进行主观赋权，然后对4个观测点得分情况进行信息总集成，得到安全共同体澳大利亚、加拿大、中国、印度、印度尼西亚、日本、南非、美国的总得分情况，如图7所示。结果显示：澳大利亚、加拿大、中国、印度、印度尼西亚、日本、南非、美国的总得分分别为0.386、0.695、0.256、0.520、0.194、0.536、0.120、0.711。在我们初步选择的8个国家中，安全共同体各国总得分依次排序分别为：美国、加拿大、日本、印度、澳大利亚、中国、印度尼西亚、南非，其中美国与加拿大、日本与印度的总得分相近、相差较小（见表9）。

3) Observation points where the gap is moderate: The gap in social security between Canada and Australia is moderate, and both countries far exceed India and Indonesia in this respect. This shows that the unemployment rate in Canadian and Australian is lower than that in India and Indonesia, and the people in these two countries feel happier;

4) Observation points where the gap is small: The gap in ecological security between Australia, Canada, the United States and Japan is moderate and decreases in descending order. These countries produce smaller amounts of CO_2 emissions and perform better in terms of the ecological footprint.

5) Observation points where the gap is big: India, the United States and Canada are among the top three in terms of international security, way ahead of the latter three. Canada and the United States also rank among the top three in terms of social security, and are ahead of other countries in terms of international security and economic security. South Africa and Indonesia fall behind other countries in terms of international security, social security, ecological security and economic security. This deserves attention.

2.3 Total scores of all countries in the security community

The analytic hierarchy process is adopted to subjectively attach weights to the four observation points of international security, economic security, social security and ecological security. And the information about the scores of the four observation points is integrated to obtain the ecological community total scores of Australia, Canada, China, India, Indonesia, Japan, South Africa and the United States, as shown in Figure 7. The total scores of Australia, Canada, China, India, Indonesia, Japan, South Africa and the United States are 0.386, 0.695, 0.256, 0.520, 0.194, 0.536, 0.120 and 0.711, respectively. The eight countries we preliminarily selected for this study of the security community are ranked in the order of the United States, Canada, Japan, India, Australia, China, Indonesia and South Africa. The total score of the United States is close to that of Canada, Japan and India, as shown in Table 9.

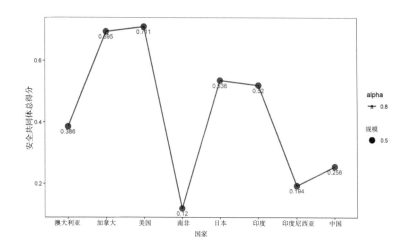

图 7 安全共同体各国总得分情况

表 9 各国安全共同体总得分排名

国家	美国	加拿大	日本	印度	澳大利亚	中国	印度尼西亚	南非
排名	1	2	3	4	5	6	7	8
得分	0.711	0.695	0.536	0.520	0.386	0.256	0.194	0.120

3. 方法二：主成分分析法（PCA）建模及结果分析

3.1 数据降维

同样，利用熵值法模型中使用的 8 个国家、4 个观测点、18 个三级指标进行分析，考虑到观测点的数量分布参差不齐，故采用主成分分析法进行降维，并利用归一化、和同向化处理的数据。

数据降维，基本思想是设法将原来众多的具有一定相关性的多个指标，重新组合成一组新的较少的互不相关的综合指

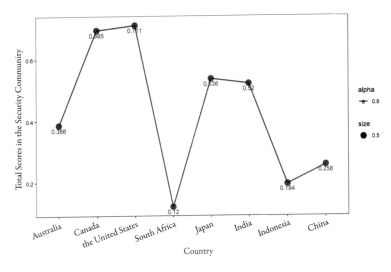

Figure 7 Total Scores of All Countries in the Security Community

Table 9 Ranking of Security Community Total Scores

Country	the United States	Canada	Japan	India	Australia	China	Indonesia	South Africa
Ranking	1	2	3	4	5	6	7	8
Score	0.711	0.695	0.536	0.520	0.386	0.256	0.194	0.120

3. Method 2: Principal component analysis (PCA) modeling and analysis of results

3.1 Data dimensionality reduction

Similarly, the eight countries, four observation points and 18 Tier 3 indicators used in the entropy evaluation method model are applied in our analysis. Considering the irregularity of the number of the observation points, principal component analysis is used to reduce the dimensionality, and normalized and isotropic data are used in the meantime.

Data dimensionality reduction is basically the regrouping of the original numerous interrelated indicators into a new, smaller set of unrelated compre-

标来代替原来指标，在损失信息量较小情形下，将指标量大大缩减，从而实现降维。主成分分析数学原理见附录。

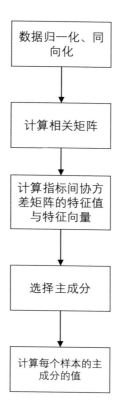

图8 主成分分析计算流程图

这里使用了SPSS来进行主成分分析，计算出特征向量与方差贡献率，经验表明，累计方差贡献到80%以上即可，运行结果如表10。

可见只需保留三个主成分，累计的方差贡献达到了约84.9%。最后根据原特特征矩阵计算在成分得分系数矩阵下的投影即可得到每个国家在各个主成分下的得分。

hensive indicators. The number of indicators is greatly reduced without losing much of the information to reduce the dimensionality. See the appendix for the mathematical principle for principal component analysis.

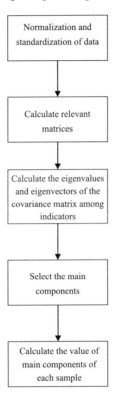

Figure 8 Flow Chart of Principal Component Analysis

SPSS is used in principal component analysis to work out the feature vector and the variance contribution rate. Experience shows that a cumulative variance contribution rate of over 80% is acceptable. Results of the analysis are shown in the following Table 10.

Only three principal components need to be retained, and the cumulative variance contribution rate reaches about 84.9%. The score of each country on all principal components can be finally obtained by working out the projection in the component score coefficient matrix according to the original characteristic matrix.

表 10　SPSS 方差解释

成分	总计	初始特征值方差百分比	累积 %	总计	提取载荷平方和方差百分比	累积 %
1	9.583	52.990	52.990	9.583	52.990	52.990
2	3.032	16.845	69.835	3.032	16.845	69.835
3	2.712	15.069	84.904	2.712	15.069	84.904

3.2 安全共同体得分结果分析

首先将国际安全、经济安全、社会安全、生态安全等4个观测点下的三级指标数据混合在一起，然后利用主成分分析法（使用相关矩阵法），提取三个主成分（提取信息量达到84%），根据各主成分与各指标之间的相关系数，将三个主成分分别命名为环境因子，产业因子，关税因子，利用这三个因子对三级指标进行信息总集成，得到安全共同体澳大利亚、加拿大、中国、印度、印度尼西亚、日本、南非、美国的总得分情况，见图9。结果显示：澳大利亚、加拿大、中国、印度、印度尼西亚、日本、南非、美国的总得分分别为 0.976、1.279、0.942、0.810、0.579、1.422、0.254、1.301。在我们初步选择的 8 个国家中，安全共同体各国总得分依次排序分别为：日本、美国、加拿大、澳大利亚、中国、印度、印度尼西亚、南非，其中日本、美国与加拿大的总得分相近、相差较小并且占据前三的位置，澳大利亚与中国次之，南非的情况最不乐观。

Table 10 SPSS Variance Explained

Component	Aggregate	Initial eigenvalue Percentage of variance	Accumulate (%)	Aggregate	Extracted payload of quadratic sum Percentage of Variance	Accumulate (%)
1	9.583	52.990	52.990	9.583	52.990	52.990
2	3.032	16.845	69.835	3.032	16.845	69.835
3	2.712	15.069	84.904	2.712	15.069	84.904

3.2 Analysis of security community scores

Firstly, the Tier 3 indicators for the four observation points of international security, economic security, social security and ecological security are mixed together, and then the principal component analysis method (using the correlation matrix method) is used to extract 84% of the information about three principal components. The three principal components are named environmental factor, industry factor and tariff factor according to the correlation coefficient between the principal components and the indicators. These three factors are used to integrate the information about the Tier 3 indicators to obtain the total scores of Australia, Canada, China, India, Indonesia, Japan, South Africa and the United States in the security community, as shown in the figure above. The total scores of Australia, Canada, China, India, Indonesia, Japan, South Africa and the United States are 0.976, 1.279, 0.942, 0.810, 0.579, 1.422, 0.254 and 1.301, respectively. The eight countries we preliminarily selected for this study of the security community are ranked in the order of Japan, the United States, Canada, Australia, China, India, Indonesia and South Africa. Japan, the United States and Canada have similar total scores and rank among the top three, followed by Australia and China. The situation in South Africa is the worst-case scenario.

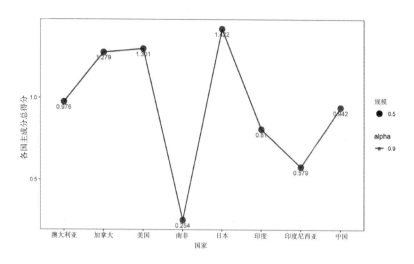

图 9　安全共同体得分情况

表 11　主成分分析下安全共同体总得分排名

国家	日本	美国	加拿大	澳大利亚	中国	印度	印度尼西亚	南非
排名	1	2	3	4	5	6	7	8
得分	0.976	1.279	0.942	0.810	0.579	1.422	0.254	1.301

四、模型的对比

1. 层次分析法

优点在于把研究对象作为一个系统，按照分解、比较判断、综合的思维方式进行决策，将定性方法与定量方法有机结合，使复杂的系统分解，将多目标、多准则又难以全部量化处理的决策问题化为多层次单目标问题；缺点是定量数据较少、定性成分偏多，且不能为决策提供新的方案。

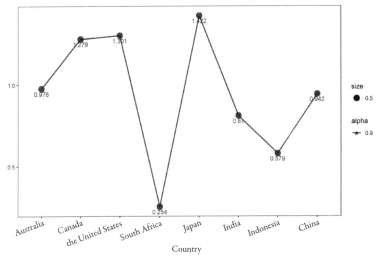

Figure 9 Security Community Scores

Table 11 PCA Ranking of Security Community Total Scores

Country	Japan	the United States	Canada	Australia	China	India	Indonesia	South Africa
Ranking	1	2	3	4	5	6	7	8
Score	0. 976	1.279	0.942	0.810	0.579	1.422	0.254	1.301

IV. Comparison of Models

1. Analytic hierarchy process

The advantage of the analytic hierarchy process is that the object of study is regarded as a system, and decisions are made after disintegration, comparison and judgment, and synthesis. Qualitative methods and quantitative methods are combined to disintegrate the complex system, and multi-objective, multi-criteria decision-making difficult to be completely quantified is converted into a multi-level, single-objective issue. The disadvantage is that the amount of quantitative data is small, the number of qualitative components is big, and it cannot provide new solutions for decision-making.

通过此方法我们得到了各个国家安全共同体总分，即得分排名为美国 0.711、加拿大 0.695、日本 0.536、印度 0.52、澳大利亚 0.386、中国 0.256、印度尼西亚 0.194、南非 0.120。

2. 主成分分析法

优点在于利用降维技术，用少数几个综合指标来代替原始多个变量，这些综合变量集中了原始变量的大部分信息，其次通过计算综合主成分函数得分，对其进行科学评价，再次在应用上侧重于信息贡献影响力综合评价；缺点则是当主成分的因子负荷的符号有正负时，综合评价函数意义就不明确，且命名清晰性较低。

通过此方法我们得到了各个国家安全共同体总分，即得分排名为日本 1.422、美国 1.301、加拿大 1.279、澳大利亚 0.976、中国 0.942、印度 0.810、印度尼西亚 0.579、南非 0.254。

3. 结论

通过两模型的结果对比得出，安全共同体总分排名前三的国家均为美国、日本、加拿大，其次南非与印度尼西亚均是倒数一、二名，中国、澳大利亚、印度的排名则在中间进行浮动，整体上两种模型并未有太多误差，如图 10 所示，两者曲线图趋势相近，故可以使安全共同体总分排名结果得到相互验证。

In this method, we get the total security community scores of the eight countries: the United States, 0.711; Canada, 0.695; Japan, 0.536; India, 0.52; Australia, 0.386; China, 0.256; Indonesia, 0.194; South Africa, 0.120.

2. Principal component analysis

The advantage of principal component analysis is that a few comprehensive indicators replace the original multiple variables after the application of the dimension reduction technology. These comprehensive variables contain most of the information about the original variables. Secondly, the scores of comprehensive principal component functions are worked out to carry out scientific evaluations and once again make comprehensive evaluations of information contribution on the application dimension. The disadvantage is that when the sign of the factor load of the principal components is positive or negative, the meaning of the comprehensive evaluation functions will become vague and the names will not be able to denote things in a transparent way.

In this method, we get the total security community scores of the eight countries: Japan, 1.422; the United States, 1.301; Canada, 1.279; Australia, 0.976; China, 0.942; India, 0.810; Indonesia, 0.579; South Africa, 0.254.

3. Conclusion

Comparison of the results of the two models shows that the three top-ranking countries are the United States, Japan and Canada, South Africa and Indonesia rank last or second from last, and China, Australia and India rank in the middle. On the whole, the two models don't make many errors. As shown in Figure 10, the two curve charts display a similar trend, making the total security community scores mutually verifiable.

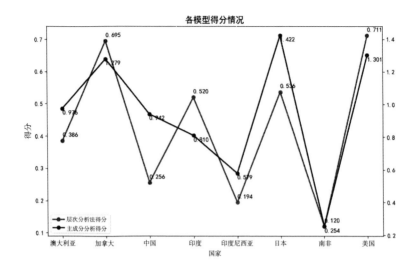

图 10　模型得分情况对比

表 12　层次分析与主成分分析结果对比排名

国家	日本	美国	加拿大	澳大利亚	中国	印度	印度尼西亚	南非
层次分析法排名	1	2	3	4	5	6	7	8
主成分分析排名	3	1	2	5	6	4	7	8

相关内容

1. 各指标归类情况

1.1 国际安全：安全峰会的召开［次］、军费（占 GDP 的比例）［%］、驻联合国部队人数［个］。

1.2 生态安全：属于生产中的二氧化碳排放量［吨］、可持续竞争能力［2013—2017=100］、经济自由度［2013—

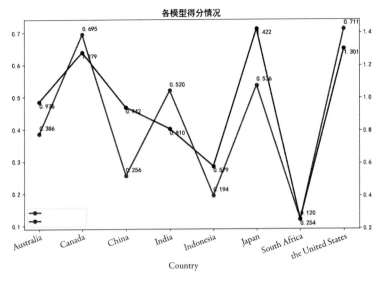

Figure 10 Comparison of Model Scores

Table 12 Comparative Ranking of AHP and PCA Results

Country	Japan	the United States	Canada	Australia	China	India	Indonesia	South Africa
Ranking of AHP results	1	2	3	4	5	6	7	8
Ranking of PCA results	3	1	2	5	6	4	7	8

Related Content

1. Classification of indicators

1.1 International security: number of security summits held, military expenditure (as a percentage of GDP), number of troops sent on UN peace-keeping missions.

1.2 Ecological security: carbon dioxide emissions in production [ton], sustainable competitiveness [2013-2017=100], economic freedom [2013-2017

2017=100］、城市人口（占人口的百分比）[%]、真实进步指数［2013—2017=100］、人类发展指数［2013—2017=1］、生态足迹指数［2013—2017=10］、对外经济贸易依存度[%]。

1.3 经济安全：自由贸易协定［个］、平均税率[%]、反倾销措施［个］、对外直接投资贡献变化率[%]。

1.4 社会安全：和平指数［2013—2017］、失业率[%]、幸福指数［2013—2017］。

2. 熵值法

2.1 算法简介

熵值法是一种客观赋权法，其根据各项指标观测值所提供的信息的大小来确定指标权重。设有个待评方案，项评价指标，形成原始指标数据矩阵 $X=(X_{ij})_{m \times n}$，对于某项指标，m 指标值的差距越大，n 则该指标在综合评价中所起的作用越大；如果某项指标的指标值全部相等，则该指标在综合评价中不起作用。

在信息论中，熵是对不确定性的一种度量。信息量越大，不确定性就越小，熵也就越小；信息量越小，不确定性就越大，熵也越大。根据熵的特性，我们可以通过计算熵值来判断一个方案的随机性及无序程度，也可以用熵值来判断某个指标的离散程度，指标的离散程度越大，该指标对综合评价的影响越大。因此，可根据各项指标的变异程度，利用信息熵这个工具，计算出各个指标的权重，为多指标综合评价提供依据。

=100], urban population (as a percentage of the total population) [%], genuine progress index [2013-2017=100], human development index [2013-2017=1], ecological footprint index [2013-2017=10], degree of foreign trade dependence [%].

1.3 Economic security: number of free trade agreements signed, average tax rate [%], number of anti-dumping measures, rate of change in contribution of outward foreign direct investment [%].

1.4 Social security: global peace index [2013-2017], unemployment rate [%], happiness index [2013-2017].

2. The entropy evaluation method

2.1 Introduction to algorithm

The entropy evaluation method is an objective way of determining indicator weight according to the size of the information provided by the observed value of each indicator. m evaluation programs and n indicators are developed to form the original indicator data matrix $X=(X_{ij})_{m \times n}$. For indicator x_j, the greater the gap in the indicator value X_{ij}, the greater the role that the indicator plays in overall evaluation; if all the values of an indicator are equal, the indicator does not play any role in overall evaluation.

In information theory, entropy is a measure of uncertainty. The greater the amount of information, the smaller the uncertainty and the entropy; the smaller the amount of information, the greater the uncertainty and the entropy. These characteristics of the entropy allow us to judge the randomness and disorderliness of a scheme by calculating the entropy value and to judge the dispersion degree of an indicator. The greater the dispersion degree of an indicator, the greater the impact of the indicator on comprehensive evaluations. Therefore, we can, according to the degree of variation of each indicator, work out the weight of each indicator using the information entropy and provide a basis for multi-indicator comprehensive evaluations.

2.2 算法实现过程

2.2.1 数据矩阵

对 n 个样本，m 个指标，x_{ij} 则为第 i 个样本的第 j 个指标的数值 i

$$A = \begin{pmatrix} x_{ij} & \cdots & x_{1m} \\ \vdots & \vdots & \vdots \\ x_{n1} & \cdots & x_{nm} \end{pmatrix}_{n \times m}，其中 x_{ij} 为第个样本第个指标的数值$$

2.2.2 数据的非负数化处理

由于各项指标的计量单位并不统一，因此在用它们计算综合指标前，先要进行标准化处理，即把指标的绝对值转化为相对值，从而解决各项不同质指标值的同质化问题。另外，正向指标和负向指标数值代表的含义不同（正向指标数值越高越好，负向指标数值越低越好），因此，对于正向负向指标需要采用不同的算法进行数据标准化处理。并且，为了避免求熵值时对数的无意义，需要进行移动轴的方法：

对于越大越好的指标：

$$x_{ij}^{'} = \frac{x_{ij} - \min(x_{1j}, x_{2j}, \cdots, x_{nj})}{\max(x_{1j}, x_{2j}, \cdots, x_{nj}) - \min(x_{1j}, x_{2j}, \cdots, x_{nj})} + 1 \quad , i = 1, 2, \cdots, n; j = 1, 2, \cdots, m$$

对于越小越好的指标：

$$x_{ij}^{'} = \frac{\max(x_{1j}, x_{2j}, \cdots, x_{nj}) - x_{ij}}{\max(x_{1j}, x_{2j}, \cdots, x_{nj}) - \min(x_{1j}, x_{2j}, \cdots, x_{nj})} + 1 \quad , i = 1, 2, \cdots, n; j = 1, 2, \cdots, m$$

为了方便起见，仍然记非负化处理后的数据为 x_{ij}

2.2 Algorithm implementation

2.2.1 Data matrix

For n samples and m indicators, x_{ij} is the value of Indicator j of Sample i

$$A = \begin{pmatrix} x_{ij} & \cdots & x_{1m} \\ \vdots & \vdots & \vdots \\ x_{n1} & \cdots & x_{nm} \end{pmatrix}_{n \times m}, \text{ here } x_{ij} \text{ is the value of Indicator } j \text{ of Sample } i$$

2.2.2 Nonnegative number processing of data

Because the units of measurement of the indicators are not uniform, so before using them to calculate comprehensive indicators, we should standardize them first. That is, convert the absolute value of indicators into relative values to avoid homogeneity of the different indicator values. In addition, positive indicators and negative indicators mean differently (the higher the positive indicator, the better, and the lower the negative indicator, the better). For positive and negative indicators, therefore, different algorithms should be used for data standardization. To prevent the evaluation of entropies from producing meaningless logarithms, the moving-axis method is required.

For indicators that should be preferably big:

$$x'_{ij} = \frac{x_{ij} - \min(x_{1j}, x_{2j}, \cdots, x_{nj})}{\max(x_{1j}, x_{2j}, \cdots, x_{nj}) - \min(x_{1j}, x_{2j}, \cdots, x_{nj})} + 1 \quad , i=1,2,\cdots,n;\ j=1,2,\cdots,m$$

For indicators that should be preferably small:

$$x'_{ij} = \frac{\max(x_{1j}, x_{2j}, \cdots, x_{nj}) - x_{ij}}{\max(x_{1j}, x_{2j}, \cdots, x_{nj}) - \min(x_{1j}, x_{2j}, \cdots, x_{nj})} + 1 \quad , i=1,2,\cdots,n;\ j=1,2,\cdots,m$$

For convenience, data that has undergone nonnegative number processing is still recorded as x_{ij}

2.2.3 计算第 j 项指标下第 i 个样本占该指标的比重

$$p_{ij} = \frac{x_{ij}}{\sum_{i=1}^{n} x_{ij}} \quad (j=1,2,\cdots,m)$$

2.2.4 计算第 j 项指标的熵值

$e_j = -k * \sum_{i=1}^{n} p_{ij} \ln(p_{ij})$，其中 $k>0$，$\ln \geqslant$ 自然对数，$e_j \geqslant 0$ 句式中常数 k 与样本数 m 有关，一般令 $k=\dfrac{1}{\ln m}$，则 $0 \leqslant e \leqslant 1$

2.2.5 计算第 j 项指标的差异系数

对于第 j 项指标，指标值 x_{ij} 的差异越大，对方案评价的作用越大，熵值就越小 $g_j=1-e_j$，则：g_j 越大，指标越重要。

2.2.6 求权数

$$w_j = \frac{g_j}{\sum_{j=1}^{m} g_j} \quad (j=1,2,\cdots,m)$$

2.2.7 计算各方案的综合得分

$$S_i = \sum_{j=1}^{m} w_j * p_{ij} \quad (i=1,2,\cdots,n)$$

2.3 熵值法的优缺点

熵值法是根据各项指标值的变异程度来确定指标权数的，这是一种客观赋权法，避免了人为因素带来的偏差，但由于忽略了指标本身重要程度，有时确定的指标权数会与预期的结果相差甚远，同时熵值法不能减少评价指标的维数。

2.2.3 Work out the ratio of Sample i under Indicator j

$$p_{ij} = \frac{x_{ij}}{\sum_{i=1}^{n} x_{ij}} \quad (j=1,2,\cdots,m)$$

2.2.4 Work out the entropy value of Indicator j

$e_j = -k * \sum_{i=1}^{n} p_{ij} \ln(p_{ij})$, in which $k>0$, ln is natural logarithm; in the inequation of $e_j \geqslant 0$, the constant of k is related to the sample number of m; if $k = \frac{1}{\ln m}$, then $0 \leqslant e \leqslant 1$

2.2.5 Work out the difference coefficient of Indicator j.

For Indicator j, the greater the difference in the indicator value x_{ij}, the greater its evaluating role on the scheme and the smaller the entropy value $g_j = 1 - e_j$. The bigger g_j is, the more important the indicator is.

2.2.6 Work out the weight

$$w_j = \frac{g_j}{\sum_{j=1}^{m} g_j} \quad (j=1,2,\cdots,m)$$

2.2.7 Work out the overall score of each scheme

$$S_i = \sum_{j=1}^{m} w_j * p_{ij} \quad (i=1,2,\cdots,n)$$

2.3 Advantages and disadvantages of the entropy evaluation method

The entropy evaluation method is an objective way of determining indicator weight according to the degree of variation of each indicator value, and it avoids human errors. Downplaying the importance of the indicator itself, however, sometimes causes the indicator weight determined to differ vastly from the anticipated result. In addition, the entropy evaluation method cannot reduce the dimensionality of indicators.

3. 层次分析法

层次分析法（Analytic Hierarchy Process, AHP），简称 AHP，是指将与总是有关的元素分解成目标、准则、方案等层次，在此基础之上进行定性和定量分析的决策方法。该方法是美国运筹学家匹兹堡大学教授萨蒂（Thomas Saaty）于 20 世纪 70 年代初，在为研究"根据各个工业部门对国家福利的贡献大小而进行电力分配"课题时，应用网络系统理论和多目标综合评价方法，提出的一种层次权重决策分析方法。

层次分析法是一种定性和定量相结合的、系统的、层次化的分析方法。这种方法的特点就是在对复杂决策问题的本质、影响因素及其内在关系等进行深入研究的基础上，利用较少的定量信息使决策的思维过程数学化，从而为多目标、多准则或无结构特性的复杂决策问题提供简便的决策方法。是对难以完全定量的复杂系统做出决策的模型和方法。

层次分析法的原理：层次分析法根据问题的性质和要达到的总目标，将问题分解为不同的组成因素，并按照因素间的相互关联影响以及隶属关系将因素按不同的层次聚集组合，形成一个多层次的分析结构模型，从而最终使问题归结为最低层 (供决策的方案、措施等) 相对于最高层 (总目标) 的相对重要权值的确定或相对优劣次序的排定。

3. Analytic hierarchy process

The Analytic Hierarchy Process (AHP) refers to the decision-making method whereby elements that are always related to decision-making are

broken down into objectives, criteria and schemes to carry out qualitative and quantitative analysis. AHP is a hierarchical weight decision analysis method put forward by Prof. Thomas Saaty, an American operational research expert from the University of Pittsburgh, in the early 1970s. It involves the network system theory and the multi-objective overall evaluation method when "studying the distribution of power according to the contribution of industrial sectors to national welfare".

AHP is a systematic and hierarchical method of qualitative and quantitative analysis. The characteristic of this method is that, on the basis of an in-depth study of the nature, factors and

internal relations of complex decision-making issues, it uses small amounts of quantitative

information to make the decision-making process mathematical and provide simple decision-making methods for multi-objective and multi-criteria complex issues or complex issues without structural property. It is a model and method for making decisions about complex systems which are difficult to be completely quantified.

The basic principle of AHP is to break down the problem into different components according to the nature of the problem and the general goal to be achieved, and combine the factors at different levels depending on the relations between the factors and their affiliation to form a multi-level analytical structure model so that the problem can be boiled down to the determination of key weights at the lowest level (programs, measures, etc. for decision making) relative to the highest level (overall goals) or the arrangement in the order of relative merit or demerit.

表13 重要性标度含义表

重要性标度	含 义
1	表示两个元素相比,具有同等重要性
3	表示两个元素相比,前者比后者稍重要
5	表示两个元素相比,前者比后者明显重要
7	表示两个元素相比,前者比后者强烈重要
9	表示两个元素相比,前者比后者极端重要
2, 4, 6, 8	表示上述判断的中间值
倒数	若元素 i 与元素 j 的重要性之比为 a_{ij},则元素 j 与元素 i 的重要性之比为 $a_{ji}=1/a_{ij}$

R 程序:

```
A<- c (1, 5,3,2,1/5,1,1/2,1/3,1/3,2,1,1/2,1/2,3,2,1)
A_m<- matrix (A, nrow = 4, ncol = 4)
A_1<- t(A_m)
A_1
judgeMatix <- matrix (A_1, ncol=4)
judgeMatix


weight <- function (judgeMatrix, round=3) {
  n = ncol(judgeMatrix)
  cumProd <- vector(length=n)
  cumProd <- apply(judgeMatrix, 1, prod)  ## 求每行连乘积
  weight <- cumProd^(1/n)  ## 开 n 次方 ( 特征向量 )
```

Table 13 Significance Indicators Explained

Significance Indicators	Explained
1	The two elements are of equal significance
3	The former element is slightly more significant than the latter
5	The former element is fairly more significant than the latter
7	The former element is considerably more significant than the latter
9	The former element is critically more significant than the latter
2, 4, 6, and 8	are medians of the above judgments
Reciprocal	If the ratio between the importance of Element i and that of Element j is a_{ij}, then a_{ji}, the ratio between the importance of Element j and that of Element i, will be $1/a_{ij}$

R program:

```
A<- c (1, 5,3,2,1/5,1,1/2,1/3,1/3,2,1,1/2,1/2,3,2,1)

A_m<- matrix (A, nrow = 4, ncol = 4)

A_1<- t(A_m)

A_1

judgeMatix <- matrix (A_1, ncol=4)

judgeMatix


weight <- function (judgeMatrix, round=3) {
    n = ncol(judgeMatrix)
    cumProd <- vector(length=n)
    cumProd <- apply(judgeMatrix, 1, prod)   ## Find the continued product of each row
        weight <- cumProd^(1/n)   ## Get the Nth root (eigenvector)
```

```
    weight <- weight/sum(weight)  ## 求权重
    round (weight, round)
}
weight(judgeMatix)

CRtest <- function (judgeMatrix, round=3){
    RI <- c(0, 0, 0.58, 0.9, 1.12, 1.24, 1.32, 1.41, 1.45, 1.49, 1.51) # 随机一致性指标
    Wi <- weight(judgeMatrix)  ## 计算权重
    n <- length (Wi)
    if (n > 11) {
        cat ("判断矩阵过大，请少于 11 个指标 \n")
    }
    if (n > 2) {
        W <- matrix (Wi, ncol = 1)
        judgeW <- judgeMatrix %*% W
        JudgeW <- as. vector(judgeW)
        la_max <- sum (JudgeW/Wi)/n
        CI = (la_max - n)/ (n - 1)
        CR = CI/RI[n]
        cat ("\n CI=", round (CI, round), "\n")
        cat ("\n CR=", round (CR, round), "\n")
        if (CR <= 0.1) {
            cat ("通过一致性检验 \n")
            cat ("\n Wi:", round (Wi, round), "\n")
        }
```

```
    weight <- weight/sum(weight) ## Find the weight
    round (weight, round)
}
weight(judgeMatix)

CRtest <- function (judgeMatrix, round=3){
    RI <- c(0, 0, 0.58, 0.9, 1.12, 1.24, 1.32, 1.41, 1.45, 1.49, 1.51) # Random consistency index
    Wi <- weight(judgeMatrix)  ## Judge Matrix
    n <- length (Wi)
    if (n > 11) {
        cat ("Judge Matrix is too large, please make it less than 11 indicators \n")
    }
    if (n > 2) {
        W <- matrix (Wi, ncol = 1)
        judgeW <- judgeMatrix %*% W
        JudgeW <- as. vector(judgeW)
        la_max <- sum (JudgeW/Wi)/n
        CI = (la_max - n)/ (n - 1)
        CR = CI/RI[n]
        cat ( "\n CI=" , round (CI, round), "\n" )
        cat ( "\n CR=" , round (CR, round), "\n" )
        if (CR <= 0.1) {
        cat ( "Pass the consistency test \n" )
        cat ( "\n Wi: ", round (Wi, round), "\n" )
    }
```

```
    else {
      cat ("请调整判断矩阵,使 CR<0.1 \n")
      Wi = NULL
      }
    }
    else if (n <= 2) {
      return (Wi)
    }
    consequence <- c (round (CI, round), round (CR, round))
    names(consequence) <- c ("CI","CR")
    consequence
    }
    CRtest(judgeMatix)
```

4. 主成分分析简介

在处理信息时，当两个变量之间有一定相关关系时，可以解释为这两个变量反映此课题的信息有一定的重叠，例如，高校科研状况评价中的立项课题数与项目经费、经费支出等之间会存在较高的相关性；学生综合评价研究中的专业基础课成绩与专业课成绩、获奖学金次数等之间也会存在较高的相关性。而变量之间信息的高度重叠和高度相关会给统计方法的应用带来许多障碍。

主成分分析以最少的信息丢失为前提，将众多的原有变量综合成较少几个综合指标，通常综合指标（主成分）有以下几个特点。

```
    else {
      cat ( "Please adjust judge Matrix, to have CR<0.1 \n" )
      Wi = NULL
      }
    }
    else if (n <= 2) {
      return (Wi)
    }
    consequence <- c (round (CI, round), round (CR, round))
    names(consequence) <- c ( "CI" , "CR" )
    consequence
  }
  CRtest(judgeMatix)
```

4. Introduction to principal component analysis

When two variables are interrelated to each other during information processing, then there is some overlap in the information about the research project. For example, there is a high correlation between the number of approved projects and project funds and project expenditure in the assessment of scientific research at colleges and universities; there is also a high correlation between the scores for basic program courses and the scores for program courses and the number of scholarships in the comprehensive evaluation of students. Considerable overlap in and correlation between the information about variables pose obstacles to the application of statistical methods.

In principal component analysis, multiple original variables are synthesized into a few comprehensive indicators without losing much of the information. The comprehensive indicators (principal components) have the following characteristics:

（1）主成分个数远远少于原有变量的个数

原有变量综合成少数几个因子之后，因子将可以替代原有变量参与数据建模，这将大大减少分析过程中的计算工作量。

（2）主成分能够反映原有变量的绝大部分信息

因子并不是原有变量的简单取舍，而是原有变量重组后的结果，因此不会造成原有变量信息的大量丢失，并能够代表原有变量的绝大部分信息。

（3）主成分之间应该互不相关

主成分分析具体计算步骤：

（1）计算协方差矩阵

计算样品数据的协方差矩阵：$\Sigma = (s_{ij}) p \times p$，其中

$$s_{ij} = \frac{1}{n-1} \sum_{k=1}^{n} (x_{ki} - \overline{x}_i)(x_{kj} - \overline{x}_j) \quad i, j = 1, 2, \cdots, p$$

（2）求出 Σ 的特征值 λ_i 及相应的正交化单位特征向量 a_i

Σ 的前 m 个较大的特征值 $\lambda_1 \geq \lambda_2 \geq \cdots \lambda_m > 0$，就是前 m 个主成分对应的方差，λ_i 对应的单位特征向量 a_i 就是主成分 F_i 的关于原变量的系数，则原变量的第 i 个主成分 F_i 为：

$$F_i = a_i^{'} X$$

主成分的方差（信息）贡献率用来反映信息量的大小，a_i 为：

$$\alpha_i = \lambda_i / \sum_{i=1}^{m} \lambda_i$$

(1) The number of principal components is far fewer than that of the original variables.

After the original variables are synthesized into a handful of factors, the factors can take the place of the original variables and participate in data modeling. This will greatly reduce the computational workload in the analysis process.

(2) Principal components contain most of the information about the original variables.

Factors are not randomly chosen original variables; they are the regrouping of the original variables. So not much information about the original variables will be lost. Factors contain most of the information about the original variables.

(3) Principal components should be independent of each other.

Specific steps of principal component analysis:

(1) Calculate the covariance matrix

Calculate the covariance matrix of the sample data: $\Sigma = (s_{ij})\, p \times p$, where

$$s_{ij} = \frac{1}{n-1}\sum_{k=1}^{n}(x_{ki} - \bar{x}_i)(x_{kj} - \bar{x}_j) \quad i, j = 1, 2, \cdots, p$$

(2) Find the eigenvalu λ_i of Σ and the corresponding orthogonalized unit a_j eigenvector

The first m large eigenvalues $\lambda_1 \geq \lambda_2 \geq \cdots \lambda_m > 0$ of σ are the variances corresponding to the first λ_i m principal components, and the corresponding unit a_j eigenvectors are the coefficients of principal component F_i about the original variable. The ith principal component F_i of the original variable is:

$$F_i = a_i' X$$

The variance (information) contribution rate of principal components is used to reflect the amount of information, a_j is:

$$\alpha_i = \lambda_i / \sum_{i=1}^{m}\lambda_i$$

（3）选择主成分

最终要选择几个主成分，即 $F_1, F_2, \cdots, F_m$ 中 m 的确定是通过方差（信息）累计贡献率 G (m) 来确定

$$G(m) = \sum_{i=1}^{m} \lambda_i / \sum_{k=1}^{p} \lambda_k$$

当累积贡献率大于 85% 时，就认为能足够反映原来变量的信息了，对应的 m 就是抽取的前 m 个主成分。

（4）计算主成分载荷

主成分载荷是反映主成分 F_i 与原变量 X_j 之间的相互关联程度，原来变量 $X_j(j=1, 2, \cdots, p)$ 在诸主成分 $F_i(i=1, 2, \cdots, m)$ 上的荷载 l_{ij}（$i=1, 2, \cdots, m; j=1, 2, \cdots, p$）：

$$l(Z_i, X_j) = \sqrt{\lambda_i} a_{ij} (i=1,2,\cdots,m; j=1,2,\cdots,p)$$

在 SPSS 软件中主成分分析后的分析结果中，"成分矩阵"反应的就是主成分载荷矩阵。

（5）计算主成分得分

计算样品在 m 个主成分上的得分：

$$F_i = a_{1i}X_1 + a_{2i}X_2 + \cdots + a_{pi}X_p \quad i=1, 2, \cdots, m$$

实际应用时，指标的量纲往往不同，所以在主成分计算之前应先消除量纲的影响。消除数据的量纲有很多方法，常用方法是将原始数据标准化，即做如下数据变换：

$$x_{ij}^* = \frac{x_{ij} - \overline{x}_j}{s_j} \quad i=1,2,\cdots,n; j=1,2,\cdots,p$$

(3) Select principal components

Finally, several principal components should be selected. That is, m in $F_1, F_1, ..., F_1$ is determined by the variance (information) cumulative contribution rate G (m).

$$G(m) = \sum_{i=1}^{m} \lambda_i / \sum_{k=1}^{p} \lambda_k$$

A cumulative contribution rate greater than 85% can reflect the information about the original variables, and the corresponding m is the first m principal components extracted.

(4) Calculate the principal component load

Principal component load reflects the degree of correlation between principal component F_i and the original variable X_j. The original variable X_j ($j = 1, 2, ..., p$) loads l_{ij} ($i = 1, 2, ..., m$) on all principal components F_i; $j=1, 2, ..., p$.):

$$l(Z_i, X_j) = \sqrt{\lambda_i} a_{ij} (i = 1, 2, \cdots, m; j = 1, 2, \cdots, p)$$

Principal component analysis carried out by the SPSS software shows that "component matrix" reflects the principal component load matrix.

(5) Calculate the principal component score

Calculate the scores of samples on m principal components:

$$F_i = a_{1i} X_1 + a_{2i} X_2 + \cdots + a_{pi} X_p \quad i = 1, 2, \cdots, m$$

In actual applications, the dimensions of indicators are often different, so the influence of dimensions should be eliminated before the principal component calculation. There are many ways to eliminate the dimensions of data. A common method is to standardize the original data, i.e., to undergo the following data transformation:

$$x_{ij}^* = \frac{x_{ij} - \overline{x}_j}{s_j} \quad i = 1, 2, \cdots, n; j = 1, 2, \cdots, p$$

其中：

$$\bar{x}_j = \frac{1}{n}\sum_{i=1}^{n} x_{ij}, \quad s_j^2 = \frac{1}{n-1}\sum_{i=1}^{n}(x_{ij} - \bar{x}_j)^2$$

根据数学公式知道，①任何随机变量对其作标准化变换后，其协方差与其相关系数是一回事，即标准化后的变量协方差矩阵就是其相关系数矩阵。②另一方面，根据协方差的公式可以推得标准化后的协方差就是原变量的相关系数，亦即，标准化后的变量的协方差矩阵就是原变量的相关系数矩阵。也就是说，在标准化前后变量的相关系数矩阵不变化。

根据以上论述，为消除量纲的影响，将变量标准化后再计算其协方差矩阵，就是直接计算原变量的相关系数矩阵，所以主成分分析的实际常用计算步骤是：

（1）计算相关系数矩阵

$$R = \begin{bmatrix} r_{12} & r_{12} & \cdots & r_{1p} \\ r_{21} & r_{22} & \cdots & r_{2p} \\ \vdots & \vdots & & \vdots \\ r_{p1} & r_{p2} & \cdots & r_{pp} \end{bmatrix}$$

$r_{ij}(i,j=1,2,\cdots,p)$ 为原变量 X_i 与 X_j 的相关系数，$r_{ij}=r_{ji}$，其计算公式为

$$r_{ij} = \frac{\sum_{k=1}^{n}(x_{ki}-\bar{x}_i)(x_{kj}-\bar{x}_j)}{\sqrt{\sum_{k=1}^{n}(x_{ki}-\bar{x}_i)^2 \sum_{k=1}^{n}(x_{kj}-\bar{x}_j)^2}}$$

（2）计算特征值与特征向量

In which,

$$\bar{x}_j = \frac{1}{n}\sum_{i=1}^{n} x_{ij} \quad s_j^2 = \frac{1}{n-1}\sum_{i=1}^{n}(x_{ij} - \bar{x}_j)^2$$

The mathematical formula shows that ① the covariance and correlation coefficient of any standardized random variable are essentially the same — the standardized covariance matrix of variables is the correlation coefficient matrix. ② On the other hand, it can be deduced from the covariance formula that the standardized covariance is the correlation coefficient of the original variable — the standardized covariance matrix of variables is the correlation coefficient matrix of the original variable. In other words, the correlation coefficient matrix of variables does not change before and after standardization.

Accordingly, to eliminate the influence of dimensions, standardizing variables and calculating their covariance matrix is actually the process of calculating the correlation coefficient matrix of the original variables. So, the common steps of principal component analysis are:

(1) Calculate the correlation coefficient matrix

$$R = \begin{bmatrix} r_1 & r_2 & \cdots & r_{1p} \\ r_2 & r_2 & \cdots & r_{2p} \\ \vdots & \vdots & & \vdots \\ r_{p1} & r_{p2} & \cdots & r_p \end{bmatrix}$$

r_{ij} $(i, j = 1, 2, ..., p)$ is the correlation coefficient of the original variables X_i and X_j, $r_{ij} = r_{ji}$, and its calculation formula is

$$r_{ij} = \frac{\sum_{k=1}^{n}(x_{ki} - \bar{x}_i)(x_{kj} - \bar{x}_j)}{\sqrt{\sum_{k=1}^{n}(x_{ki} - \bar{x}_i)^2 \sum_{k=1}^{n}(x_{kj} - \bar{x}_j)^2}}$$

(2) Calculate eigenvalues and eigenvectors

解特征方程 $|\lambda_I - R| = 0$，常用雅可比法（Jacobi）求出特征值，并使其按大小顺序排列 $\lambda_1 \geqslant \lambda_2 \geqslant \cdots \geqslant \lambda_p \geqslant 0$；

分别求出对应于特征值 λ_i 的特征向量 $e_i (i=1,2,\cdots,p)$，要求 $\|e_i\|=1$，即 $\sum\limits_{j=1}^{p} e_{ij}^2 = 1$

其中 e_{ij} 表示向量 e_i 的第 j 个分量。

（3）计算主成分贡献率及累计贡献率

贡献率：

$$\frac{\lambda_i}{\sum\limits_{k=1}^{p} \lambda_k} \quad (i=1,2,\cdots,p)$$

累计贡献率：

$$\frac{\sum\limits_{k=1}^{i} \lambda_k}{\sum\limits_{k=1}^{p} \lambda_k} \quad (i=1,2,\cdots,p)$$

一般取累计贡献率达 85%—95% 的特征值，$\lambda_1, \lambda_2, \cdots, \lambda_m$ 所对应的第1、第2、…、第 m（$m \leqslant p$）个主成分。

（4）计算主成分载荷

$$l_{ij} = p(z_i, x_j) = \sqrt{\lambda_i} e_{ij} (i,j=1,2,\cdots,p)$$

（5）各主成分得分

$$Z = \begin{bmatrix} z_{11} & z_{12} & \cdots & z_{1m} \\ z_{21} & z_{22} & \cdots & z_{2m} \\ \vdots & \vdots & & \vdots \\ z_{n1} & z_{n2} & \cdots & z_{nm} \end{bmatrix}$$

Solve the characteristic equation $|\lambda_I - R| = 0$. The Jacobi method is often used to find the eigenvalues and arrange them in order of size $\lambda_1 \geqslant \lambda_2 \geqslant \cdots \geqslant \lambda_p \geqslant 0$;

Find the eigenvectors e_i ($i=1, 2, \ldots, p$) corresponding to the eigenvalue λ_i respectively. The requirement is $\|e_i\|=1$, that is, $\sum_{j=1}^{p} e_{ij}^2 = 1$

in which e_{ij} is the jth component of the vector e_i.

(3) Calculate the principal component contribution rate and cumulative contribution rate

Contribution rate:

$$\frac{\lambda_i}{\sum_{k=1}^{p} \lambda_k} \quad (i = 1, 2, \cdots, p)$$

Cumulative contribution rate:

$$\frac{\sum_{k=1}^{i} \lambda_k}{\sum_{k=1}^{p} \lambda_k} \quad (i = 1, 2, \cdots, p)$$

$\lambda_1, \lambda_2, \ldots, \lambda_m$ Generally, eigenvalues with a cumulative contribution rate of 85%—95% are taken; they correspond to the 1st, 2nd, …, mth ($m \leqslant p$) principal components.

(4) Calculate the principal component load

$$l_{ij} = p(z_i, x_j) = \sqrt{\lambda_i} e_{ij} (i, j = 1, 2, \cdots, p)$$

(5) Score of all principal components

$$Z = \begin{bmatrix} z_1 & z_2 & \cdots & z_{1m} \\ z_2 & z_2 & \cdots & z_{2m} \\ \vdots & \vdots & & \vdots \\ z_{n1} & z_{n2} & \cdots & z_m \end{bmatrix}$$

五、特殊条件对比国家的指标体系模型的建立与分析

1. 研究对象与选择

因数据有限,"特殊条件"在此只对中国,美国进行可持续范畴的研究。

$$r_{ij} = \frac{\sum_{k=1}^{n}(x_{ki}-\bar{x}_i)(x_{kj}-\bar{x}_j)}{\sqrt{\sum_{k=1}^{n}(x_{ki}-\bar{x}_i)^2 \sum_{k=1}^{n}(x_{kj}-\bar{x}_j)^2}}$$

2. 指标数据描述

2.1 指标分类

可持续范畴一共包括两个部分,其分别为:(1)建立普遍安全的世界测度;(2)建立卫生健康安全的世界测度,其中又可细分为各项低级指标,详情见表14:

表14 各级指标

一级指标	二级指标	三级指标
可持续的范畴	建立普遍安全的世界测度	1.建立安全事务协调机制的测度
	建立卫生健康安全的世界测度	1.建立全球公共卫生安全合作治理框架
		2.建立公开透明的防控体系
		3.建立国际医疗卫生物资供应体系

V. Establishment and analysis of the indicator system model for comparison of countries meeting special conditions

1. Objects of study and the choice of them

Due to data shortage, "special conditions" apply only to the study of the sustainability of China and the United States

$$r_{ij} = \frac{\sum_{k=1}^{n}(x_{ki} - \overline{x}_i)(x_{kj} - \overline{x}_j)}{\sqrt{\sum_{k=1}^{n}(x_{ki} - \overline{x}_i)^2 \sum_{k=1}^{n}(x_{kj} - \overline{x}_j)^2}}$$

2. Description of indicators

2.1 Indicator classification

The category of sustainability includes two parts: (1) measure of a world with universal security (2) measure of a world with health security. Lower indicators can be derived from these two parts, as shown in Table 14 below:

Table 14 Indicators across All Levels

Tier 1 indicators	Tier 2 indicators	Tier 3 indicators
Category of sustainability	Measure of creating a universally safe world	1. Measure of establishing a security affairs coordination mechanism
	Measure of creating a world of health security	1. Establishment of a cooperative governance framework for global public health security
		2. Establishment of an open and transparent prevention and control system
		3. Establishment of an international medical and health supply system

2.2 数据分析

2.2.1. 建立安全事务协调机制的测度

中国与美国对外联合声明次数对比

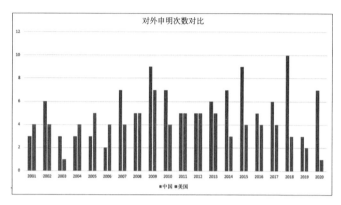

图 11　中国与美国联合声明次数对比图

通过对比中美两国对外申明的次数来刻画两国的国际影响能力，其中中国的对外申明由著名的和平组织上海合作组织（SCO）的活动情况所度量，美国的对外申明次数由其国际上的公开军事活动所度量。根据不完全数据统计，得到如图 12 所示情况，显然中国的对外申明次数逐年呈上升趋势，但在 2010 年前 10 年里低于美国的数据，为平均 3—6 次，在 2010 年的后 10 年里，中国逐渐超越美国，为 6—10 次，呈明显的领先地位。而美国的对外声明次数逐年呈下降趋势，虽然在 2010 年前 10 年里高于中国，为 4—7 次，但在后 10 年里，逐步下降且低于中国的数据，为 1—4 次，与中国的趋势呈现出明显的对比效果。足以证实近几年中国在国际上的影响力逐步扩大，并超过了美国的影响力的事实。

2.2 Data analysis

2.2.1. Measure of establishing a security affairs coordination mechanism

Comparison of the number of joint statements made by China and the United States

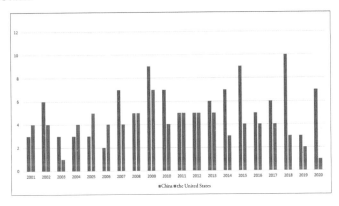

Figure 11 Comparison of the number of joint statements made by China and the United States

Comparison of the number of public political statements made by China and the United States reflects their respective international influence. China's public political statements are measured by activities undertaken by the well-known peace organization Shanghai Cooperation Organization (SCO), and the public political statements of the United States are measured by its military operations in the world. An inexhaustive statistical survey indicates that, as shown in Figure 12, the number of public political statements made by China rises year by year but averaged 3-6 in the 10 years before 2010, lower than the United States. In the 10 years after 2010, China gradually surpassed the United States with 6-10 public political statements, way ahead of the United States. The number of public political statements made by the United States declines year by year. Though higher than China with 4-7 public political statements in the 10 years before 2010, it declined gradually and fell behind China with 1-4 public political statements in the 10 years after 2010, a stark contrast to China. This is proof that China is extending its international influence and surpassing the United States in this regard.

2.2.2 建立全球公共卫生安全合作治理框架

中美与世界卫生组织互动对比

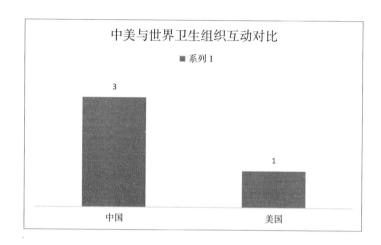

图 12 中美与世界卫生组织活动对比图

中国：① 2020 年 1 月 10 日世界卫生组织总干事与中华人民共和国国家卫生委员会负责人进行了交谈。他还致电与中国疾病预防控制中心主任分享信息。② 2020 年 2 月 9 日世卫组织与中华人民共和国签署了协议，并为世卫组织–中国联合特派团部署了一支先遣队。1 月底，世卫组织代表团访华期间，先遣队与中国国家卫生委员会，中国疾病预防控制中心，当地合作伙伴和相关实体以及世卫组织中国国家代表处共同完成了为期五天的深入准备工作。③ 2020 年 1 月 27—28 日由总干事率领的世卫组织高级代表团抵达北京，会见了中国领导人，进一步了解了中华人民共和国的对策，并提供了技术援助。

2.2.2 Establishment of a cooperative governance framework for global public health security

Comparison of the World Health Organization's Interaction with China and the United States

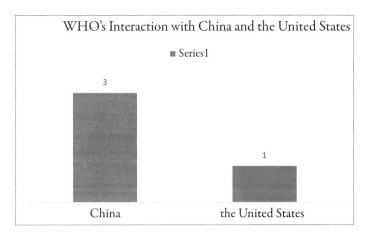

Figure 12 Comparison of the World Health Organization's Interaction with China and the United States

China: ① On January 10, 2020, Director-General Tedros Adhanom Ghebreyesus had a conversation with the head of the National Health Commission of the People's Republic of China. He also shared information with the director of the Chinese Center for Disease Control and Prevention on the phone. ② On February 9, 2020, WHO signed an agreement with the People's Republic of China and deployed a task force for the WHO-China joint mission. In late January, during the WHO delegation's visit to China, the task force made a five-day-long thorough preparation together with the National Health Commission of China, the Chinese Center for Disease Control and Prevention, local partners and entities, and the WHO Representative Office in China. ③ On January 27-28, 2020, a high-level WHO delegation led by Director-General Tedros Adhanom Ghebreyesus arrived in Beijing, met with Chinese leaders, was briefed on China's

美国：①泛美卫生组织（PAHO）主任敦促美洲国家做好准备以发现、隔离和护理感染新型冠状病毒的患者，以防接收来自不断传播新型冠状病毒病例的国家的旅行者。主任在泛美卫生组织在华盛顿向美洲国家组织（OAS）的大使作简报时发表了讲话。

据不完全统计，可从中美与世界卫生组织的主要互动次数对比看出，中国与世界卫生组织的关系更加亲密，已经达到了会见的程度，这对中国的可持续发展有着重要意义。而世界卫生组织对美国仅仅只是督促，由此可见，美国与世界卫生组织的关系并不那么紧密，甚至有些抵触，这或许会对美国的可持续发展产生影响。

2.2.3 建立公开透明的防控体系

①中国与美国过去的每日疫情发展态势变化对比

从图13中可以看出，中国的总新增病历确诊数整体呈现着下降趋势，曲线从刚开始的陡峭到如今的平缓，说明中国在短时间内可以做到对疫情蔓延的遏制，同时也从侧面说明了中国疫情防控体系的成熟。中国对待疫情始终秉持着公开透明的原则，对内而言，中华人民共和国国家卫生健康委员会对国家以及各省、市、区、县等严格把关，实时反馈疫情的相关情况；对外而言，中国与世界卫生组织等国际组织进行友好合作，愿意将本国最新的疫情概况以及新的研究成果进行上报，从而达到双赢。

measures against COVID-19, and provided China with technical assistance.

The United States: ① PAHO director urged American countries to get ready to discover, isolate and care for patients infected with COVID-19 and to prevent travelers from countries where COVID-19 is rampant from coming. PAHO director delivered a speech at the briefing that PAHO arranged for the ambassadors to the Organization of American States (OAS) in Washington.

Though available statistics are not exhaustive, a comparison of WHO's interactions with China and the United States shows that China has a closer working relationship with WHO than the United States — so close that WHO officials met with Chinese officials. This is of great significance to China's sustainable development. What WHO did regarding the United States was simply supervision. This shows the relationship between the United States and WHO is not close — there are even conflicts between them. This may have a negative impact on the sustainable development of the United States.

2.2.3 Establishment of an open and transparent prevention and control system

① Comparison of the daily spread of COVID-19 in China and the United States

According to Figure 13, the total number of confirmed COVID-19 cases in China was on the decline, and the original sharp curve is now a gentle one. This shows that China has curbed the spread of the epidemic in a short time, an indication that China has a mature epidemic prevention and control system. China has been transparent about COVID-19. Internally, the National Health Commission adopts a strict policy at the state, province, city, district and county levels and reports the latest developments without any delay. Externally, China cooperates with WHO in a friendly manner and pledges to report the latest developments in the epidemic and China's new research results with a view to achieving win-win results.

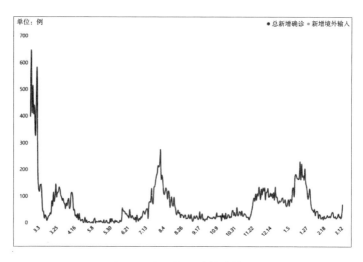

图 13　中国每日疫情走势图

相反,从图 14 中可以看出,美国的总新增病历确诊数整体呈现着上升趋势,曲线从刚开始的平缓到如今变化幅度较为严重,说明美国对待疫情的态度并不重视,确诊数最高达到了30 多万的峰值,从侧面可以看出,美国一开始有意隐瞒疫情,

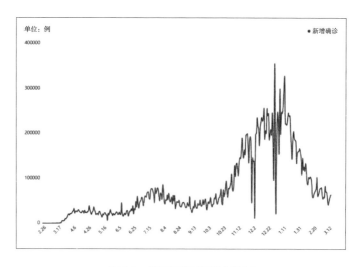

图 14　美国每日疫情走势图

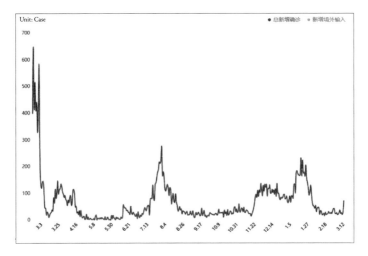

Figure 13 Daily Spread of COVID-19 in China

On the contrary, as can be seen from Figure 14, the total number of confirmed COVID-19 cases in the United States is on the rise, and the original gentle curve is now a sharp one. This indicates that the United States doesn't take the pandemic seriously — the number of confirmed cases reached a record high of over 300,000. The United States intentionally concealed the epidemic situation at the beginning,

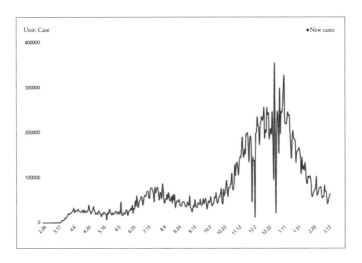

Figure 14 Daily Spread of COVID-19 in the United States

导致疫情堆积，致使在后来一特定时间段爆发，这种做法既是对国家的失职，也是对民众的不负责，倘若早一点对疫情公开透明并建立完整的防控体系，所造成的损失将会降至最低。

②中国与美国政府反映严格指数对比

政府反应严格指数是指在 2020 年疫情期间，衡量政府应对措施的差异。从政府反应严格指数对比图（见图 15）中可以看出，从疫情被发现时，中国政府反应迅速，即刻开始做出各种应对措施，抑制疫情的扩散。而美国政府虽然同时期也发现疫情，却不以为然，没有对其重视，等到 2 月才开始做出防范措施。且从政府反应严格指数持续峰值可看出，中国对疫情持有高防范意识的时期更长。由此可以看出中国的防控体系更加完善。

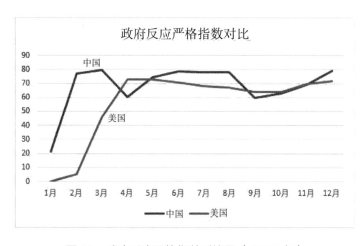

图 15　政府反应严格指数对比图（2020 年）

2.2.4　建立国际医疗卫生物资供应体系

2020 年，中国与美国对外捐赠医疗器材折合价格对比如图 16 所示。

which led to the accumulation of cases and massive infections. It is a dereliction of duty to the country and the people. The harm to human health would have been reduced to a minimum if the United States government had been transparent about the disease and established a sound prevention and control system.

② Comparison of the government response stringency indexes of China and the United States

The government response stringency index is a measure of the differences in government responses during the spread of COVID-19. Figure 15 shows that the Chinese government responded quickly and took various measures to curb the spread of COVID-19. The US government discovered the epidemic during the same period, but it didn't take it seriously until February 2020. And the sustained peak level of the government response stringency index shows that China's high awareness of epidemic prevention lasts longer. This indicates that China's prevention and control system is more perfect.

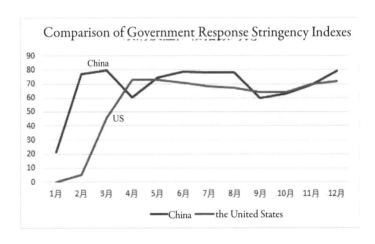

Figure 15　Comparison of Government Response Stringency Indexes (2020)

2.2.4 Establishment of an international medical and health supply system

Comparison of the equivalent prices of medical equipment donated by China and the United States during the spread of COVID-19, as shown in Figure 16.

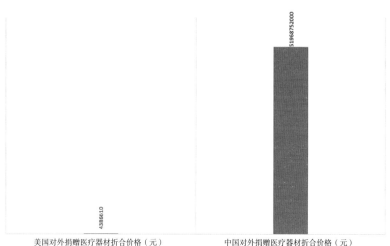

图 16 中国与美国对外捐赠医疗器材折合价格对比（2020 年）

根据上述统计数据，中国对国外包括韩国、日本、以色列、意大利等国家捐赠的 N95 口罩，一次性医用口罩，防护服，呼吸机等医疗器材比美国多得多，美国主要为一些非营利机构自行组织对国外的捐赠。将这些医疗器材按照专家评判法给予权重折合成人民币的对比情况见图 16，美国大约为438.661 万元，中国大约为 519.688 亿元，中国在对外捐赠情况远超美国，在世界性的防疫上中国对于人类命运共同体可持续发展的支持强于美国。

3. 建立模型及结果分析

3.1 模型的建立

根据收集到的有关可持续的范畴的数据，发现中美两国的数据较为完整，所以在此只对中国、美国进行相关研究。

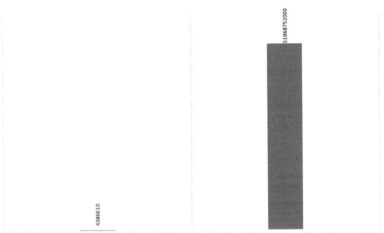

Figure 16 Comparison of the Equivalent Prices of Medical Equipment Donated by China and the United States (2020)

Above statistics statistics indicate that China donated far more N95 masks, disposable medical masks, protective clothing, and ventilators to Korea, Japan, Israel and Italy than the United States. In the United States, non-profit organizations are the main organizer of donations to foreign countries. Experts attached weights to these medical devices and worked out their prices in RMB. The comparison is shown in the above figure. The United States donated about 4,386,610 yuan of medical devices while China donated about 51,968,800 yuan of medical devices to other countries. China is way ahead of the United States in terms of donations, and it makes greater contributions to the sustainable development of the Community with a Shared Future for Mankind than the United States in the worldwide fight against COVID-19.

3. Model building and results analysis

3.1 Model building

According to available data on the category of sustainability, it is found that the data about China and the United States are complete, so only China and the United States are studied here.

关于可持续的范畴研究的技术路线图如图 17 所示。具体数据预处理有如下三种方法：①数据归一化：为了消除数据特征之间的量纲和数量级的影响，本文需要对特征进行归一化处理，使得不同指标之间具有可比性。②数据同向化：如安全共同体一样，某些数据越大越好，而有些数据则越小越好，在这里也需要做一个统一，将数据统一成同指标同趋势化，即越大越好，此处每日疫情态势变化回归分析得到的系数为负反而更好，说明疫情是下降趋势，此处综合得分需与其他指标一样，变成为正并且越大越好，此处直接将拟合的系数取相反数即可。③专家评判法总得分：鉴于各项指标之间的测度不同，难以直接比较，因此听取相关专家建议，以此对各项指标进行打分，使其具有一定的可比性。

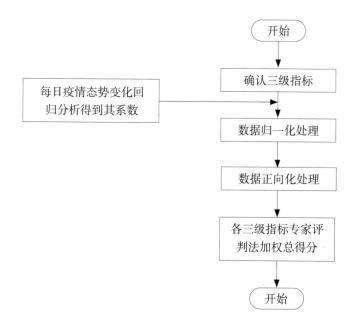

图 17　技术路线图

See Figure 17 for the technical roadmap for the research of sustainability There are three specific data preprocessing methods: ① Data normalization: To eliminate the influence of dimensions and order of magnitudes on data features, this paper needs to normalize the features and make different indicators comparable. ② Data isotropization: Similar to the security community, some data are preferably big, and some are preferably small. Here, we need to convert all the data in such a way that the bigger the indicator, the better. If the coefficient obtained through the regression analysis of the change in the daily spread of COVID-19 is negative, it will be considered a good indicator for its shows that the number of cases is on the decline. The comprehensive score should be positive and big, as is the case with other indicators. The fitted relation coefficient should be an opposite figure. ③ Total scores given in expert evaluations: In view of the difference in the measures of the indicators, it is difficult to compare them directly. Therefore, the advice should be taken from the experts and scores all the indicators to make them comparable.

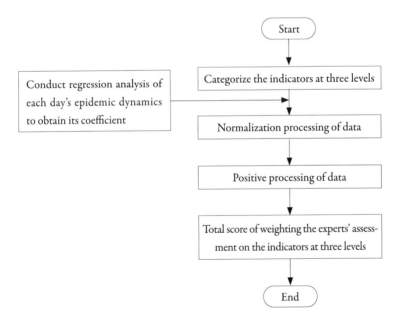

Figure 17 Technology Roadmap

首先对数据同向化处理：

$$x_i = -y_i (i = 1, 2) \tag{1}$$

接着本文对数据进行归一化处理：

$$\frac{x_i}{\max(X)} (i = 1, 2) \tag{2}$$

由此建立如下专家评判得分模型：

$$F(x) = A \cdot x_1 + B(a \cdot x_2 + b \cdot x_3 + c \cdot x_4 + d \cdot x_5) \tag{3}$$

3.2 结果分析

获得的原始数据如下：

表 15 可获得的数据

类别	中国	美国
对外捐赠器材折合价格（元）	51 968 752 000	4 386 610
与世卫组织互动（次）	3	1
政府反映严格指数（年平均）	65.99 479 888	55.17 202 747
对外联合声明次数（次）	111	78
每日疫情态势变化回归系数	-1.922 962 581	401.1 458 253

两国数据同向化后如下：

表 16 同向化后数据

类别	中国	美国
对外捐赠器材折合价格	51 968 752 000	4 386 610
与世卫组织互动	3	1
政府反映严格指数	65.99 479 888	55.17 202 747
对外联合声明次数	111	78
每日疫情态势变化系数	1.922 962 581	-401.1 458 253

Data isotropization:

$$x_i = -y_i (i = 1, 2) \qquad (1)$$

Data normalization:

$$\frac{x_i}{\max(X)} (i = 1, 2) \qquad (2)$$

Expert evaluation model:

$$F(x) = A \cdot x_1 + B(a \cdot x_2 + b \cdot x_3 + c \cdot x_4 + d \cdot x_5) \qquad (3)$$

3.2 Analysis of results

The raw data obtained are as follows:

Table 15 Available Data

Category	China	the United States
Equivalent price of donated medical equipment (yuan)	51,968,752,000	4,386,610
Number of interactions with WHO	3	1
Government response stringency index (annual average)	65.99,479,888	55.17,202,747
Number of joint statements made	111	78
Regression coefficient of daily spread of COVID-19	-1.922,962,581	401.1,458,253

Isotropic data of the two countries:

Table 16 Isotropic Data of the Two Countries

Category	China	the United States
Equivalent price of donated medical equipment	51,968,752,000	4,386,610
Interactions with WHO	3	1
Government response stringency index	65.99,479,888	55.17,202,747
Number of joint statements made	111	78
Variation coefficient of daily spread of COVID-19	1.922,962,581	-401.1458,253

两国数据归一化后如下：

表17 归一化后数据

类别	中国	美国
对外捐赠器材折合价格	1	0.000 084 4
与世卫组织互动	1	0.333 333 333
政府反映严格指数	1	0.836 005 691
对外联合声明次数	1	0.702 702 703
每日疫情态势变化系数	0.004 793 675	-1

根据建立的专家评判得分模型法给予权重打分之后，中国与美国得分对比如图18所示。

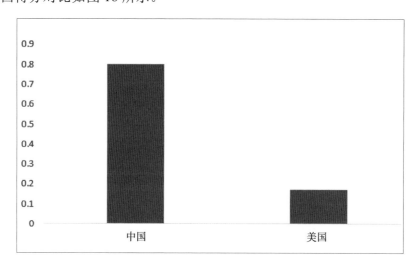

图18 美国与中国总得分对比图

综合各项指标之后，美国总得分为0.18，中国总得分为0.82，中国高于美国，可以看出中国在可持续发展方面做得比美国好，值得推崇。

Anisotropic data of the two countries:

Table 17 Anisotropic Data

Category	China	the United States
Equivalent price of donated medical equipment	1	0.000,084,4
Interactions with WHO	1	0.333,333,333
Government response stringency index	1	0.836,005,691
Number of joint statements made	1	0.702,702,703
Variation coefficient of daily spread of COVID-19	0.004,793,675	-1

Weights and scores are given to China and the United States according to the expert evaluation model, as shown in Figure 18.

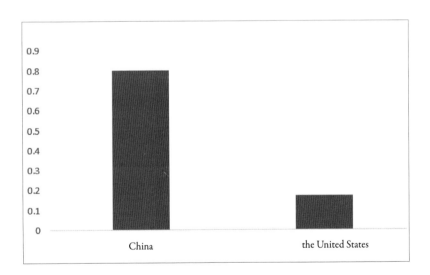

Figure 18 Comparison of the Total Scores of the United States and China

The United States' total score is 0.18, and China's total score is 0.82, on all indicators. China's total score is higher than that of the United States, an indication that China does commendably better than the United States in sustainable development.

4. 结论

通过专家评判模型的结果得出,安全共同体进程的可持续范畴的得分,中国不管是各项指标还是总得分都全部高于美国,鉴于数据的真实性和专家的可靠评判,这里建立的专家评判模型及其结果具有较高的可信度。

习近平主席指出:"当今世界,安全问题的联动性、跨国性、多样性更加突出。中国愿同各国政府及其执法机构、各国际组织一道,共同构建普遍安全的人类命运共同体。""应该树立共同、综合、合作、可持续的安全观。"2017年1月,习近平主席在联合国日内瓦总部发表了题为《共同构建人类命运共同体》的主旨演讲,再次主张为建设一个普遍安全的世界,各方应该树立共同、综合、合作、可持续的安全观,从而使可持续安全观成为共建人类命运共同体的有机组成部分。这是可持续安全观的又一次发展。由此,可持续安全观已成为中国向世界提出的系统、完整的有关国际安全的新理念,具有重要的国际指导意义,同时也对中国方案、中国贡献赋予全方位的时代蕴涵。

可持续安全观是一个开放、发展的安全理念。在构建人类命运共同体之中,可持续的内容涵盖了既成的安全状况,也包含了正在发生与有可能发生的情况,以可持续反观安全共同体的构建,将更好地测度如何构建持续安全的发展环境,使得人类命运共同体进程指标更加体现出对未来的指向。

4. Conclusion

The results produced by the expert evaluation model show that the scores given to the category of sustainability in the security community process of China are higher than the United States — on all indicators and in terms of the total score. The data are genuine, and the expert evaluation is reliable, so the expert evaluation model and the results it produces are relatively valid.

President Xi Jinping says, "Security issues are increasingly interconnected, transnational and diverse in today's world. China will work with other countries (including their law enforcement agencies) and international organizations to build a universally safe Community with a Shared Future for Mankind." "We should develop a concept of security that highlights commonality, comprehensiveness, cooperation and sustainability." In January 2017, President Xi Jinping delivered a keynote speech entitled "Build a Community with a Shared Future for Mankind" at the United Nations Headquarters in Geneva. To build a universally safe world, he reiterated, all countries should develop a concept of security that highlights commonality, comprehensiveness, cooperation and sustainability so that the concept of sustainable security can become an integral part of the Community with a Shared Future for Mankind. This is another development of the concept of sustainable security. The concept of sustainable security is a new, systematic and complete concept of international security that China frames for the world. It is an important international guideline that has redefined the Chinese approach and China's contribution.

The concept of sustainable security is an open, developing concept. In the Community with a Shared Future for Mankind, the concept of sustainable security defines the existing security situation, as well as ongoing and possible security situations. Developing the guideline of sustainability for the building of a security community will help measure what is a development environment with sustainable security and make the indicators for measuring the building of a Community with a Shared Future for Mankind more forward-looking.

后　记

2018年，汪明义教授参加中央党校第70期市厅级领导干部进修班学习，与同班学员祝灵君、姚涵组成"人类文明进程排行榜指标体系"研究小组，大家对如何评价人类文明进程进行了充分讨论。在此基础上，四川师范大学成立了"人类命运共同体构建进程指标体系"课题组，组长由校长汪明义教授担任，副组长由四川省委宣传部副部长高中伟、四川师范大学副校长张海东两位同志担任。课题组成员除了前面三位之外，还包括四川师范大学吕京教授、孙勇教授、谭光辉教授、雷勇教授、郑涛教授、陈丽静副教授及甘娜副教授。

课题组成立以来，成功申请了四川省社科重大课题"人类命运共同体构建进程指标体系研究"（编号：SC19ZD11）及全国教育科学"十三五"规划2020年度国家级课题"大

Postscript

Prof. Wang Mingyi attended the 70th Training Workshop for the Leaders at Municipal and Department Levels organized by the Central Party School of the Communist Party of China in 2018. Prof. Wang established a research team on the Indicators System on the Ranking List of Human Civilizations Process, together with Zhu Lingjun and Yao Han, who also attended the training workshop. They held discussions on how to assess the human civilizations process. On this basis, the Task Force on the Indicators System on the Process of Building a Community with a Shared Future for Mankind was established by Sichuan Normal University (SICNU). In the Task Force, Prof. Wang Mingyi, president of SICNU, served as the team leader, while Gao Zhongwei, deputy director of the Publicity Department of the CPC Sichuan Provincial Committee, and Zhang Haidong, vice president of SICNU, served as the deputy team leaders. Apart from the above-mentioned members, members of the Task Force also include Profs. Lyu Jing, Sun Yong, Tan Guanghui, Lei Yong, Zheng Tao and associate professor Chen Lijing and Gan Na from SICNU.

Since the inception of the Task Force, it has successfully applied for eight projects. These projects include: the Indicators System on Building a Community with a Shared Future for Mankind (No. SC19ZD11), a major project

学推动人类命运共同体建设的理论依据及实践研究"（编号BIA200176）等 8 个项目。同时，课题组积极推动四川师范大学（Sichuan Normal University）与巴基斯坦卡拉奇大学（University of Karachi）和韩国延世大学（Yonsei University）成立"SKY"大学联盟，邀请国内外专家学者定期举办人类命运共同体构建进程高峰论坛，现已举办两届。

课题研究过程中，得到了教育部原党组副书记、副部长，中国高等教育学会会长杜玉波同志的大力支持。

课题还得到了许多专家的悉心指导，包括四川大学宋志辉教授、蒋瑛教授、蒋国庆教授、周维东教授、丁忠毅教授，西南财经大学刘世强教授、王翔宇副教授，西南民族大学尹忠明教授、郑长德教授，西南交大王鹏飞教授、段从学教授，电子科技大学冯文坤教授、李泉副教授，四川省工程咨询研究院张义方教授，四川师范大学王川教授、傅林教授、唐代兴教授、邓伟教授，成都山地所朱万泽教授，西华大学李玲教授，成都理工大学黄寰教授，四川轻化工大学黄英杰教授及成都师范学院卢阳春教授等。

吕京教授负责本书的"汉译英"工作。

of social sciences in Sichuan; and Theoretical Rationale and Practice of Colleges and Universities to Promote the Building of Community with a Shared Future for Mankind (No. BIA200176), a project at the national level in 2020 under the National 13th Five-Year Plan for Education Science, among others. Meanwhile, the Task Force has actively advanced SICNU, China, University of Karachhi, Pakistan and Yonsei University, South Korea to establish "SKY" University Alliance. Domestic and foreign experts and scholars in this discipline are brought together to hold summits on a regular basis on the process of building a community with a shared future for mankind. To date, two sessions have already been organized.

We would like to thank Du Yubo, former deputy secretary of the Party Leadership Group and former vice minister of China's Ministry of Education, and president of China Association of Higher Education, for his strong support during the process of the project implementation.

Our thanks also go to many professors and associate professors who have provided guidance in the process. They include: Profs. Song Zhihui, Jiang Ying, Jiang Guoqing, Zhou Weidong and Ding Zhongyi from Sichuan University; Prof. Liu Shiqiang and associate professor Wang Xiangyu from the Southwestern University of Finance and Economics; Profs. Yin Zhongming and Zheng Changde from Southwest Minzu University; Profs. Wang Pengfei and Duan Congxue from Southwest Jiaotong University; Prof. Feng Wenkun and associate professor Li Quan from University of Electronic Science and Technology of China; Prof. Zhang Yifang from Sichuan Engineering Consulting and Research Institute; Prof. Wang Chuan, Prof. Fu Lin, Prof. Tang Daixing and Prof. Deng Wei from SICNU; Prof. Zhu Wanze from the Institute of Mountain Hazards and Environment, CAS; Prof. Li Ling from Xihua University; Prof. Huang Huan from Chengdu University of Technology; Prof. Huang Yingjie from Sichuan University of Science & Engineering; Prof. Lu Yangchun from Chengdu Normal University, and more.

Prof. Lyu Jing took the lead in translating the book from Chinese into

周贤林博士、吴良平博士、陈琴博士承担了人类命运共同体构建进程安全维度指标体系排序案例的推演工作。

本书得以出版离不开北京大学中国战略研究中心邵春堡研究员及中国出版集团中译出版社社长乔卫兵先生、范伟女士、张孟桥先生的大力支持！

谨向上述各位领导专家学者致以诚挚谢意！

因时间和水平有限，书中难免有不少疏漏之处，欢迎各位读者批评指正！

2022 年 3 月 18 日

English.

Drs. Zhou Xianlin, Wu Liangping and Chen Qin from SICNU were responsible for deducing the cases of ranking the indicators system of building a community with a shared future for mankind: Security Dimension.

The publication of the book could not have been made possible without the strong support of Prof. Shao Chunbao from Peking University's China Center for Strategic Studies, Mr. Qiao Weibing, president of China Translation & Publishing House, Ms. Fan Wei and Mr. Zhang Mengqiao from the Publishing House.

Finally, we would like to express our sincere gratitude to all the leaders, scholars and experts for their support.

Your comments and suggestions on the book are welcome.

March 18, 2022

图书在版编目（CIP）数据

人类命运共同体构建进程指标体系研究 = The Indicators System on the Process of Building a Community with a Shared Future for Mankind：汉英对照 / 汪明义等著. -- 北京：中译出版社，2022.3
ISBN 978-7-5001-7016-7

Ⅰ. ①人… Ⅱ. ①汪… Ⅲ. ①国际关系－研究－汉、英 Ⅳ. ①D82

中国版本图书馆CIP数据核字(2022)第044217号

出版发行 / 中译出版社
地　　址 / 北京市西城区新街口外大街 28 号普天德胜科技园主楼 4 层
电　　话 / (010)68005858, 68358224（编辑部）
传　　真 / (010)68357870
邮　　编 / 100088
电子邮箱 / book@ctph.com.cn
网　　址 / http://www.ctph.com.cn

责任编辑 / 张孟桥　范　伟
封面设计 / 潘　峰

排　　版 / 北京竹页文化传媒有限公司
印　　刷 / 北京顶佳世纪印刷有限公司
经　　销 / 新华书店

规　　格 / 710 毫米 ×1000 毫米　1/16
印　　张 / 21
字　　数 / 260 千字
版　　次 / 2022 年 3 月第一版
印　　次 / 2022 年 3 月第一次

ISBN 978-7-5001-7016-7　定价：128.00 元

版权所有　侵权必究
中 译 出 版 社